Soviet and Post-Soviet Politics and Society (SPPS)

ISSN 1614-3515

Founded in 2004 and refereed since 2007, SPPS makes available affordable English-, German-, and Russian-language studies on the history of the countries of the former Soviet bloc from the late Tsarist period to today. It publishes between 5 and 20 volumes per year and focuses on issues in transitions to and from democracy such as economic crisis, identity formation, civil society development, and constitutional reform in CEE and the NIS. SPPS also aims to highlight so far understudied themes in East European studies such as right-wing radicalism, religious life, higher education, or human rights protection. The authors and titles of all previously published volumes are listed at the end of this book. For a full description of the series and reviews of its books, see www.ibidem-verlag.de/red/spps.

Editorial correspondence & manuscripts should be sent to: Dr. Andreas Umland, DAAD, German Embassy, vul. Bohdana Khmelnitskoho 25, UA-01901 Kyiv, Ukraine. e-mail: umland@stanfordalumni.org

Business correspondence & review copy requests should be sent to: *ibidem* Press, Leuschnerstr. 40, 30457 Hannover, Germany; tel.: +49 511 2622200; fax: +49 511 2622201; spps@ibidem.eu.

Authors, reviewers, referees, and editors for (as well as all other persons sympathetic to) SPPS are invited to join its networks at www.facebook.com/group.php?gid=52638198614 www.linkedin.com/groups?about=&gid=103012 www.xing.com/net/spps-ibidem-verlag/

Recent Volumes

130   *Konstantin Sheiko, Stephen Brown*
History as Therapy
Alternative History and Nationalist Imaginings in Russia, 1991-2014
ISBN 978-3-8382-0565-6

131   *Elisa Kriza*
Alexander Solzhenitsyn: Cold War Icon, Gulag Author, Russian Nationalist?
A Study of the Western Reception of his Literary Writings, Historical Interpretations, and Political Ideas
With a foreword by Andrei Rogatchevski
ISBN 978-3-8382-0689-9 (Paperback edition)
ISBN 978-3-8382-0690-5 (Hardcover edition)

132   *Serghei Golunov*
Elephant in the Room
Corruption and Cheating in Russian Universities
ISBN 978-3-8382-0670-7

133   *Manja Hussner, Rainer Arnold (Hrsg.)*
Verfassungsgerichtsbarkeit in Zentralasien I
Sammlung von Verfassungstexten
ISBN 978-3-8382-0595-3

134   *Nikolay Mitrokhin*
Die "Russische Partei"
Die Bewegung der russischen Nationalisten in der UdSSR 1953-1985
Aus dem Russischen übertragen von einem Übersetzerteam unter der Leitung von Larisa Schippel
ISBN 978-3-8382-0024-8

135   *Manja Hussner, Rainer Arnold (Hgg.)*
Verfassungsgerichtsbarkeit in Zentralasien II
Sammlung von Verfassungstexten
ISBN 978-3-8382-0597-7

136   *Manfred Zeller*
Das sowjetische Fieber
Fußballfans im poststalinistischen Vielvölkerreich
Mit einem Vorwort von Nikolaus Katzer
ISBN 978-3-8382-0787-2

137   *Kristin Schreiter*
Stellung und Entwicklungspotential zivilgesellschaftlicher Gruppen in Russland
Menschenrechtsorganisationen im Vergleich
ISBN 978-3-8382-0673-8

138   *David R. Marples, Frederick V. Mills (Eds.)*
Ukraine's Euromaidan
Analyses of a Civil Revolution
ISBN 978-3-8382-0700-1 (Paperback edition)
ISBN 978-3-8382-0740-7 (Hardcover edition)

David R. Marples,
Frederick V. Mills (Eds.)

UKRAINE'S EUROMAIDAN

Analyses of a Civil Revolution

ibidem-Verlag
Stuttgart

Bibliographic information published by the Deutsche Nationalbibliothek
Die Deutsche Nationalbibliothek lists this publication in the Deutsche Nationalbibliografie; detailed bibliographic data are available in the Internet at http://dnb.d-nb.de.

Bibliografische Information der Deutschen Nationalbibliothek
Die Deutsche Nationalbibliothek verzeichnet diese Publikation in der Deutschen Nationalbibliografie; detaillierte bibliografische Daten sind im Internet über http://dnb.d-nb.de abrufbar.

ISSN: 1614-3515
ISBN-13 Paperback edition: 978-3-8382-0700-1
ISBN-13 Hardback edition: 978-3-8382-0740-7
© *ibidem*-Verlag / *ibidem* Press
Stuttgart, Germany 2015

Contents

Acknowledgements

The editors owe a great debt to the Canadian Institute of Ukrainian Studies, University of Alberta, which helped to sponsor the project and provided critical funding. For most of the period under study, it was also the home of the Stasiuk blog site "Current Politics in Ukraine," which provided regular analyses of the situation during Euromaidan and subsequently, with CIUS funding. CIUS held a number of seminars and conferences on events in Ukraine in 2013–14, organized chiefly by Bohdan Harasymiw, head of the Centre for Regional and Political Studies. We owe a great debt to CIUS director Volodymyr Kravchenko for his enthusiasm and support for this project, which continued, one should add, after David Marples formally left CIUS at the end of August 2014.

Much of the editorial work undertaken by Dr. Marples took place while he was a Visiting Scholar with the Slavic and Eurasian Research Center (SRC) at the University of Hokkaido, Sapporo, Japan, during the summer of 2014. That work was facilitated and enhanced by the members of SRC, and in particular its director Osamu Ieda. Aya Fujiwara, one of the contributors to this book, presented a version of her paper at SRC in August 2014. We are also grateful to Marta Dyczok for providing photographs and to *The King's Review*, an online magazine publishing academic journalism based in King's College, University of Cambridge, for permitting us to republish a new version of Tanya Zaharchenko's paper. We would like to thank Sofia Dyak, for alerting us to the work of Natalia Otrischenko and Anna Chebotariova of the Lviv Center for Urban History in East-Central Europe, who agreed to contribute to this volume.

Lastly, we are grateful to *ibidem*-Verlag for their patience and helpfulness at various stages, especially to Valerie Lange, Florian Boelter, and Chris Schoen. Having a cooperative publisher is a tremendous asset for any project and this one has been exemplary.

David R. Marples
Frederick V. Mills

Edmonton, Alberta, Canada
January 2015

Introduction

David R. Marples

From November 2013 to the end of February 2014, protesters gathered on Kyiv's central square, in a series of demonstrations known as the Euromaidan. These protests involved several distinct stages, culminating in what some analysts have called a national revolution that removed the government and presidency of Viktor Yanukovych. As a historian who has followed Ukraine since Soviet times, I recall in particular two earlier civic protests of importance. The first was the occupation of the Maidan by Kyiv's university students in 1990, demanding the resignation of then Prime Minister Vitalii Masol. Though widely condemned by Communist officials, it ended with the removal of the unpopular figure. The second was known as the Orange Revolution, and arose as a protest against the doctored results of the 2004 presidential election. Ironically, this event served to prevent the same Yanukovych from winning the presidency. He did, however return as Prime Minister under the Yushchenko presidency, and then won the 2010 elections, narrowly defeating Yulia Tymoshenko.

In late November 2013, Yanukovych had signaled his willingness to commit Ukraine to signing an Association Agreement with the European Union at the EU summit in Vilnius, an event that represented the culmination of an agreement made in 2012, and the high point to date of the Eastern Partnership initiative of 2008.[1] The Europeans had demanded in return that he release Tymoshenko from captivity (she had served 2.5 years of a 7-year jail sentence for signing an agreement with Russia on energy prices in 2009, when she was Prime Minister), and start constitutional and legal reforms. After a visit to Moscow, where he spoke with President Vladimir Putin, Yanukovych made the decision to postpone the signing of the agreement and seek better terms. It seemed once again that Ukraine would remain within the Russian orbit, and would most likely commit itself to future membership in the Eurasian Economic Union, which was to come into force on January 1, 2015, and currently involves Russia, Kazakhstan, and Belarus, with Armenia a likely additional member.

---

1   For the full text of the agreement, see http://eeas.europa.eu/ukraine/assoagreem ent/assoagreement-2013_en.htm (accessed August 18, 2014).

9

On November 24, protesters came to the streets, motivated by anger at the change of direction. They were mainly youth, alerted by social networks and text messages. What occurred was essentially a civil protest on the future of Ukraine and it took the authorities completely by surprise. Though the daily numbers would dwindle, every weekend saw masses come out on the streets. At its peak, the numbers were so vast that it was impossible to count them. In several cities of Ukraine, especially in the western regions, the events in Kyiv were replicated. On the whole, the authorities reacted cautiously, deploying the *Berkut* riot police but without any serious confrontations. But on the night of November 30 and the morning of December 1, the order was given for the *Berkut* to clear the square by force. The *Berkut* descended on the Maidan, clubbing and beating demonstrators.

The protests were re-energized by this clumsy and thoughtless assault. The numbers rose sharply again. On December 16, Putin offered Ukraine $15 billion in loans and reduced gas prices to offset Ukraine's financial crisis, sparked by the near depletion of its hard currency reserves.[2] More than anything the offer seemed to emphasize that without Russia, Ukraine could not survive. Moreover, the sum was far more than the EU or the IMF was prepared to consider. In truth it was probably more than Russia could afford. The situation was exacerbated further by the quasi-legal rushing through parliament of draconian laws—the so-called "anti-protest laws" on January 16.[3] Their goal appeared to be to curb freedom of speech and assembly, the outlawing of NGOs and the establishment of a dictatorship under Yanukovych. The laws were the brainchild of two deputies from the Party of Regions, Vadym Kolesnychenko and Volodymyr Oliinyk. Though repealed only twelve days later, these laws heralded the culmination of the Euromaidan protests.

The protests were now less about the EU and more about the future of Ukraine. More attention was paid to the innate and grotesque corruption of the ruling regime, of the prevalence of oligarchs who had enriched them-

---

2   See, for example, "Russia Promises Ukraine Cheaper Gas, $15 Billion Loan," *Voice of America*, December 17, 2013, http://www.voanews.com/content/russia-promises-ukraine-cheaper-gas-15-billion-loan/1811836.html (accessed August 18, 2014).

3   "Rehionaly ta komunisty 'pryinialy' paket zakoniv dlya borotby z hromadyanamy Ukrainy [Party of Regions and Communists "passed" a set of laws to take measures against the citizens of Ukraine]," *Texty.org.ua*, January 1, 2014, http://texty.org.ua/pg/news/devrand/read/51058/Regionaly_ta_komunisty_pryjnaly_paket_za koniv_dla (accessed August 19, 2014).

selves at the expense of the state, and the lack of legal reforms. These protests had two immediate results. One was the agreement of Yanukovych to sacrifice his Prime Minister, Nikolay Azarov (who promptly fled to Vienna on an Austrian passport) and try to make a compromise with opposition leaders by bringing them into the ruling administration.[4]

On January 25, the Prime Minister's position was offered to Arsenii Yatsenyuk, the former Economy and Foreign Minister of Ukraine and leader of the Batkivshchyna [Fatherland] Party following the incarceration of Tymoshenko. That of Deputy Prime Minister for "humanitarian questions" was offered to Vitalii Klychko (Vitaly Klitschko), the former world champion boxer and leader of the party UDAR [the Fist], which ran third in the 2012 parliamentary elections. Both refused to take up these posts, possibly because they could detect the growing weakness of the government, but more likely because to have done so would have cost them influence on the square. Moreover, Yatsenyuk was insistent that the new government should be formed through the parliament rather than the presidency.[5]

In reality, these leaders, and to some extent the third opposition leader Oleh Tyahnybok of Svoboda, had never led the protests. Rather they reacted to the moves on the Maidan. As the situation polarized, both sides changed character and personnel. On the government side, gangs of thugs were bussed into Kyiv from other cities, principally Kharkiv and Donetsk, simply to cause mayhem. Batkivshchyna formed its own self-defense group. The average protester—if one can deduce such a thing—was no longer the 20-something student, but more hardened 30 and 40-year olds, not only ready for a fight but unprepared to compromise. Many were from western Ukraine. In their local regions, the government of Yanukovych no longer existed. Elsewhere the government deployed gangs to carry out drastic actions. They set fire to cars, beat up protesters, kidnapped people, and targeted prominent journalists.

---

4   On his Facebook page, Azarov declared that he was in need of "a rest." Cited in "Azarov na chastnom samolete uletel v Venu—Avstriyskie [Azarov flew to Vienna on a private plane—Austria media]," NB News, January 16, 2014, http://nbnew s.com.ua/ua/news/112015/ (accessed August 18, 2014).
5   Vira Karpinska, "Yatsenyuk rozpoviv za yakykh umov pohodytsya ocholyty uryad [Yatsenyuk states under what circumstances he would agree to lead the government]," Zaxid.net, February 5, 2014, http://zaxid.net/news/showNews.do?yatse nyuk_rozpoviv_za_yakih_umov_pogoditsya_ocholiti_uryad&objectId=1302025 (accessed August 18, 2014).

On the opposition side, several local militias formed, based partly on rightist groups like *Pravyi Sektor* (hereafter Right Sector). The latter initially comprised soccer fan "ultras," mainly Russophones who were nonetheless fanatical nationalists. Though relatively small in numbers, Right Sector's members were prominent in a number of radical actions, commencing with an attack on Ministry of Internal Affairs (MVS) police and *Berkut* on December 1, on which date a bulldozer was deployed close to the presidential administration. On January 19, Right Sector led an assault on police at Hrushevskyi Street. During attacks, members used Molotov cocktails as well as incendiary devices, which they flung into the ranks of police forces. The extremists rejected the conciliatory tactics of politicians like Klychko and Yatsenyuk, who they regarded as cowardly and inflamed the confrontation on several critical occasions.[6]

The EU finally returned to active involvement. On February 21, 2014, as the EU agreed to introduce sanctions against Ukrainian leaders, the foreign ministers of Poland (Radoslaw Sikorski), France (Laurent Fabius), and Germany (Frank-Walter Steinmeier) arrived in Kyiv. Working into the night, they brokered a deal between the government and the three parliamentary opposition leaders. It would have introduced a temporary administration, constitutional reforms to be introduced by September to reduce the powers of the presidency—returning to the situation as it was in 2004—and new presidential and parliamentary elections by the end of the year. The opposition was to cease using "forceful measures" and the government would not apply a state of emergency. Government buildings and occupied squares in cities across Ukraine were to be vacated. The stipulation, which was supported by the United States, was that in the interim, Yanukovych would remain as president.[7] That provision proved unacceptable to those on the Maidan. Russia, which was present at the discussions, declined to sign the agreement, but would refer constantly to the

6   "Chto takoe 'Pravyi Sektor': fakty i domysly o radikalnoi organizatsii [Just what is 'Right Sector': Facts and Speculation about this Radical Organization]," *112.UA*, January 23, 2014, http://112.ua/analityka/chto-takoe-pravyy-sektor-13388.html (accessed August 18, 2014).
7   "21 lyutoho ts.r. u Kyiv pidpysano Uhodu z vrehylyuvannya kryzy v Ukraini [On February 21, an agreement was signed in Kyiv to end the crisis in Ukraine]," *Ministry of Foreign Affairs of Ukraine*, February 21, 2014, http://mfa.gov.ua/ua/press-center/news/18110-21-lyutogo-cr-u-kijevi-pidpisano-ugodu-z-vregulyuvannya-krizi-v-ukrajini (accessed August 19, 2014).

failed agreement thereafter as evidence of the uncompromising attitude of the protesters.

In the center of Kyiv, the situation began to resemble the final scene of the musical *Les Miserables*, with barricades piled high, burning tires that set off thick black smoke, and the accumulation of a variety of weapons— mostly Molotov cocktails, but some guns and clubs. The struggle was now for control of Ukraine. It ended with carnage and bloodshed, as the government—Yanukovych and Minister of Internal Affairs Vitalii Zakharchenko are usually cited—reportedly ordered troops to fire on protesters using live ammunition, situating snipers on rooftops who picked off targets at will. Other reports suggest that both Russian agents and opposition forces played roles in the massacre.[8] But perhaps the most authoritative account came from Hennadii Moskal, a lawyer and former Deputy Minister of Internal Affairs.

Moskal noted, inter alia, the involvement of SBU members in disguise on the Maidan. Snipers were given orders to fire not only on protesters, but also on militia. The goal was to escalate the conflict and justify a forceful "cleansing" of the square. The security forces were already demoralized and unwilling to fight. Two operations were prepared, called "Wave" and "Boomerang." There were several groups of snipers including Alfa forces of the SBU and the MVS special force "*Sokil*" [Falcon]. Only Defense Minister Zakharchenko had the authority to order the latter to use weapons, something he admitted to doing, according to Moskal, in his statement of February 20. Alfa were under the control of head of the SBU Oleksandr Yakymenko. The permission to activate the two operations, however, was ordered personally by President Yanukovych. Moskal dismisses claims that a third force of "foreigners" (presumably Russians) was involved as an attempt to whitewash the actions of the SBU and MVS. It is clearly established, in his view, that the snipers were in combat positions when people were killed and the evidence was later destroyed or else removed to Russia.[9]

---

8 BBC reporter Daniel Sandford is cited in this source as stating that the first victims he saw were members of police forces. Interim Interior Minister Arsen Avakov declared that twelve members of the *Berkut* were suspects in the deaths of seventeen victims. See Daniel Sandford, "Ukraine Crisis: What we Know about the Snipers," *BBC*, April 3, 2014, http://www.bbc.com/news/world-europe-26866069 (accessed August 18, 2014).

9 "'Snaipery otrymaly vid vlady vkazivku rozstrilyuvaty ne lyshe protestuyuchykh, ale i militsioneriv'—Moskal ['Snipers received orders from the government to shoot not

It was the moment of no return. The number of dead approached 100; hundreds more were wounded, many severely. But the assault, remarkably, failed and the protesters remained in place. The immediate outcome was the flight of the president and most of his Cabinet. The government of Ukraine fell on February 22. On the previous evening Yanukovych had fled the capital from his opulent Mezhyhirya residence (it later became a tourist attraction), first to Kharkiv, and ultimately to Russia, where he has remained, used alternatively as a symbol of Russia's position that the government in Ukraine is illegal, and as a pawn in Vladimir Putin's strategy for the neighboring country, but not one that was considered a likely catalyst of anything decisive. Putin has never had much time for Yanukovych. The former president maintained that he had been removed by a coup d'état, though an analysis published in January 2015 suggests, quite feasibly, that he was abandoned by his security forces and left with no alternative but to depart.[10] His departure was reportedly not premeditated, though it took several days to remove his goods.[11]

Ukraine selected a temporary president, appointed by a parliament in which many deputies of the Party of Regions had abandoned their affiliation with the former incumbent. The acting president was the new parliamentary speaker, Oleksandr Turchynov, a 49-year old economist from *Batkivshchyna* Party. Yulia Tymoshenko was freed, also on February 22, and declared her intention to run for president, though reactions to her on the Maidan, where her photograph had featured on the huge Christmas tree for weeks, were mixed as some protesters linked her with the "old regime." New presidential elections were brought forward from December 2014—as agreed to in the deal between the old government, the opposi-

only the protesters, but the police'—Moskal]," *Prestupnosty.net*, March 11, 2014, https://news.pn/ua/politics/98896 (accessed August 19, 2014). Other sources disagree with this analysis and claim that the instigators of the massacre were members of the protest movement. See, for example, Ivan Katchanovski, "The 'Snipers' Massacre on the Maidan in Ukraine," https://www.academia.edu/8776021/The_Snipers_Massacre_on_the_Maidan_in_Ukraine (accessed November 23, 2014).

10 Andrew Higgins and Andrew E. Kramer, "Ukraine Leader Was Defeated Even Before He Was Ousted," *The New York Times*, January 3, 2015, http://www.nytimes.com/2015/01/04/world/europe/ukraine-leader-was-defeated-even-before-he-was-ousted.html?smid=fb-share&_r=0 (accessed January 4, 2015).

11 "Yanukovich prinjal reshenie bezhat iz Kyiva posle dvukh zvonkov—Malomuzh [Yanukovych decided to flee Kyiv after two calls]," *Delo.ua*, July 24, 2014, http://delo.ua/ukraine/janukovich-prinjal-reshenie-bezhat-iz-kieva-posle-dvuh-zvonkov-m-242434/ (accessed August 18, 2014).

tion, and EU leaders—to May 25. The frontrunner from the outset was an oligarch, chocolate manufacturer Petro Poroshenko who, according to analyst Taras Kuzio, one of the authors in this volume, is a political chameleon.[12]

In contrast to the Orange Revolution, the president had been overthrown, only ten months ahead of the end of his term in office. Ukraine had entered a new phase in its development. Ostensibly, Euromaidan had resulted in a victory for the protesters. Russia, initially, was left on the sidelines, seemingly preoccupied with the Sochi Winter Olympic Games. The EU and the United States had also failed to influence the course of events in the later stages. The provisional government was making up rules as it proceeded. The *Svoboda* Party, still only a minor party in parliamentary elections took over three key positions in the Cabinet: Oleh Makhnitskiy as Prosecutor-General; Ihor Tenyukh, the former Commander of the Ukrainian Navy, as Minister of Defense; and Oleksandr Sich as Vice Prime Minister (subordinate to the Deputy Prime Minister). Of the three, only Sych remained in place after the election of Poroshenko as president. Threats from anti-Maidan elements to split the country initially proved futile. The Right Sector, as noted an integral part of the more violent aspects of the Euromaidan, was removed from its headquarters in the central Kyiv Dnipro Hotel by the Ukrainian police after a shooting incident.[13] Essentially, despite the handful of rightists, the Cabinet was dominated by members of *Batkivshchyna* Party, which had finished second to the Party of Regions in the previous elections.[14]

Revolutions are never black and white; they all have shades of gray. The Euromaidan was no exception. The innocence of its first days was very different from February 20–21, the most violent days in the history of independent Ukraine. The country removed some of the legacies of

---

12 See the YouTube interview with Taras Kuzio at "Beware of Petro Poroshenko, a serial flip-flopper," *Kyivpost.com*, March 29, 2014, http://www.kyivpost.com/opinion/op-ed/taras-kuzio-beware-of-petro-poroshenko-a-serial-flip-flopper-video-341313.html (accessed August 19, 2014).

13 Some details can be found at "Avakov: 'Pravyi Sektor' vyishov z hotelyu 'Dnipro' bez zbroi [Avakov: 'Right Sector left the Hotel 'Dnipro' unarmed]," *BBCUkraina*, April 1, 2014, http://www.bbc.co.uk/ukrainian/politics/2014/04/140401_kyiv_fire_arr est_dk.shtml (accessed August 19, 2014).

14 "Karty pro parlamentski vybory 2012 po dilnytsyakh [Maps of the 2012 Parliamentary Elections according to districts]," http://statistika.in.ua/vybory2012/ (accessed August 19, 2014).

1991—a Donetsk-based regime of apparatchiks and gangsters with their own private mansions and assets abroad—but it was by no means clear that the interim government could offer unity and compromise. The financial crisis of late February was much worse than it had been in late November. Russia had as expected withdrawn the loan offered to Yanukovych. And it was at this stage that Vladimir Putin decided to make a retaliatory move against what he perceived as a Western-directed coup d'état in Ukraine.

Euromaidan entered its second phase on February 27, when armed units in uniforms without markings took over the Crimean parliament and government buildings in Simferopol. They installed a new prime minister, Sergey Aksionov, whose party had received only about 4% in the most recent Crimean elections. Only forty-seven deputies were present during his "election" meaning that it was well short of a quorum.[15] Troops, who were supplemented by the 25,000 sailors of the Russian Black Sea Fleet, took over government buildings and military installations, forcing the surprised Ukrainian units to surrender. The Ukrainians did not respond with force, and the attackers (later clearly identified as Russians) did not suffer any losses during the takeover. The annexation of Crimea was solidified by a referendum on March 16,[16] during which it was reported that over 96% supported the peninsula joining the Russian Federation[17]—the alternative on the ballot, confusingly, would have led to the re-adoption of the Constitution adhered to briefly in 1992.

Russia and Ukraine then engaged in a war of words about what was happening. The Ukrainians, backed by most of the democratic world (USA, Canada, and most of the EU countries) and the UN, maintained that Russia had invaded their territory, violating international treaties signed in Budapest in 1994 and Kyiv in 1997, the latter a treaty of friendship and coop-

---

15 Dmitriy Volchek, "Premer po klichke 'Goblin' [A premier nicknamed 'Goblin']," *RadioSvoboda*, March 1, 2014, http://www.svoboda.org/content/article/25281940.html (accessed August 19, 2014).

16 Details of the organization of the election can be found at "V Krymu 16 Marta na referendum vynesut vopros o vkhozhdenii v RF [The March 16 referendum will ask the question about joining the Russian Federation]," *ZN.UA*, March 6, 2014, http://zn.ua/POLITICS/v-krymu-16-marta-na-referendum-vynesut-vopros-o-vhozh denii-v-rf-140498.html (accessed August 19, 2014).

17 See "Krym vybral Rossiyu [Crimea has chosen Russia]," *Gazeta.ru*, March 15, 2014, http://www.gazeta.ru/politics/2014/03/15_a_5951217.shtml (accessed August 19, 2014).

eration between the two states that agreed to existing boundaries. This treaty had been revised by the 2010 Kharkiv Accords, which had extended Russia's lease on the Sevastopol base for the fleet for a further twenty-five years (i.e. from 2017 to 2042). In return Russia agreed to a rent of $100 million per year as well as to provide discounts to Ukraine for purchases of Russian gas.[18] Russian president Putin officially revoked the 2010 treaty. The Russian version of events, soon to be propagated by a barrage of propaganda, was that an illegal pro-Nazi junta had taken over Ukraine and was persecuting Russians and Russian speakers.

Aside from sanctions and travel bans, however, the Western response to events was somewhat subdued. US president Barack Obama ruled out any form of military response to Russian intrusions into Ukraine.[19] Russia amassed a large military force on Ukraine's borders and was believed to have some involvement in the mass disturbances in several Ukrainian cities. Small groups of around 200 people began to take over administrative buildings in Donetsk and Luhansk and erected barricades around them. They later declared the formation of autonomous republics. A similar attempt in Kharkiv failed. Russian political leaders expressed their support for the introduction of a "federal system" in Ukraine, including in talks with United States. Ukraine's richest oligarch Rinat Akhmetov supported this position, with the proviso that Donbas should remain in Ukraine.[20] It might be termed a form of "Finlandization."

Thus Ukraine found itself in a critically unstable position and the threat of a Russian invasion of the mainland seemed quite serious. Its interim leadership acted cautiously and timidly, albeit insisting that Russia had no right to make demands on Ukraine as to its form of government. Though in the long term, international sanctions imposed by United States and the

---

18 The text of the document can be found at "Dohovir Yanukovycha i Medvedyeva pro bazuvannya flotu do 2042 roku. Tekst dokumentu [Agreement between Yanukovych and Medvedev about the basing of the Fleet until 2042. Text of the Document]," *Ukrainska Pravda*, April 22, 2014, http://www.pravda.com.ua/articles/2010/04/22/4956018 (accessed August 20, 2014).

19 Katie Zezima, "Obama—No Military Excursion in Ukraine", *Washington Post*, March 19, 2014, http://www.washingtonpost.com/blogs/post-politics/wp/2014/03/19/obama-no-military-excursion-in-ukraine/ (accessed August 20, 2014).

20 See the video feed at http://ukrstream.tv/en/videos/zvierniennia_rinata_akhmietova_shchaslivii_donbas_v_iedinii_ukrayini#.U_PppbySxss. The statement established the position of Ukraine's richest man as one supporting a unified, rather than federated or divided, Ukraine and at the same time distanced him from the anti-Kyiv separatists.

European Union may imperil Russia's energy-centered economy, in the short term, there was no doubt that Putin's position was the more powerful in the spring of 2014. The West was unable to predict his next move and NATO was belatedly bolstering its position in the eastern borderland member states. What was the Russian president's thinking in escalating an international crisis? Why did a politician, whom many considered to be a rational actor, choose to intervene in Ukraine?

Analyzing the mind of the Russian president is not a simple task. His statements are often contradictory. He maintains, for example, that Ukraine's new leaders should have adhered to the deal brokered by the European foreign ministers on February 21 that would have entailed former President Viktor Yanukovych remaining in office until new presidential elections in December 2014. Yet, as we have noted, Russia took no part in that discussion nor did it sign that agreement, and perhaps even more significant, it has not advocated the return of Yanukovych, despite the fact that the latter has fled to Russian territory. Putin also maintained that there had been no invasion of Crimea. The forces were simply volunteers who had acquired Russian weapons and wore uniforms without insignia.

Much has been said and written in Western circles about violations of international law. But President Putin maintains that because of the collapse of the EU-brokered deal, and the formation of a government in Ukraine based on mob rule by neo-Nazis, Russia was no longer bound by the terms of the 1994 Budapest Memorandum, by which Russia, the United States, and the United Kingdom committed themselves to guaranteeing the security of Ukraine. Presumably that statement also applies to the 1997 Treaty of Friendship between Ukraine and Russia, which divided the Black Sea Fleet and ended the impasse over the port of Sevastopol, both of which were cited earlier. It may also pertain to the agreement of November 1990, when Russia's first president recognized the borders of Ukraine; and even the Belavezha Agreement of December 1991 that effectively ended the Soviet Union. None of these agreements, of course, bore the signature of Vladimir Vladimirovich Putin.

In essence, according to this line of reasoning, the Euromaidan leaders, following the lead of extremist pro-Nazi forces, had carried out a coup. Yet Yanukovych had lost his majority support in the Ukrainian parliament as many of the Party of Regions deputies deserted to the opposition. Moreover, although the Right Sector had played a prominent role in some of the more radical actions, its influence overall was relatively small, as became evident from the results of the May presidential elections. When combined with *Svoboda*, it failed to break 1% of the electoral vote.[21] Thus insofar as its actions had been decisive, it lacked support to take over the government. In many respects it appeared quite dissatisfied with the results of the protests. On the other hand, and taking into account the fact that it was very difficult for voters to go to the polls in the Donbas region, the "pro-Russian" votes had fallen to a new low. The majority of voters now seemed oriented toward Europe and the EU, and for a Ukrainian future away from the Russian-lead Customs Union.[22]

Putting these illogicalities aside, what else do we know about Putin's thinking on the situation in Ukraine? What can have prompted him to flout the Budapest Memorandum and perpetuate and give new credibility to the old canard of Russian aggression against Ukraine? If we assume for the moment that we are inside Putin's head,[23] then the logic might run something like the following.

The Western powers, in his view, had refused to accept Yanukovych's decision not to sign the Association Agreement with the European Union in November 2013 in Vilnius. That decision, it will be recalled, came after Putin's meeting with the Ukrainian president in Moscow on November 9. Thus, outraged, they financed and openly supported a mass protest in the streets of Kyiv during which violent protesters, organized by nationalist extremists, set afire their own police with Molotov cocktails. As evidence of US involvement the Russian leadership could cite the following: US Ambassador to Ukraine Geoffrey Pyatt and Victoria Nuland were overheard in a phone conversation choosing the next government of Ukraine; and Senator John McCain appeared in the Maidan, standing, outrageously, alongside the *Svoboda* leader Oleh Tyahnybok, a man whom even Yush-

---

21 The main results of the election can be found at "TsVK oholosyla Poroshenka prezydentom Ukrainy [The Central Election Commission announced Poroshenko as the president of Ukraine]," *UNIAN*, June 2, 2014, http://www.unian.ua/politics/924 621-tsvk-ogolosila-poroshenka-prezidentom-ukrajini.html (accessed August 20, 2014).
22 See, for example, the analysis of the elections at http://h.ua/story/404229/ (accessed August 20, 2014).
23 One scholar who has tried to do this consistently is Stephen F. Cohen, Professor Emeritus at Princeton University, whose writings have sometimes been met with anger and derision on the part of other Western analysts. A typical example is http://www.thenation.com/article/180942/new-cold-war-and-necessity-patriotic-heresy (accessed August 20, 2014).

chenko had thrown out of Our Ukraine over a decade ago for his racist views on Russians and Jews.[24]

Once the insurgents had attained the removal of Yanukovych, they elected their own government composed mainly of supporters of Euromaidan, and one devoid of any members of the Regions or Communist Parties, the parties traditionally supported by Russian-speaking Eastern Ukrainians. Moreover, the interim Cabinet promptly banned the controversial language law that had permitted Russian-speaking parts of Ukraine to conduct business in their own language.[25] The "Fascist" leaders in Kiev had declared war on Russian and Russian-speaking residents of Ukraine and over the past twenty years had managed to establish only a "pseudo-democratic" system.[26] Thus might run the position taken by Russian President Putin in late February 2014.

But to understand fully Putin's perspective, one would need to delve deeper. Here is a politician that would fit neatly into what Lenin perceived as the Russian chauvinist of 1922 when the Soviet Union was first forming: an adherent of the view that Kyiv—or more correctly Kiev—is the ancestral and founding city of the Rus', the East Slavic nation that accepted Christianity in 988 and eventually divided into three component parts of the same family: Russians, Ukrainians, and Belarusians, united also by the Russian Orthodox Church.[27] On several visits to Ukraine over the past few years,

24 Nuland also used a vulgarity with regard to the European Union in a telephone conversation with US ambassador to Ukraine Geoffrey Pyatt that was recorded. See "Nuland Denies U.S. Training Ukraine Militants, Suggests Aid Possible," *RFE/RL*, February 7, 2014, http://www.rferl.org/content/nuland-ukraine-russia-protests/25256 496.html (accessed August 18, 2014). On McCain's meeting with Tiahnybok, see "Far-right group at heart of Ukraine protests meet US senator," *Channel 4 News*, December 16, 2013, http://www.channel4.com/news/ukraine-mccain-far-right-svo boda-anti-semitic-protests (accessed August 18, 2014).

25 This ban was soon lifted. However, on March 3, Acting President Turchynov announced that he would not sign the decree banning the language law. See "Turchynov pidtverdzhyie, shcho ne pidpyshe skasuvannia movnoho zakonu [Turchynov confirms he will not change the language law]," *RadioSvoboda.ua*, March 3, 2014, http://ww w.radiosvoboda.org/content/article/25284231.html (accessed August 20, 2014).

26 See "Putin vystavil ukraintsev fashistami, a sebya—Iley Muromtsem [Putin exposes Ukrainian fascists, and himself—Iley Muomtsem]," *Inotv*, May 13, 2014, http://russian.rt.com/inotv/2014-05-13/Putina-vistavil-ukraincev-fashistami-a (accessed August 20, 2014).

27 This was the official position of the historical past of Russia, Belarus, and Ukraine during the Soviet period. It should be added that the antithetical view, as expressed by historian Mykhailo Hrushevskyi, that Ukraine has a continuous and clearly dis-

Putin has made it plain that in his view, Ukraine is not a foreign country. One can take that further—in his view it is not even a country, but rather, to cite what Metternich wrote about Italy in 1849, a "geographical expression." It is an anomaly that derived from what the Russian leader perceives as the greatest tragedy in history: the collapse of the Soviet Union in 1991.

During Putin's visit to Kyiv in late July 2013 for the 1025th anniversary of the establishment of Christianity in Rus', he made reference to the Treaty of Pereyaslav in 1654, when Russia and the Ukrainian Cossacks under Bohdan Khmelnytskyi signed a treaty in a war against the Poles.[28] Ironically, it was on the 300th anniversary of that treaty that Nikita Khrushchev, in what some sources have described as a drunken moment, chose to give Crimea to Ukraine as a "gift" from Russia. It is of course quite reasonable to give a prized possession to one's brother. But if that brother subsequently leaves home and then renounces all family ties (Ukraine in 1991), then the gift becomes a theft.

For Putin, Crimea, and especially its port of Sevastopol, is sacred Russian soil. The port survived two great sieges after its conquest in 1783: one in the Crimean War of 1853–56; and another during the "Great Patriotic War" of 1941–45 against Hitler. Sevastopol was one of the original Hero Cities designated by Stalin in May 1945, alongside Leningrad, Stalingrad, and Odesa—many others were added subsequently as well as a new designation in the Putin era, "Cities of Military Glory." Equally important Crimea is the one place in Ukraine that he can claim is ethnically Russian—though that perception implies a striking lack of recognition for the rights of the Crimean Tatars, deported by Stalin at the end of the war and still struggling for their rights today.[29]

But I think we must delve further. Russia's intrusions went beyond Crimea even in early March. Russian forces occupied a gas factory in the Kherson region on the Ukrainian mainland. Unknown gangs began to take

---

cernible historical past dating back to Kyivan Rus', and thus some ten centuries of history during its national development, seems equally flawed.

28 Kira Latukhina, "Vladimir Putin prinyal uchastie v prazdnovaniy yubileya Kreshcheniya Rusi [Vladimir Putin participated in the celebration of the anniversary of the Baptism of Rus']," *RG.RU*, July 29, 2013, http://www.rg.ru/2013/07/27/kreshenie-site.html (accessed August 20, 2014).

29 See, for example, David Marples and David F. Duke, "Crimean Tatars—tragic past and uncertain present," *ODr Russia and Beyond*, March 3, 2014, https://www.opendemocracy.net/od-russia/david-marples/who-are-crimean-tatars-tragic-past-and-uncertain-present (accessed August 20, 2014).

over the headquarters of the Donetsk security forces. There were clashes in Kharkiv, and further signs of trouble brewing in Luhansk and Odesa. In fact the only secure parts of Ukraine were the capital Kyiv and the western regions—what was once known as Right-Bank Ukraine west of the Dnipro River that divides the country more or less into two equal halves.

Russia had intervened in Moldova in 1992, where the breakaway pro-Russian region called Transnistria has survived for more than twenty years, unrecognized by most of the world. Russia has also ensured the survival for more than six years of two regions of Georgia, which declared independence after a war in 2008 in which Russia also intervened, South Ossetia and Abkhazia. It is thus playing the role of a regional power in what it terms the "Near Abroad," i.e. the republics formed from the old Soviet Union. And there have been fears, particularly among Western analysts, that it wishes to go much further in securing the rights of large enclaves of Russians wherever they live, including Latvia, Estonia, and northern Kazakhstan, and that Western powers lack the will and resolve to prevent it.[30]

But this redressing of old wounds is based on at best a misreading—deliberate or otherwise—of history. One could equally point to the anomaly of Kaliningrad region, a Russian enclave deep behind the borders of the European Union. Or to the rights of several regions of Russia that were ridden over roughshod since Putin came to power in 2000, including not only the well-known ones like Chechnya and Ingushetiya, but the extremely rich Tatarstan and Sakha (formerly known as Yakutiya) in eastern Siberia—the latter comprises about 20% of Russian territory. In the summer of 2014, various marches in support of the federalization of Siberia were halted by Russian police, which prevented gatherings in parks and squares. The main organizer was reportedly arrested.[31] Putin's Russia is extremely sensitive to such calls within its own federation. By raising the issue of the rights of Crimea in 1992, Russia has also reminded its own citizens of some of its past dubious constitutional maneuvers.

---

30 See, for example, Richard Rozwadowski, "Putin is not going to stop," *KyivPost*, August 19, 2014, https://www.kyivpost.com/opinion/op-ed/richard-rozwadowski-putin-is-not-going-to-stop-361144.html (accessed August 20, 2014).

31 "Politsiya Rossii sorvala marshi za federalizatsiyu Sibiri [Russian police disrupted marches for the federalization of Siberia]," *LigaNovosti*, August 17, 2014, http://news.liga.net/news/world/2957734-politsiya_rossii_sorvala_marshi_za_federalizatsiyu_sibiri_.htm (accessed August 20, 2014).

The responses of the international community and Ukraine appeared confused and muted. Both the EU and United States have applied sanctions on individuals, and some institutions. President Barack Obama, in what can only be described as an unfortunate moment in his leadership, declared openly that the United States would not use military force in Ukraine.[32] With that statement, he effectively provided Putin with affirmation that the conquest of Crimea was secure and that the US would not respond to further adventurism on his part.

The Ukrainian government essentially was in transition during this period. Thus the old regime had disappeared, but there was no clarity as to its replacement. The temporary President Oleksandr Turchynov, the Speaker of the Parliament, lacked leadership skills and was a stopgap figure. The more dynamic Prime Minister, the then-38-year old Arsenii Yatsenyuk, is an economist from a family of professors. He was linked with former Prime Minister Yulia Tymoshenko and the *Batkivshchyna* Party but had never been a nationally popular figure. The people who guided Ukraine through its most difficult days—they also included Acting Foreign Minister Andrii Deshchytsia—might be described as "unwilling revolutionaries." They were prepared to assist their country, but they had not been elected.

The interim Cabinet was a mixture of centrist and right-wing politicians with a large proportion from western Ukraine, almost none from Donetsk (the region that dominated and controlled the previous cabinet), and devoid of members from two political parties that decided not to take part in it: the Party of Regions—formerly the largest and most powerful party in Ukraine; and *UDAR*, led by Klychko. Presidential elections took place in late May and brought a businessman (Petro Poroshenko) to the presidency. The country was almost bankrupt, its army barely mobile, and its new leaders initially could do little but respond with angry rhetoric to each new move by the Russians. The survival of Ukraine as a viable independent nation seemed very much in question.

In this sense, assuming that his purpose was to destabilize an adversary and halt the progress of Euromaidan, Vladimir Putin had attained a series of resounding successes, and unsurprisingly his popularity in Russia rose to its highest in three years, at more than 71%, as is often the case

---

32 Michael D. Shear, "Obama Rules Out Military Force Over Ukraine," *The New York Times*, March 20, 2014, http://www.nytimes.com/2014/03/21/world/europe/obama-ukraine.html (accessed August 18, 2014).

when a political leader conducts a small but victorious war against an infe-
rior foe.[33] Moreover, the choice of Crimea was apposite since aside from
the Crimean Tatars, most of the population might have supported Russian
rule even in a referendum that was free and fair. Indeed there have been
earlier calls for referenda by local politicians starting in the early 1990s.

Yet what was also clear is that nothing in Vladimir Putin's world would
ever be the same. His moves could not be reversed. He had destroyed any
illusions that Western statespersons might have once held about him, including George W. Bush (who famously looked into his eyes and saw his
soul) and Angela Merkel. The newly released Yulia Tymoshenko, as presidential candidate, declared that she would remove the Russian Black Sea
Fleet from Sevastopol at the earliest opportunity and denounce the Kharkiv
Accords—a statement more important for its sentiment that potential reality. Putin seemed to have taken Russia back into the sort of isolated Sla-
vophilism that once prevailed in the 19th century.[34] The man who was nom-
inated for a Nobel Peace Prize for his plan to scrap Syria's chemical
weapons[35] will surely not be on the next list of potential recipients in Oslo.

Moreover, he has managed to convince doubters of what some "Moscow skeptics" have tried to claim for years: that Russia in essence has retained its imperialist outlook, and is a predatory state that seeks to swallow
its neighbors: that it operates less like Russia and more like *Rossiya*, seeking to regain its lost empire through the creation of integrationist schemes
such as the Eurasian Economic Community.[36] Such comments before

33 "Reyting Vladimira Putina dostig samoy vysokoy otmetki za tri goda [Vladimir
Putin's approval rating hits three year high]," *Peterburgskiy Dnevnik*, March 13,
2014, http://www.spbdnevnik.ru/news/2014-03-13/reyting-putina-dostig-samoy-vys
okoy-otmetki-za-tri-goda/ (accessed August 20, 2014). It continued to rise, despite
increasing difficulties in the summer of 2014, reaching a record 87% by early August. See "Reyting populyarnosti Putina vykhodit na rekordno vysokiy uroven v
87% [Putin's popular approval reaches high of 87%]," *inoSMI.ru*, August 8, 2014,
http://inosmi.ru/russia/20140808/222247845.html (accessed August 20, 2014).
34 "Tymoshenko rozpovila pro pershi kroky pislya vyboriv prezydenta [Tymoshenko
spoke about the first steps after the presidential election]," *Tyzhden.ua*, March 4,
2014, http://tyzhden.ua/News/104031 (accessed August 20, 2014).
35 See http://www.huffingtonpost.com/2014/03/05/putin-nobel-prize_n_4904768.html
(accessed November 23, 2014).
36 See, for example, Vladimir Socor, "Russia Preparing to Buy Allies Through Anti-
Crisis Assistance," *Eurasia Daily Monitor* 6, no. 27, February 10, 2009, http://www.j
amestown.org/single/?tx_ttnews%5Btt_news%5D=34484&no_cache=1#.U_Qp0ryS
xss (accessed August 20, 2014). The author is one of the leading proponents of this
perspective.

2014 sounded far-fetched. Putin single-handedly has succeeded in giving weight to even the most outlandish of such claims.

Perhaps such policies worked in Chechnya in 2000 and Georgia in 2008; they seem doomed to fail in the long term in Ukraine because for once, the Russian president followed his heart rather than his head. Ukraine's residents may or may not be disturbed by the events of November-February in Kyiv; but there is no evidence whatsoever that more than a handful of residents sought or welcomed a Russian invasion. Perhaps more to the point, there has been no indication that the interim Ukrainian government had targeted Russian-speakers for persecution. Even the controversial language law, which was repealed after the Kyiv events, was quickly reinstalled giving Russians language rights in areas where they constitute more than 10% of the population.

To return to Euromaidan, the departure of Yanukovych from Kyiv represented its culmination point. The barricades remained in place and were only removed from the capital in August 2014 and it also became in part a commemorative site for those who died there, who were christened "the heavenly hundred." In one sense it had succeeded, namely the departure of the president and some of his Cabinet, but success cannot be measured so simply because its goals were changing and never expressly stated. It represented the wishes of a new generation of Ukrainians who are oriented toward Europe and sought to break the old ties with the former Soviet countries (other than the Baltic States) and avoid integration with Russia, whether in the Customs Union or other structures. Again, however, it is difficult to assert that such was a clear goal of all participants, as many joined in response to particular events and measures.

The goal of this book is to offer new interpretations of events that comprise a genuine 21st century revolution. Some of the contributors were on the square and took an active role on a regular basis, others visited Euromaidan at various times, still others watched from afar or from neighboring states. Likewise some were and remain emotionally involved in the events, others began as political analysts but became increasingly connected with civil activists in the Maidan, and still others remained on the sidelines observing history being made. Thus not every author can be said to offer a truly objective approach and that fact should surprise no one. It is far too much to ask when one's country appears to be in danger of disappearing from the map of Europe as was the case for Ukraine at several junctures in the tumultuous 2014 year. The book has no claim to be a definitive account, and no doubt it has its deficiencies, like any other publication. Nonetheless, it can be argued that this is a unique collection of papers that provide valuable and essential insights into events. It is also one that comprises—as it turned out, since this was not a goal from the outset—the contributions of mainly younger scholars: PhD students, newly minted PhDs, and younger professors. Just as Euromaidan represented in part a movement of a younger generation away from the former Soviet sphere, so also the collection represents the opinions of many younger Ukrainian scholars and researchers, together with scholars from the West. Together these chapters provide a detailed and intriguing portrayal of one of the 21st century's great civil uprisings, one that continues to have repercussions, especially in Eastern Ukraine and Crimea.

Maidans Past and Present: Comparing the Orange Revolution and the Euromaidan

Olga Onuch

Introduction—Déjà Vu: a Ukrainian Revolution

It happened again! On November 21, 2013, Ukrainians began protesting. The, at first, small protests, triggered by the government's refusal to sign the EU-Ukraine Association Agreement, assumed the name Euromaidan. On November 24, the protests—organized by opposition political parties, student organizations, as well as long-time activists—grew in size to approximately 250,000 in Kyiv.[1] Tens of thousands of "ordinary" Ukrainians joined in Lviv (and across western Ukraine), and a few hundred to a few thousand joined in eastern and southern cities like Odesa, Simferopol, Kharkiv, and Sumy.[2] By December 1, it was estimated that up to 800,000 ordinary Ukrainians joined protest events in Kyiv, and even more when including those that protested in other cities across Ukraine, such as in Donetsk and Luhansk, both considered Yanukovych strongholds.

At first, the Euromaidan seemed like something we have seen before: the Orange Revolution. We returned to November 23, 2004, when observers of Ukrainian politics were shocked to witness a sea of ordinary Ukrainians, joined by activists and opposition party members, in a moment of mass mobilization.[3] While Ukraine had previously experienced several

---

1 Activists are more engaged and more formalized members of social movement organizations (SMOs). They are connected to activist networks, and as I and other scholars have defined them—they are "in the business of protest." An "ordinary" citizen can become an activist, but this is rather infrequent. Olga Onuch, *Mapping Mass Mobilizations: Understanding Revolutionary Moments in Ukraine and Argentina* (London: Palgrave Macmillan, 2014), 39–46.

2 "Ordinary" Ukrainians or "ordinary" citizens are used by the author to denote the non-activist, non-politicized citizens of a polity, who tend to be regularly disengaged from politics, other than when (and if) they vote in elections. Generally, they have not been active members of an SMO, nor have they consistently participated in previous protests. Included are individuals of all socio-economic, employment, and education levels. "Ordinary" citizens draws on Nancy Bermeo's (2003) use of the term "ordinary people." The term is used to avoid "the masses," "average people/citizens," or even "median voter," as they depict a different concept of actors.

3 Mass mobilizations are "proportionally larger than other protest events..." in which the balance of participation shifts away from activists...to a...majority made of 'ordi-

27

smaller protest events, such as those surrounding the 1986 Chornobyl disaster, the 1991 Revolution on the Granite, and the 2001 Ukraine Without
Kuchma protests, the sheer size of the 2004 protests, and the fact that the
majority of the protesters were ordinary Ukrainians was unprecedented.[4]
The protests were first heralded as a democratic awakening and a step
towards "Europeanization." After the election of the villain of the Orange
Revolution, Viktor Yanukovych, as president in 2010, however, academics
agreed that for a variety of reasons, including protest fatigue, Ukraine
would not soon see another mass mobilization.[5] Thus, when the November
2013 protests grew to 800,000 strong, political scientists returned to the
drawing board. Mass mobilization against an unrepresentative regime was
happening again, and again scholars did not see it coming. While it
seemed like *déjà vu,* the Euromaidan was very different, not least because
it was preceded by the events of 2004.

This formidable moment of mass mobilization quickly descended into
violence unprecedented in post-Soviet Ukraine. Like the prying open of
Pandora's box, the Euromaidan protests divided the country, creating opportunities for radical voices—on both sides of the spectrum—to take center stage. As of summer 2014, the crisis included the annexation of Crimea
by the Russian Federation, the rise of Russian-sponsored guerrilla-
separatist conflicts in eastern Ukraine—which military experts interviewed
defined as a low level war—and a presidential election plagued by violence
and a record low[6] turnout of 59.48% (national average excluding Donbas
where the estimated turnout was 20%).[7] Thus, when a moment of mass

---

nary' citizens." Mass mobilizations involve broad cross-sections of society and "are
moreextemporaneous...undirected and lack a clear leadership." Onuch, *Mapping
Mass Mobilizations*, 3–4.

4   Ibid.

5   Adam Meirowitz and Joshua A. Tucker, "People Power or a One-Shot Deal? A Dynamic Model of Protest," *American Journal of Political Science* 57, no. 2 (2013):
478–90.

6   The first round average voter turnout for presidential elections since independence
is 73.2% and 74.0% for first and second rounds. In 1991, 1994, 1999, 2004, and
2010 first round turnout was 84.2%, 70.4%, 70.1%, 74.5%, and 67.0% respectively.
In 1994, 1999, 2004, and 2010 second round turnout was 71.6%, 74.9%, 81.1%,
and 69.0% respectively. (all turnout data taken from Central Election Commission,
Presidential Election Reports, 1991–2014. (Kyiv, Ukraine, 2014),
http://www.cvk.gov.ua (accessed August 25, 2014).

7   Ibid. Michel Chossudovsky, "Ukraine Presidential Elections. Low Turn-Out. Poroshenko Declares Victory," *Global Research*, May 25, 2014, http://www.globalre
search.ca/ukraine-presidential-elections-low-turn-out-poroshenko-declares-

mobilization like the Euromaidan surprises the academe, the regime, and even participants, we must first identify the temporal boundaries of the protest events, who participated in them, how, and why? Moreover, as the events and outcomes of the 2004 and 2013–14 mass mobilizations in Ukraine were so different, it is necessary to place Euromaidan into comparative perspective and through process tracing to identify how the two protest movements were similar and different.[8] This chapter is the first attempt to tackle systematically the different aspects of mobilization for the case of the Euromaidan, and compare it against a previous case of mobilization that ended peacefully and resulted in relative stability, the Orange Revolution.

Outline

This chapter aims to analyze and contextualize critically the Euromaidan as a case of mass protest, by comparing it to the Orange Revolution. First, it will briefly outline the data used. Second, it will highlight some key writing on mobilization and activism in Ukraine, and will identify potential contributions of this analysis to the literature. The majority of the text will assess the Euromaidan mobilization. Employing interview and focus group data that I collected, we will compare and contrast the parameters and trajectories of two protest waves, including their duration, location, and geographical diffusion. This study will also compare the central actors involved in the mobilization process and their main claims. At each step, this chapter will explore the differences and similarities between the 2004 and 2013–14 mass mobilizations. Finally, once the main boundaries of the mobilization have been mapped out, the chapter will address the recent focus of the

---

victory/5383777 (accessed September 2, 2014). Gwendolyn Sasse, "The Only Chance to Rebuild Ukraine," *Carnegie Europe*, May 6, 2014, http://www.carnegie europe.eu/strategiceurope/?fa=55508 (accessed September 2, 2014).

8 This chapter uses process-tracing methodology to analyze its data. Such an approach was influenced by Beissinger in his study of *Nationalist Mobilization and the Collapse of the Soviet State* (2002), and by methodological insights presented therein; Andrew Bennett, "Process Tracing and Causal Inference"; David Collier, "Understanding Process Tracing," *PS: Political Science & Politics* 44, no. 4 (2011): 823–30. Process-tracing includes meticulously identifying, tracing, mapping, and triangulating first-hand accounts, focus group materials and debates, and documentary evidence. The events and actors' participation were first traced in reverse, simultaneously mapping both the actors' interaction and cooperation, and the various stages of the mobilization process, until the origin of mass-mobilization was identified.

media and social scientists alike on the rise of the right, the use of violence, and the new role of social media in the Euromaidan mobilizations. This initial analysis seeks to provide a schema for larger studies of Euromaidan mobilizations and in the conclusion will highlight key hypotheses for future testing.

Methodology and Data

The empirical findings discussed below consist of data collected during two periods. The data were collected by the author and her team of research assistants between November 26, 2013, and July 24, 2014, in Kyiv, Ukraine. This includes data from on-site surveys (n=1475), rapid on-site interviews with protest participants, digital photos of slogans and posters held by protesters in the first four weeks of the protests, and twenty-one interviews and correspondences with activists, journalists, and politicians, including both opposition and regime insiders.[9] Due to the continuing nature of the crisis, interviewees have been anonymized, and I use Chatham House rules to protect the informants' identities. To provide the comparison, I rely on interview (n=98) and focus group (n=15) data collected between 2005 and 2010, covering the 2004 mass protests, past mobilizations, and activism in Ukraine.[10] Process tracing methodology was employed by the author to comparatively analyze the data.[11]

9   For more information about the survey, see: Olga Onuch, "Social Networks and Social Media in Ukrainian 'Euromaidan' Protests," *Washington Post*, January 2, 2014, http://www.washingtonpost.com/blogs/monkey-cage/wp/2014/01/02/social-networks -and-social-media-in-ukrainian-euromaidan-protests-2/ (accessed September 2, 2014); Olga Onuch, "The Puzzle of Mass Mobilization: Conducting Protest Research in Ukraine, 2004–2014," *Reviews & Critical Commentary: Council of Europe*, May 22, 2014, http://councilforeuropeanstudies.org/critcom/the-puzzle-of-mass-mobilization-conducting-protest-research-in-ukraine-2004–2014/ (accessed September 2, 2014); Olga Onuch, "'Who Were the Protesters?,'" *Journal of Democracy*, 2014.
10 For more information about the data, see: Olga Onuch, "Why Did They Join En Masse? Understanding 'ordinary' Ukrainians' Participation in Mass-Mobilisation in 2004," *New Ukraine/Nowa Ukraina*, no. 11 (2011): 89–113; Onuch, *Mapping Mass Mobilizations*.
11 For more on process tracing, see: Bennett, "Process Tracing and Causal Inference"; David Collier, "Process Tracing: Introduction and Exercises," *Beta Version*, September 22 (2010): 2010.

Contributing to the Literature on Ukrainian Activism and Protest

Ukrainian activism and mobilization is rarely examined until a mass protest occurs (be it in 2001, 2004, or 2013). Moreover, most analyses fail to provide either historical context or a comparative perspective. That said, there are several valuable studies on mobilization in Ukraine. I should note that this is far from, and is not intended to be, a conclusive list. Key studies include research on the Ukrainian labor movement,[12] women's movements,[13] and dissident activism.[14] Still, the vast majority of studies focusing on activism and protest in Ukraine have been limited to the Orange Revolution. I have argued elsewhere[15] that the three dominant types of studies of the Orange Revolution are those focusing on the role of intra-regional knowledge transfer,[16] those arguing that foreign actors helped finance, train, and or coordinate the activists, their organizations, and the protests,[17] and those that focus on the role of elites in both the formation of SMOs and in masterminding the protests.[18] Several recent studies have also attempted to problematize micro-level participation in Ukrainian mobilizations, but these have relied on perception based rather than experiential data, and we have previously been unable to get at the actual protest-

---

12 Stephen Crowley, *Hot Coal, Cold Steel: Russian and Ukrainian Workers from the End of the Soviet Union to the Post-Communist Transformations* (Ann Arbor: University of Michigan Press, 1997); David R. Marples, *Ukraine under Perestroika: Ecology, Economics and the Workers' Revolt* (New York: St. Martin's Press, 1991).

13 Alexandra Hrycak, "Foundation Feminism and the Articulation of Hybrid Feminisms in Post-Socialist Ukraine," *East European Politics & Societies* 20, no. 1 (2006): 69–100; Tamara Martsenyuk, "What Is The Maidan Talking About," 2005.

14 Yehven Zakharov, "History of Dissent in Ukraine," Virtual Museum, *Virtual Museum of the Dissident Movement in Ukraine*, (2004), http://archive.khpg.org/en/index.php?id=1127288239 (accessed September 2, 2014).

15 Onuch, *Mapping Mass Mobilizations*.

16 Beissinger 2007; Bunce and Wolchik 2007

17 Anders Åslund and Michael McFaul, *Revolution in Orange: The Origins of Ukraine's Democratic Breakthrough* (Brookings Institution Press, 2006); Michael McFaul, "Ukraine Imports Democracy: External Influences on the Orange Revolution," *International Security* 32, no. 2 (October 2007): 45–83; Andrew Wilson, "Ukraine's Orange Revolution, NGOs and the Role of the West," *Cambridge Review of International Affairs* 19, no. 1 (2006): 21–32.

18 Åslund and McFaul, *Revolution in Orange*; Paul D'Anieri, *Understanding Ukrainian Politics: Power, Politics, and Institutional Design*, (M.E. Sharpe Inc., 2006); Lucan Way, "The Real Causes of the Color Revolutions," *Journal of Democracy* 19, no. 3 (2008): 55–69.

ers when they are in the streets.[19] Recent survey work by the Ukrainian Protest Project, the Kyiv Institute of Strategic Studies, and a National Science Foundation-sponsored research team headed by Henry Hale at The George Washington University, will continue to fill this gap. This chapter combines and addresses the different above-noted perspectives on mobilization in Ukraine, and by doing so helps bridge empirical gaps. By comparing it to the Orange Revolution, this chapter will allow us to understand better not only the Euromaidan, but will also further elucidate the patterns and politics of mobilization in Ukraine. Perhaps, this will help us better understand why the Orange Revolution ended peacefully and why the Euromaidan resulted in a geopolitical crisis. First, we need to understand better the nature of the Euromaidan, and then we can contrast and compare it to the Orange Revolution.

What was the Euromaidan?

To facilitate a deep understanding of extra-institutional political behavior, activism, social mobilization, and democratization more broadly in Ukraine, it is crucial to address briefly a question central to our puzzle: what was the Euromaidan The 2013–14 Euromaidan was both an instance of mass mobilization and a wave of protest. Thus, there are, as is the case with most moments of mass mobilization, two separate phenomena that require our attention. The first is a longer mobilization *process* pursued by and one in which activists and the political opposition participated. The second, a simultaneous event in the case of the Euromaidan, was the phenomenon of a large protest, a moment of mass mobilization, in which "ordinary" citizens joined the activists in the streets *en masse*.

---

19 Mark R. Beissinger, "The Semblance of Democratic Revolution: Coalitions in Ukraine's Orange Revolution," *American Political Science Review* First View (2013): 1–19; David Lane, "The Orange Revolution: 'People's Revolution' or Revolutionary Coup?," *The British Journal of Politics & International Relations* 10, no. 4 (2008): 525–49; Meirowitz and Tucker, "People Power or a One-Shot Deal?"; Olga Onuch and Gilles Serra, "The Protest Calculus: Why Ordinary People Join-in Post-Electoral Protests?" (presented at the Oxford workshop: Comparing Transitions, Nuffield College, Oxford, UK, 2010); Onuch, "Why Did They Join En Masse?"; Onuch, *Mapping Mass Mobilizations*; Onuch, "'Who Were the Protesters?'"; Joshua A. Tucker, "Enough! Electoral Fraud, Collective Action Problems, and Post-Communist Colored Revolutions," *Perspectives on Politics* 5, no. 3 (2007): 535–551.

More Similar than Different, or Visa-Versa: the Euromaidan and Orange Revolution Compared

Several crucial points of similarity and difference exist between the Euromaidan and the Orange Revolution. First, we can compare the duration, location, and size of the protests. This will provide us with clarity as to what series of protest events the analysis refers.[20] The chapter will pay specific attention to how the 2004 and 2013–14 protest waves differed geographically. We will explore how, from the first weekend, the mobilization spread to regions that previously did not see any serious protest events; contrary to some media reports, protests were not confined to the center and west of the country. Secondly, we will discuss the different actors involved in the mobilization process, and identify their roles. Here, we will highlight how the composition of the protesters shifted throughout the different phases of the protests. Through process-tracing, which includes survey and interview data, we will explore which actors are perceived to have spearheaded protests and compare that to the actors who actually took the lead in the events of 2004 and 2013–14. We will also investigate how the role of SMOs differed during the two protests. Next, we will query the central demands, claims, and repertoires[21] employed by the protesters. While there has been much ado in the media about the role of Ukraine's nationalist right in the Euromaidan, this paper explores, using posters and signage from the protests, onsite rapid interviews, and focus group responses, whether "integral nationalists" received the same, more, or less support in 2013–14 than they did in 2004. Moreover, the dramatic and unprecedented use of violence will be clarified. Lastly, the use of new Information Communication Technologies (ICTs) and specifically the use of social media[22] in the 2013–14 protests will be problematized.

---

20 A series of connected protests are often referred to as a wave of protests.
21 Repertoires of contention refers to the set of protest-related tools and actions available to activists. Donatella Della Porta, "Repertoires of Contention," *The Wiley-Blackwell Encyclopedia of Social and Political Movements*; Charles Tilly, "Repertoires of Contention in America and Britain, 1750–1830"; Charles Tilly, *Regimes and Repertoires* (Chicago: University of Chicago Press, 2006).
22 *Vkontakte*, Twitter, internet news streams, and Facebook

Size, Spatiality[23] and Geographic Diffusion of Protest Events

The Euromaidan was reported in mainstream news to be a longer and significantly larger mobilization compared to the Orange Revolution.[24] Also reported was the claim that the Euromaidan manifests the same east-west Ukrainian geographic divide. Thus, first we must address the length of the Euromaidan mobilizations and assess if this greatly differed from the mobilizations in 2004. Second, we must assess the location, both spatially and geographically, of participants. Lastly, we must attempt to account for the size of the mobilizations.

When? And How Long?

As we know, the initial day of protest of the Euromaidan was November 21, 2013. The following Sunday, November 24, was the first day the protests assumed a 'mass' quality. Yet, it was not until the weekend of November 30, and specifically December 1 that the Euromaidan became a mass mobilization, in which we see a broad cross section of Ukrainian society take to the streets and squares of most large cities in Ukraine. While meetings of the Euromaidan continued, we can consider the date Yanukovych fled the country, February 21, 2014, the final day of the Euromaidan mobilization (even if the crisis continued, shifted and expanded thereafter). Thus, the multiple protest waves lasted three months.

Euromaidan went through four distinct phases and at least four waves of protest and repressions.[25] The first phase, November 21–30, was sparked by the government's volte-face on the EU Association Agreement. The second phase began after *Berkut* violently beat students and journalists, and cleared the Square. This also marked the first escalation of pro-

---

23 Spatiality means any property relating to or occupying space. Here I am referring to the spaces that the protests occupied. Helga Leitner, Eric Sheppard, and Kristin M. Sziarto, "The Spatialities of Contentious Politics," *Transactions of the Institute of British Geographers* 33, no. 2 (2008): 157–72; Deborah G. Martin and Byron Miller, "Space and Contentious Politics," *Mobilization: An International Quarterly* 8, no. 2 (2003): 143–56; William H. Sewell Jr, "Space in Contentious Politics," *Silence and Voice in the Study of Contentious Politics* 78 (2001): 18.

24 Author's notes on BBC World News Report January 21, 2014, and CNN International Report February 19, 2014.

25 Olga Onuch and Gwendolyn Sasse, "What Does Ukraine's #Euromaidan Teach Us about Protest?," *Washington Post*, February 27, 2014, http://www.washingtonpost.com/blogs/monkey-cage/wp/2014/02/27/what-does-ukraines-euromaidan-teach-us-about-protest/ (accessed September 3, 2014).

test repertoires and an increase in militia violence—protests grew in size until mid-December. The third wave of protests began after the announcement of the anti-protest laws on January 16 by the *Verkhovna Rada* [Supreme Soviet, or Parliament] making it illegal to protest and lasted until January 19. Some protesters, who were organized in smaller groups of *sotnya* [groups of 100], employed more violent tactics. The state escalated its use of repression—army and special forces militia used live ammunition, resulting in four deaths. The most violent encounters took place on Hrushevskyi Street, approximately 600 meters from Independence Square. Other protest zones, however, remained relatively peaceful. This phase particularly saw the spread of protests, including regional direct action campaigns,[26] road blockades, and government building takeovers, to the east and south of the country.[27] The fourth and final wave of mass repression began on February 18, 2014, when the regime attempted to clear the Square in a military operation that included snipers employing live ammunition. This final phase of protests and violence ended when Yanukovych fled to Crimea, and when protesters stormed the Presidential Administration Building in Kyiv.

In the case of the Orange Revolution, most analysts agree that while planning for the protest events took several months, activists and opposition mobilized around the time of the first round of presidential elections on October 21, 2004.[28] Observers generally agree that the protests turned into a moment of mass mobilization approximately on November 23, 2004, after the official announcement of the fraudulent election results on November 21. This mobilization ended on or close to December 27 following a revote of the second round of the presidential elections and the election of Viktor Yushchenko as President. Thus, the Orange Revolution lasted approximately two months. While the length of the Orange Revolution and

26 Direct action is political activity that bypasses normal political channels, by directly and even physically engaging with politic-economic elites. Barbara Epstein, *Political Protest and Cultural Revolution: Nonviolent Direct Action in the 1970s and 1980s* (Los Angeles: University of California Press, 1991); David Graeber, *Direct Action: An Ethnography* (AK Press, 2009); Tim Jordan, *Activism!: Direct Action, Hacktivism and the Future of Society* (London: Reaktion Books, 2002).

27 Onuch and Sasse, "What Does Ukraine's #Euromaidan Teach Us about Protest?"

28 Beissinger, "The Semblance of Democratic Revolution"; Bunce and Wolchik, "Transnational Networks, Diffusion Dynamics, and Electoral Revolutions in the Postcommunist World"; Olena Nikolayenko, "The Revolt of the Post-Soviet Generation: Youth Movements in Serbia, Georgia, and Ukraine," *Comparative Politics* 39, no. 2 (January 1, 2007); Onuch, *Mapping Mass Mobilizations*.

the Euromaidan are similar, the events of October 2004 were neither a large protest nor a mass mobilization. It was only on November 23, 2004, a full month after initial protests that ordinary Ukrainians joined *en masse*. This escalation and expansion of the protests happened at a much faster rate in 2013. Moreover, while the beginning of the longer mobilization process in 2004 can be traced back to at least January 2004, when SMO networks began to coordinate protest groups[29] and to develop a plan of action for the fall election, there is little evidence that activists and the opposition anticipated the events of Euromaidan. Thus, one could argue that while the mass mobilization component and the crisis resulting from the Euromaidan lasted longer, the mobilization process was much more drawn out and, as we will see below, better coordinated in 2004 than in 2013–14.[30]

In the Cities

When Ukrainian politics first witnessed the crowds on *Maidan Nezalezhnosty* [Independence Square], it was assumed that the 2013 protest was a "mini" Orange Revolution. A BBC World reporter stated that it was striking how it was "the same square, same time of year, [and] same city."[31] Within days, activists erected a stage at the base of the Statue of Independence along the southern section of the Maidan, and also set up tents with food and medical supplies. From the stage, activists and politicians spoke and musicians sang. Similar demonstrations happened in Lviv and several smaller western Ukrainian towns and cities. The space in which protest took place was symbolic and historically important, connecting the past struggles (be it the Revolution on the Granite, the Ukraine Without Kuchma Protest, or the Orange Revolution) to the current one.

Crucial differences, however, existed in the spatiality of the Euromaidan protests compared to the Orange Revolution. Namely, in most cities and towns, including Kyiv, there were at least two different, though not

---

29 While social mobilization organizations are large entities, not all members are involved in the direct action. Many activists consider the *samooboronas* of the Maidan as protest groups. Another example are the *sotnya*.

30 This chapter is unable to explore fully this longer mobilization process. For a more detailed analysis of the different waves and phases of mobilization in 2004,and of the 2013–14 mobilization see Olga Onuch and Gwendolyn Sasse, "What Does Ukraine's #Euromaidan Teach Us about Protest Waves?," *Nuffield College Politics Working Paper Series* 2014, no. 1 (2014).

31 Author's notes of a *BBC World* reporter's commentary on December 1, 2013.

oppositional, protest locations. Often, however, the same square hosted at least two different protest groups. One location was for the activists, journalists, students, and self-organized members of local communities, and the other was chosen and used by opposition parties and their immediate supporters. In Kyiv, the former was immediately established on Independence Square, while the latter was at first based in the *Yevropeiska Ploshcha* [European Plaza], some 900 meters eastward. Even after protests united (in Kyiv this took place over several days from November 24 to 27), the Squares were still divided into different zones. Each group or stakeholder developed a distinct protest area. Thus, from the very beginning even the physical space of the protest zones showed divisions between different groups. For instance, the often referred to and rebranded as a political party *Pravyi Sektor* [Right Sector], was until mid-December simply a location in the Maidan protest zone. Its members were located in the right-hand corner of the Square. There, too, were a variety of SMOs, right-wing political parties and networks, and individuals who were willing to take part in frontline protests and provide security to other protesters (see image 1). The spatiality of the protest zones was important as it allowed for different groups, with different approaches and aims, to carve out their own version of the Euromaidan.

Image 1 Meeting Place of the Maidan Initially Called "The Right Sector"

(Picture taken on November 29, 2013: Ukrainian Protest Project ©, Olga Onuch and Tamara Martseniuk, 2013)

During the Orange Revolution, the Maidan was also divided between different groups, into what some would call zones. However, from the beginning of the protests activists and party coordinators were united. In 2004, as explained by the coordinators themselves, the different networks of activists and political opposition forces cooperated, coordinated, and even signed a formal deal in 2004.[32] By contrast, the coordination and cooperation between activists and organizers surrounding Euromaidan was complicated and highly contested. This was specifically the case between activist networks and politicians; but it was also a problem between different generations of activists.[33] Thus, while the setting and stage design of the Euromaidan and the Orange Revolution seemed similar, divisions were clearly visible in the architecture of the 2013–14 Maidan. The lack of coordination between the actors, as well as the prominence of self-organized "ordinary" citizens, altered the boundaries of the contentious performance.

---

32 Interview with Vladyslav Kaskiv, *Pora!* (*zhovta*) activist and National Deputy of the Pora Party, Kyiv, April 19, 2008; Interview with Volodymyr Viatrovych, *Pora!* (*chorna*) activist, Kyiv, July 10, 2007; Interview with Zoloti Vorota and Yevhen Zolotariov, *Pora!* (*zhovta*) and human rights activist, Kviv, July 9, 2008.
33 Interview with a student activist, February 25, 2014.

In the Country

Beyond this subtle shift in the spatiality of the protests at the local level, there was a more important expansion and extension of protests at the national level during the Euromaidan. While we know that protest participation differed regionally, unlike the Orange Revolution, which was certainly a phenomenon of western and central Ukraine, the Euromaidan was a national phenomenon, even though the largest protests took place in similar locations to 2004. From the very first weekend, small protests occurred in large cities in Simferopol, Odesa, Donetsk, Kharkiv, and even Donetsk, among other eastern and southern oblasts.[34] These protests not only took place in central squares and outside of local government buildings, they occurred in cities and towns that have witnessed few protests since independence. Protests also occurred in places considered strongholds for the Party of Regions and Yanukovych supporters. Thus, protests spread to places wherein the risks associated with protesting were higher than in Kyiv because the level of support for the regime was higher. This geographic diffusion of protest events was one of the most interesting and novel aspects of the Euromaidan protests.

Historically, Ukrainian activists hail from all parts of Ukraine. Elsewhere, I have described four "islands of contention," regionally based activist *tusovky* [cliques or networks] in Lviv in the west, Kyiv in the center, Kharkiv in the east, and Odesa in the south. But, protests by ordinary Ukrainians in the east and the south were and are a rare occurrence. Instances of mobilization in these regions during the Orange Revolution were exceptional. In the case of the Euromaidan, the national diffusion of the protests was instantaneous, and occurred in three waves. The first wave of protest event diffusion began around the weekend of November 24. These protests were quite small and were usually organized locally—only a handful coordinated with local political parties, typically *Blok Yulii Tymoshenko* (BYuT) [Yulia Tymoshenko Bloc], *Ukrainskyi Demokratychnyi Alians za Reformy* (UDAR) [Ukrainian Democratic Alliance for Reform], and *Svoboda* [Freedom]. On November 29, 2013, I counted thirty-eight groups on the Russian-language social media site *VKontakte* related to Euromaidan protests. The second wave of diffusion followed the violence of November 30, 2013, when *Berkut* forces attacked protesters. The state's use of violence expanded the rhetoric of the protesters to include universal

---

34 Onuch and Sasse, "What Does Ukraine's #Euromaidan Teach Us about Protest?".

civil and human rights. The continued diffusion of protests throughout the country was even more pronounced, and they grew significantly in size.

The third wave took place between January 17 and February 18, and saw the growth of radical and direct action tactics. These included the occupation of government buildings and the toppling of Lenin statues [Leninopads]. While activists and opposition parties coordinated some events, most were organized by local citizens. This development is evident in the images of shawl-wearing grannies who stumbled into local government buildings with their plastic carrier bags, alongside hoodie-clad youth—both refusing to vacate in protest. One broadcast from Krivyi Rih, a large metallurgical center southwest of Dnipropetrovsk, showed an elderly woman who claimed, "I do not know how to protest. You can take your protest, I am not interested. I am a citizen and I am not leaving until Yanukovych resigns."[35] While a more thorough quantitative analysis focusing solely on the relationship between the identities and expectations of protesters and their geographic diffusion is necessary, it is clear that "ordinary" Ukrainians who had lived in places of relative calm since independence were key participants in the Euromaidan.

What is yet to be adequately documented, however, is the extent of the internal migration of protesters to Kyiv during the Euromaidan.[36] While it is assumed that most migrants came to Kyiv from western oblasts, survey data that I collected from protesters contend that a significant proportion came from central and eastern oblasts. Moreover, many of the most radical protesters, including the leaders of Pravyi Sektor, came from eastern oblasts. Dmytro Yarosh and many of his closest colleagues hail from Dnipropetrovsk. This departs from 2004, when the leaders of Pora! (zhovta) [It's Time! (yellow)] and Pora! (chorna) [It's Time! (black)], came from western and central oblasts. Thus, the Euromaidan is distinguished from the Orange Revolution by not only its trajectory and outcome, but to the extent that eastern based SMO networks and ordinary Ukrainians participated in protests.

How Many?

The size and scale of protests in 2004 and 2013–14 are comparable. At their height approximately 800,000 people took part in the protests in Kyiv

---

35 Author's notes and recordings of broadcast.
36 Interview with a Maidan activist, Kyiv February 22, 2014.

and close to 1.5 million across all of Ukraine. Depending on the time and location, the protest count varied considerably. Recent work from the Center for the Study of Society, located in Kyiv, Ukraine, which has counted protests and estimated sizes, is a good reference.[37] As noted by the Center, it is not the size of the protests that distinguish the Euromaidan from the Orange Revolution. Rather, it is the number of protests and incidents. The Center estimates that just under 4,000 protests took place during a three-month period of Euromaidan. This high number is likely linked to the lack of coordination between different types of actors and protesters, and to the geographic diffusion and self-organized nature of the many of the protests. The next section will look at the roles and responsibilities of key actors during the mobilization process.

Actors Involved in Euromaidan Mobilization Processes

While identifying the dates, waves, boundaries, frequency, size, and location of protests helps us better understand the Euromaidan, let us now turn our attention to how and when important actors influenced protest events. Elsewhere, I have identified four types of actors that are integral to the mass mobilization process: activists and SMOs, political elite, "ordinary" citizens, and foreign actors. Each category of actor can be further divided. For instance, activists and SMOs can consist of diverse and even competing networks, while "ordinary" citizens can represent a broad cross-section of society or it can be limited to a particular sub-group or electorate. Importantly, political elite should be divided between those strongly tied to the regime and those in opposition with few or no links. Foreign actors include supranational institutions, individual states, foreign leaders, politicians, bureaucrats, foreign activists and SMOs, journalists and citizens from neighboring countries or expatriates, and the national diaspora.

Analyses of Ukrainian and other Eastern European mobilizations have focused on foreign actors—politicians, activists, or financiers—and the ways in which they can enact, guide, and manipulate the mobilization process. Ultimately, the literature concludes that mobilization is most dependent on the actions of the political and economic elite. Since civil society is generally weaker in post-Soviet regimes, the trajectory and outcomes of

---

37 Roman Hankevych, "Khto Buv Na Maydani? [Who was on the Square?]," *ZAXID.NET*, July 9, 2014, http://zaxid.net/news/showNews.do?hto_buv_na_may dani&objectId=1314409 (accessed September 3, 2014).

mobilizations are elite dependent and ordinary citizens who mobilized tended to do so out of partisanship, emotional appeals, and ethno-linguistic nationalism.[38] The next section will engage with the above framework and briefly investigate the roles of the different actors in the 2004 and 2013–14 mobilizations. I will also identify key differences that can explain the different trajectories and outcomes of these two movements.

Activists and SMOs

While a detailed and quantitative process tracing of the different activists, SMOs, and networks involved in the mobilization process is not possible here, based on a small sample of interviews with activists I seek to identify trends and patterns in activist mobilization in 2013/14. In 2004, the SMOs *Pora!* (*chorna*) and *Pora!* (*zhovta*) became household names. During the Euromaidan, no SMO was as ubiquitous. Nonetheless, activists stressed that several *tusovky* [cliques] involved in coordinating protests, and specifically the Maidan in 2013–14, were continuations or revivals of SMOs active in 2004 and 2001. They came together under umbrella groups like *Hromadskyi Sektor* [Civic Sector], *Opora* [Support], *Molodyi Opir* [Young Resistance], *Chesno* [Honestly], Coordinating Committee of the Maidan, *Zhinocha Sotnya* [Women's 100 Squadron], *Avto Maidan* [Car Maidan], *Samooborona* [Self-Defense], and *Pravyi Sektor*. Moreover, self-organization was not only a phenomenon among ordinary citizens; it was also a trend among activists who broke off from pre-existing groups and launched their own activities. Unlike in 2004, when in order to be an activist one had to join a network, this time activists created new networks around their aims, strategies, and tactics for revolution. One such example was when individual activists with long CVs of engagement joined or organized their own *sotni* or *samooborona* groups.[39] Much like in 2004, as well as in past mobilization like Ukraine without Kuchma, the boundaries between journalists, activist networks, and *tusovky* were heavily blurred in the Euromaidan. Mustafa Nayem, a well-known journalist and co-founder of Hromadske.TV, has been said to have in part initiated the events of Euromaidan when he urged Ukrainians to gather in protest on Independence

---

38 Beissinger, "The Semblance of Democratic Revolution"; Marc Morjé Howard, *The Weakness of Civil Society in Post-Communist Europe* (Cambridge: Cambridge University Press, 2003); Nicu Popescu, "The Strange Alliance of Democrats and Nationalists," *Journal of Democracy* 23, no. 3 (2012): 46–54.

39 Interview with an unnamed *Pora!* (*zhovta*) activist, August 27, 2013.

Square against Yanukovych's decision to delay the implementation of the Association Agreement. Internet television and journalism strongly reflected activist rhetoric; former coordinators of *Pora!* (*chorna*) and *Pora!* (*zhovta*), for example, served as cinematographers stationed on the Square.[40] For this reason, this discussion groups together these two actors.[41]

While it initially seemed as though activists did not play as key a role in the 2013–14 mobilization compared to 2004, most insiders highlight the role of activist-journalists in framing protest claims and sparking the initial mobilization, and then acting as connectors and intermediaries between self-organized ordinary citizens, smaller activist groups, and politicians. Several small networks of activist-journalists, via social media, polemics, and an on-the-ground presence, enabled greater mobilization. In a Facebook post, Nayem and other journalists framed the non-signing of the EU Association Agreement as illegitimate and a violation of democratic rights.[42] Yet, insiders explained as early as December 2013 that it was this willingness of certain politicians and journalist-activists to assume leadership roles without premeditation that divided the SMO networks. Activists repeatedly pointed out that, "while in 2004 leaders found common ground, in 2013 SMO networks...[were] fragmented and lacked cooperation, making much of the coordination and mobilization...much more complicated."[43] Activists stated that even though the majority of SMO leaders in 2013–14 were key figures from past mobilizations and played active leadership roles in 2004, they had to coordinate quickly not only with other activists, but also with a new generation of university-student-activists and networks. The two processes of uniting activists and incorporating the activities of student networks into a coordinated and united front, which in 2004 took months of preparation, had to take less than a few days in 2013. Even though the use of social media permitted faster mobilization, schisms and differences among and between the activist leadership, SMOs, and politicians resulted

---

40 The major online news websites are Spilno.TV, Hromadske.TV, Espreso.TV, and RadioSovoba.TV.
41 For a more detailed analysis of the media, see Dyczok's analysis in this volume and elsewhere Marta Dyczok and O. V. Gaman-Golutvina, *Media, Democracy and Freedom: The Post-Communist Experience* (Bern: Peter Lang, 2009); Marta Dyczok, "Information Wars: Hegemony, Counter-Hegemony, Propaganda, the Use of Force, and Resistance," *Russian Journal of Communication* 6, no. 2 (2014): 1–4.
42 Interview with a journalist-politician, December 17, 2013.
43 Interview with unnamed Civic Network activist #1, November 30, 2013.

in the slower than anticipated coalescence of anti-regime interests. This, in turn, created opportunities for the formation of alternative subgroups to form.

Insiders have explained that though activist leaders relied on pre-existing diffuse networks, conflicts and disagreements appeared instanta-neously on how the protests should proceed. Creating a united protest front was further complicated by egos and political differences. A former *Pora!* (*zhovta*) activist who played an important role in the Euromaidan Coordinating Committee explained that differences of "how to mobilize, were the outcome of disappointments after 2004."[44] She mentioned that, "some [activists] stressed that we should...prepare for a violent revolution, others did not want to cooperate with politicians... making it difficult to co-ordinate the protests and keep the peace."[45] She explained, contrary to some of the Ukrainian punditry, that these sentiments neither stemmed from nor were a reaction to the regime's use of violence. The fragmenta-tion of activists and the rise of violence "was not simply a cause and effect story. That is too simplistic." Ideas of violent revolution "developed over several years." Nonetheless, these tactics were, according to some activ-ists, certainly "legitimized, when the regime repressed students and jour-nalists on November 30, 2013." Other experienced activists explained that the Coordinating Committee and old guard activist leaders could not pre-vent the formation of subgroups that promoted the use of violence and de-stabilized the situation because there was no clear idea under what condi-tions this mobilization should end. Unlike in 2004 when the aim was to pre-vent further *Kuchmizm*[46] and elect Viktor Yushchenko, the goals of the Eu-romaidan were neither clear nor static. Thus, it was difficult for activists to coordinate both protests and messages, particularly as SMOs represented different constituencies with different long-term interests.

Foreign Actors

In both 2004 and 2013–14, foreign actors played an important role in the mobilization process. In the two-year period leading up to 2004, Ukrainian activists relied on funds and training from various Intergovernmental and

44 Interview with an activist, December 16, 2013.
45 Interview with an activist, December 16, 2013.
46 *Kuchmizm* is often used as shorthand, specifically by activists, for the system of corrupt (clientelistic and clan based) and semi-authoritarian (part-machine and re-pressive) rule experienced under President Kuchma.

Non-Governmental Organizations (IGOs and NGOs). Foreign actors were important, though not essential, for the mobilization process. In 2013, protests were triggered by a foreign policy issue, the geopolitical direction of Ukraine, although with domestic implications, thus making the EU, its institutions and member states key actors in the mobilization process, specifically in its trajectory and outcome. Foreign NGOs and IGOs did indeed provide some small levels of support to several independent news groups and SMOs in 2013, but this was clearly *ad hoc* and initiated by Ukrainians. Moreover, as a Kyiv-based embassy worker explained, most foreign actors, diplomats or NGOs focused on elite actors and attempted to help broker a deal.[47] Informally, Ukrainian political insiders have complained about Europe's and America's lack of initial interest and, then, later mismanagement of the Euromaidan crisis. Thus, it is difficult to discern the influence these actors had on the mobilization process.

It is possible, as I have argued elsewhere, that a focus on foreign actors often exaggerates both their ability to mobilize and to influence actors and events. Yet, it is also possible, and more likely, that during the Euromaidan, as opposed to the Orange Revolution, the Yanukovych regime was less concerned with the West. The EU and the USA lacked both carrots and sticks with which to influence the regime. Moreover, the regime was both heavily influenced by and arguably dependent on Russia and Putin by fall 2013. Unlike in 2004, in 2013 the Yanukovych regime was not composed of a broad coalition of interests. As such, it had greater freedom not to negotiate with western diplomats. Hesitant and furtive actions on the part of the West also reflect uncertainty as to the desirability of Ukraine's potential future leadership. On February 7, 2014, a telephone conversation reportedly between Assistant Secretary of State Victoria Nuland and US ambassador to Ukraine Geoffrey Pyatt was leaked to the press. In it, Nuland speaks frankly on the merits of the three main opposition leaders— Vitaliy Klychko, Oleh Tyahnybok, and Arsenii Yatsenyuk. This brings us to the political economic elite, both in power and in opposition, and their role in the mobilization process.

Political-Economic Elite

By 2013, it was clear that the Yanukovych regime was very different from Kuchma's. Yanukovych's was composed of a small inner circle of family,

---

47 Author's personal correspondence, New York City, February 14, 2014.

friends, and business associates. The Party of Regions consisted of a pa-tron-client network that heavily relied on patronage and nepotism, which made it less susceptible to defections and lessened the likelihood of inter-locutors.[48] In fact the first signs of defection came when Serhii Tihipko left the Party of Regions, and when Serhii Lyovochkin, Chief of the Presiden-tial Administration, resigned in January 2014. These actions provided cov-er for Yanukovych and enabled him to resist foreign pressure to resign. In-siders have suggested that because of differing worldviews Yanukovych was more able and willing to use repressive force than Kuchma.[49] Thus, the regime was stronger and qualitatively different from Kuchma's semi-authoritarian rule.

Furthermore, political opposition was simply not as united and coher-ent as it was in 2004. The divisions, visible conflicts, and differing policy aims of key opposition leaders, Klychko, Tyahnybok, and Yatsenyuk, also made any coordination difficult. As one Yanukovych administration insider explained, "they could not pose a legitimate political threat. They could not easily win an election. They were too different".[50] As a former SBU insider explained in 2012, the post-2010 opposition had few contacts in the re-gime, and thus had little influence on policy generally and specifically, in-cluding the violent repressions of November 2013, particularly. Unlike the formal agreements made between the opposition in 2004, the initial lack of coordination and inability to prevent the use of violence resulted in a "coali-tion of inconvenience." Moreover, opposition parties struggled to coordi-nate with activists and SMOs. Not only was the regime stronger and more willing to engage in violence, the opposition was disoriented, and for the most part incapable of coordinating with, let alone controlling, the Maidan. This is a sharp contrast to 2004, when, by December, Yushchenko's Our Ukraine party, had near total control of the Maidan, and in fact co-opted the mobilization of activists and ordinary citizens into its own.

"Ordinary" Citizens: the Median Protester

"Ordinary" citizens are the most interesting category of actors involved in mass mobilization processes. Political scientists still debate why these

---

48 Here I mean individuals who communicated between the two camps with ease and frequency.

49 Unnamed, Kuchma Presidential Administration Insider 2, February 7, 2010, Interview, Da Vinci, Kyiv.

50 Interview with a former Yanukovych administration insider, January 28, 2014.

generally disengaged individuals join activists and political opposition *en masse*. While in 2004 a clear partisan cleavage dominated the Maidan, the story of the Euromaidan is much more complex. The shifting aims of the Euromaidan reflect, in part, the diverse socio-economic and political affiliations of the protesters. The average age of Euromaidan protest participants surveyed was 36 and men outnumbered women, representing 59% of participants between November 26, 2013 and January 10, 2014. Eighty-two percent of protesters were Ukrainophones while 12% were Russophones. [51] Sixty-nine percent identified Ukrainian as the language most used in private life, while 22% identified Russian.[52] According to the 2001 Census, this is representative of the general population in central Ukraine.[53] Also, the majority of protesters surveyed were employed and had at least secondary and some post-secondary education.[54]

According to our findings as part of the Ukrainian Protest Protect, the Euromaidan protesters can be divided into three broad groups: students and youth; the employed middle-aged; and retirees and those over 50. The youth and students called themselves the initiators of the protest, and said they sought abstract goals such as "freedom" and "a 'real' democracy." They reported frustration with their parents' generation for permitting the failure of democracy in Ukraine. The middle-aged group saw themselves as the "most important" protesters as they were the "workers" and "voters" who were necessary to win elections and to keep the economy running. They explained that unlike the students, they could not be ignored because of their political and economic power. Their demands were more concrete than those of the younger cohort. Issues of economic security, travel to the EU, and ending the state's illegitimate use of violence characterized their demands. The older group saw themselves as the "guardians of the Maidan." This group of protesters, as they had no children and were retired, had "less to lose." As such, they saw it as their responsibility to protest.

A preliminary analysis of our protest participant study coincides with findings from surveys and focus groups conducted after the 2004 mass mobilization. Euromaidan protesters, like the participants of the 2004 pro-

---

51 Olga Onuch, *EuroMaidan Protest Participant Survey* (Ukrainian Protest Project. Funded by the British Academy's Newton International Fellowships and the John Fell Fund, 2014).

52 Ibid.

53 State Statistics Committee of Ukraine, *All-Ukrainian Population Census*, 2001, http://2001.ukrcensus.gov.ua/eng/results/ (accessed September 2, 2014).

54 Onuch, *EuroMaidan Protest Participant Survey*.

tests, eloquently employed a profound rhetoric of human rights to describe the central motivating factor behind their mobilization. Protesters identified the repression of November 30 and the official announcement of electoral fraud as the two moments when they "realized that this could happen to anyone and everyone."[55] In 2013, even previous supporters of the Party of Regions understood that repression and infringement of rights affected all citizens equally. In contrast, in 2004, the same realization escaped regime supporters. An interviewee explained, "anyone who had Internet and saw the videos stopped being a *BYuT* or Party of Regions supporter, and became a citizen."[56] Furthermore, a comparison of focus group discussions I conducted with participants of the Orange Revolution shows differences in how grievances were framed. In 2004, the protesters focused on civil rights, whereas in 2013 the majority of protesters seemed to focus first on human rights, next socio-economic rights, and lastly civil rights. This makes sense as the Orange Revolution was motivated by fraudulent election results. The immediacy of the violence during Euromaidan also explains different demands. As protesters described, their focus on human rights, combined with social media's ability to rapidly inform and share information, and the legitimacy of self-organization, seems to have brought a wider mix of people to the protests than in 2004.

An Expanding Protestorate?

The Ukrainian Protest Survey found that while the general participation and membership in civic organizations, unions, and political parties is quite low, surprisingly only 63% of protesters surveyed participated in the Orange Revolution.[57] Even if we account for age, a significant portion of our Euromaidan survey respondents were first time protesters or "novices." This, coupled with our knowledge that the protests were larger and more diffuse nationally than during the Orange Revolution, points to an expanded "protestorate." Moreover, among protesters almost 10% had voted for the Party of Regions or for Yanukovych in past elections. As such, these protesters should not be understood as blind partisans. Rather, they represent a type of middle class, swing voter that we have observed in other countries, like the "Soccer Mom" in the United States. I argue that not only

55 Rapid interview conducted onsite, Kyiv, December 1, 2013.
56 Rapid interview conducted onsite, Kyiv, December 1, 2013.
57 Onuch, *EuroMaidan Protest Participant Survey*.

does the Euromaidan median protester point to an expanding protestorate, but also to a less sectarian voter who will withdraw political support if they feel a leader or party has broken campaign promises or violated the social, democratic contract. The self-organizing ordinary Ukrainians, thus, are central to distinctions between the Euromaidan and the Orange Revolution. The grassroots, self-organized protestorate came out *en masse* in 2013 compared to 2004. Now that we have a better understanding of the protest events and the actors involved, we can briefly address four themes central to informed observations and media reports: ethno-linguistic issues, the state's use of violence, the rise of the right, and social media.

Protest Claims Then and Now: Foreign Policy, Civic and Ethno-linguistic Claims

Recent news coverage has focused heavily on the ethno-linguistic and ethno-nationalist component of the Euromaidan.[58] Statements like protesters were "mostly Ukrainian-speakers" frame the Euromaidan as an ethno-linguistic issue. The reality is that *most* Ukrainians speak Ukrainian. The 2001 Census found that 65% of Ukrainians are Ukrainophones. The ethno-linguistic identities of Ukrainians are complex, fluid, and generally poor predictors of political behavior; rather, region has more predicative, explanatory power in this regard.[59] The analysis of Ukrainian activism through the prism of ethno-linguistic identity is not new and was best articulated by Mark Beissinger's August 2013 article in *American Political Science Review*.[60] When we compare past focus group discussions and recent interviews, it is clear that in 2004 ethno-linguistic identity had a greater influence on protest objectives and on protesters more generally

---

58 Andrew Higgins, "A Battle in Ukraine Echoes Through the Decades," *The New York Times*, June 26, 2014, http://www.nytimes.com/2014/06/27/world/europe/world-war-i-battle-in-ukraine-echoes-through-the-decades.html (accessed September 2, 2014); "Pro-West Protesters Defy Riot Police, Shiver in Ukraine's Snowy Capital," *NBC News*, December 10, 2013, http://www.nbcnews.com/news/other/pro-west-protesters-defy-riot-police-shiver-ukraines-snowy-capital-f2D11720949 (accessed September 3, 2014); "The Eastern Wall," *The Economist*, June 28, 2014, http://www.economist.com/news/special-report/21604685-polands-poorer-less-dev eloped-east-still-has-lot-catching-up-do-eastern-wall (accessed September 3, 2014).

59 Gwendolyn Sasse, "The Role of Regionalism," *Journal of Democracy* 21, no. 3 (2010): 99–106.

60 Beissinger, "The Semblance of Democratic Revolution."

than in 2013–14. Furthermore, if we compare the digitally documented protest posters as displayed on Independence Square in 2004 and 2013–14,
we see fewer references to language and ethnic identity issues in the latter. We also observe more Russian language posters during the Euromaidan than during the Orange Revolution.

Moreover, the fact that the mobilization initially occurred over a foreign
policy issue was also somewhat novel in Ukraine. In the past we saw
smaller protests with an anti-Russia and anti-NATO focus in 2005 and
2008 respectively. Protesters, however, did not actually discuss their demands in foreign policy or geopolitical terms. Rather, they spoke about socio-economic rights that would be protected by the Association Agreement
and the illegitimacy and lack of accountability of the Yanukovych government for reneging on a promise of closer ties with the EU.[61] Nonetheless,
the media's focus on an allegedly divided Ukraine overlooked the fact that
in both 2004 and even more so in 2013–14, the majority of demonstration
placards and posters focused on the regime's corruption and on Yanukovych and his cronies' criminal behavior. Pictures of the Orange Revolution and the Euromaidan would be difficult to distinguish if not for the prevalence of "Yushchenko orange" in those from 2004 and "EU reflex blue,"
the dominant color of the EU flag, in those from 2013. Thus, while a minority of protesters were preoccupied with ethno-linguistic issues, my team
and I actually observed an expansion of protest claims in 2013–14. However, the majority of protesters, as in 2004, demanded political protection
of civil rights.

---

61 "Yanukovych Promises Reforms to EU," *The Moscow Times*, March 2, 2010, http:/
/www.themoscowtimes.com/news/article/yanukovych-promises-reforms-to-eu/4007
33.html?id=400733 (accessed September 4, 2014).

Expansion of Protest Tactics: the Rise of Violence

Although there is much continuity between 2004 and 2013–14, the use of extreme violence both by the regime and by protesters is a substantial departure from a long history of non-violence practiced by dissidents, activists, and opposition parties. I have previously mapped out the history of activism and SMO networks in Ukraine since the 1960s and found that dissidents and activists purposefully eschewed violent tactics. From the Sixtiers (*Shistdesyatnyky*) to the People's Movement of Ukraine (*Narodnyi Rukh Ukrainy*), and from the Revolution on Granite to the Ukraine without Kuchma movement, protest in Ukraine has a distinct history of nonviolence. The majority of activists previously interviewed took seriously Ukraine's tradition of non-violent protest. Former leaders of *Pora!* (*chorna*) and *Pora!* (*zhovta*) recounted how they taught tactics that would minimize protest violence and reduce the possibility of violent reappraisals from the regime. In focus groups it was remarkable how activists described their self-restraint and refusal to use violent tactics.[62] As one activist noted "any act of vandalism, drunken disorder, whatever, can give the militia an excuse to put us all in jail."[63] Non-violent tactics, to which all activists during the Orange Revolution swore allegiance, were considered sacrosanct

Such experienced activists, as a result, were frustrated during the Euromaidan by their collective inability "to control the activists, the crowds, and the provocateurs" and thus proved unable to stop the spread of violence.[64] Though only a minority of the more radical protesters used violence, they were unfortunately the most visible in the media. This does not mean to deny that the protests escalated to a "Molotov Revolution." Rather, the images of fighters, walls of fire, and masked young men did not and do not represent the peaceful, larger groups that turned out well into February to join evening demonstrations in city squares.

Still, this shift in the tactics of Ukrainian protest should be concerning, if only because previous protesters were generally peaceful. To many

---

62 Activist focus group #2 , *Pora!* (*zhovta*) organizers (only men), Kyiv, August 5, 2007. Participants included Mykhailo, 26 years-old, from Kyiv and Donetsk, Coordinator of *Pora!* (*zhovta*), Ostar, 28 years-old from Kyiv, Design Coordinator of *Pora!* (*zhovta*), Pavlo, 25 years-old from Kyiv, Design Team member of *Pora!* (*zhovta*), Yarolsav, 27 years-old from Kyiv, Design Team member of *Pora!* (*zhovta*) and Yuri, 27 years-old from Lviv, Coordinator of *Pora!* (*zhovta*).

63 Interview with Ostap Kryvdyk, *Pora!* (*zhovta*) activist and journalist, Kyiv, July 18, 2007.

64 Interview with unnamed Civic Network activist #2, November 30, 2013.

Ukrainian activists it was troubling to learn that Egyptian protesters used Ukrainian how-to videos to make Molotov cocktails.[65] But as many have explained, it was their lack of coordination and control over protest events that allowed the spread of violence. This begs the question as to who sparked it and stood to gain from its use.

The Rise of the Right and the Divisive Nature of the Protests

Recent Ukrainian focus groups reveal a belief that the Euromaidan was divisive and, according to some, did more harm than good. The state's violent tactics divided the country, they said. Yet, from mid-January onward, Russian and Western media focused increasingly on escalating violence and right-wing groups, which unfortunately were branded as the dominant groups of the Maidan.[66] This focus on "Banderite Nationalists" provided an even greater opportunity for dividing the Ukrainian population. Dyczok's recent scholarship has explained how the media manipulated these competing images to develop a fear of the enemy next door, be they violent "Banderites" or the repressive *Berkut*.[67]

The central focus has been on *Pravyi Sektor*. As noted above, and though currently an official political party, during the Euromaidan it was a coalition of several right-wing and nationalist groups. It also included individuals who wanted to assist security and frontline activities.[68] Some participants, including its leaders, were long time members of pre-existing organizations, but others had and still have no organizational affiliation.[69] While Keith Darden and Lucan Way highlighted these organizations' western Ukrainian origins, Dmytro Yarosh, the leader of *Pravyi Sektor*, and his coordinators were from Dnipropetrovsk, in the east. It was *Pravyi Sektor*,

65 Neil Ketchley, "How Social Media Spreads Protest Tactics from Ukraine to Egypt," *The Washington Post*, February 14, 2014, http://www.washingtonpost.com/blo gs/monkey-cage/wp/2014/02/14/how-social-media-spreads-protest-tactics-from-ukraine-to-egypt/ (accessed September 4, 2014).

66 Keith Darden and Lucan Way, "Who Are the Protesters in Ukraine?," *The Washington Post*, February 12, 2014, http://www.washingtonpost.com/blogs/monkey-cage/w p/2014/02/12/who-are-the-protesters-in-ukraine/ (accessed September 5, 2014).

67 Dyczok, "Information Wars."

68 Author's interview with unnamed *Pravyi Sektor* activist, February 10, 2014.

69 Such organizations include *Tryzub* (Trident), the Ukrainian National Assembly-Ukrainian National Self-Defense (UNA-UNSO), Patriots of Ukraine, the Social-National Assembly, *Karpatska Sich* (Carpathian Sich), *Volya* (Freedom) and *Bilyi Molot* (White Hammer), among others.

the party, and Yarosh, the politician, who benefited the most from the use of violence as it resulted in increased media attention taking both from obscurity and turning them into household brands. Yet, just how new was this "rise of the right"?

Of course, right wing groups exist and have existed in post-independence Ukraine. A lack of evidence, however, exists as to whether or not participation in these groups has increased or decreased. Though anecdotal and observational, the results of right-wing groups in recent elections inform that these groups have been unable to attract any substantial support. For instance in the May 2014, presidential elections, right wing and conservative candidates Oleh Tyahnybok and Dmytro Yarosh received 1.6% and 0.7% of the national vote respectively. In the 2012 Parliamentary elections *Svoboda*, a party with ethno-nationalist roots, received 10.4% of the vote.

If we compare the role of right-wing organizations in past protest events, it was certain individuals who were participants in the organizations noted above who assumed top leadership positions in the SMOs active in 2004. Thus, it is difficult to conclude that right wing participation in protests is a new development. Insiders also disagree if the number of right wing protesters increased between 2004 and 2013.[70] Yet, their visibility and their use of radical, direct, and violent tactics certainly has changed significantly. One activist explained that "there was more discipline among activists and party organizers in 2004, but with the rise of the internet, the ability of anyone to create their own group/protest event, the control of the situation by activists declined and so did their ability to stay disciplined."[71] He reminded me of a conversation we had in Kyiv in the summer of 2009, when activists were preparing for the 2010 Presidential Elections, "back then people were saying, we failed in 2004, we need to start an armed revolution... with the disarray of 'self-organization' they got their opportunity to do this." Again, this reinforces the claim that disorganization among the opposition and activist networks created the conditions necessary for the rise of right-wing elements. These conditions were simply not present in 2004.

---

70 Interview with *Pravyi Sektor* activist, February 10, 2014.
71 Interview with Civic Network activist, November 30, 2013.

New Technologies, Social Media
and Samo-orhanizatsya [Self-organization]

Finally, we turn to social media and the ability of Euromaidan protesters to self-organize. The relationship, however, between self-organization and social media use is not clear. Was self-organization more prevalent because of social media or was social media use more prevalent because of a higher propensity for self-organization? It is clear, though, that during the Euromaidan the two were positively correlated. Though able to both facilitate the spread of information quickly and democratize protest, social media "selfies" and "self-organization" more broadly are not without concern

My research has revealed that social media was not in and of itself mobilizing. It is clear, though, from initial findings that social networks specifically friendship networks, as participants attended the protest with close friends and family members, were integral to mobilizing individuals. This does not mean that social media was not influential—it certainly was and by all accounts, it aided significantly information dissemination and protest coordination. While Twitter was predominantly used by activists, organizers, politicians, and other policy practitioners, Facebook and *VKontakte* were used by "ordinary" citizens, who often created their own pages, groups, and events related to the Euromaidan. This was particularly important in the regions where people could not easily access information; social media enabled near instantaneous access. Moreover, social media work differently from internet media. With the former, you do not need to search for information *per se* since your newsfeed lets you know what your friends read and watch, and if they plan to attend certain events. Even so, social media still needs people to create posters and events. It was also far too easy to simply like and share an item and feel as if one had already participated and made a difference, a development termed "slacktivism" or "armchair activism." Changing a profile picture is a poor substitute for physical presence at a protest site. Social media activity was, for the most part, also seen as safe and free of risks. Yet, it exposed activists, real and imagined alike, to regime repression, by making them easily identifiable. Moreover, the spread of photoshopped and aggressive propaganda also created opportunities for the spread of violence. Thus, while social media may have had a democratizing effect, as noted by one activist, "there is a dark side to social media... you can safely voice radical views... you can spread misinformation... and just like it was a space to battle regime propaganda, it also allowed opponents of the Euromaidan to demonize us."[72]

Several activists explained that they viewed the self-organization and the prevalence of social media during the Euromaidan as concerns because they contributed to organizational chaos, loose discipline, and a reduced focus on the use of non-violence. Some explained in interviews that they believed that the rise of Facebook activism contributed to the rise of the right, and to the escalation of violence. While further analysis is necessary and the causal relationship is still unknown, it is certain that we can at least see a correlation between the three variables previously mentioned. This hypothesis can be tested for Ukraine and for mass mobilizations internationally.

Conclusions—Directions for Further Study

While our initial impressions of the Orange Revolution and Euromaidan lead us to believe that the two events were very similar, this chapter has identified key differences. First, while the mass mobilization and the crisis resulting from Euromaidan lasted longer, the general mobilization process was much longer, better coordinated, and better planned in 2004 than in 2013–14. In terms of space, the protest sites also differed in how they were managed. In 2013, each group or stakeholder developed their distinct protest areas. Even the physical space of the protest zones mirrored the divisions and lack of coordination among different groups of actors. It was argued that the spatiality of the protest zones was important as it allowed for diverse groups, with different approaches and aims, to carve out their own version of the Euromaidan. Furthermore, in 2004 the protests mostly occurred in Kyiv and western Ukrainian cities. In 2013, the protests quickly spread throughout the country. From the very beginning of the Euromaidan we observed—albeit small—protest events in eastern and southern oblasts. It is hypothesized that social media platforms, specifically Facebook and *VKontakte*, facilitated the spread of protests through the dissemination of important, timely information. This merits further analysis by social media experts.

Furthermore, the diffusion and geography of the protests can be better understood through the employment of spatial statistical analysis. While the actors involved in the two mass mobilizations were generally the same,

---

72 Interview with unnamed student activist, February 25, 2014.

they were not adequately able to coordinate their activity in 2013–14. While many observers and activists alike have applauded this democratization, the lack of clear boundaries and leadership offered radical voices the space to expand and even encouraged protesters to violence. This brings us to the last issue discussed in the chapter, the extremely violent nature of the protests. Unlike in 2004, Euromaidan witnessed violence from both the state and protesters. Unlike in 2004, the regime unleashed extreme force against the citizens of Ukraine. These were blatant violations of human rights and undoubtedly stoked a more aggressive and desperate response from protesters. Kuchma, unlike Yanukovych, was unwilling to use agents of the state to silence protest—a deeper analysis into the inner workings of the two presidential administrations will allow us to understand better this process. However, the use of violence was a significant shift among Ukrainian activists, who had long employed a variety of non-violent tactics. This is, in my opinion, one of the most significant differences between the Orange Revolution and the Euromaidan. The repercussions of this move to violence need to be understood within the context of the further escalation of violence, and in the delegitimization of the movement according to some Ukrainians. Recent focus groups that I conducted show Ukrainians believe that not only has the violence of the Maidan traumatized a generation of Kyivans, it has provoked the division of Ukrainian society. The regime and a small group of protesters' turn to and increasing use of violence will require study for many years to come. In order for Ukraine to move past these horrific events, we need to continue to offer evidence-based advice on how to unite Ukrainian society. This will achieve a more nuanced and sensitive understanding of the motivations of those who participated in the violence.

Vigilantes, Organized Crime, and Russian and Eurasian Nationalisms: The Case of Ukraine

Taras Kuzio

Neo-Soviet and Russian nationalism was—and remains—the biggest threat to Ukraine's democratic system and to European integration. Viktor Yanukovych's four-year presidency and the actions of the Party of Regions showed that Russian and Eurasian nationalism is violent, anti-democratic, and corrupt with ties to organized crime. The Ukrainian Prosecutor-General's office calculated Yanukovych and his team stole upwards of $100 billion during his presidency. Until the Euromaidan, Western scholars and journalists viewed nationalism in Ukraine as a sentiment held only by ethnic Ukrainians and as a dominant political force only in the west of the country, while ignoring other forms of nationalism and intolerance. In fact, the outward manifestations associated with nationalism—anti-democratic culture, racial intolerance, anti-Semitism and xenophobia—are more of a problem in eastern and southern Ukraine and Crimea than in western Ukraine. US embassy cables from Kyiv reported that neo-Nazis and skin-heads were most active in eastern and southern Ukraine.[1]

Both in opposition and in power, Yanukovych and the Party of Regions have represented, by far, the most aggressive and violent political force in Ukraine. This is evident from the violence they have meted out inside and outside parliament against opposition parliamentarians and journalists, through the imprisonment of political opponents, horrendous violence and mass murders during the Euromaidan, widespread use of vigilante skinhead sportsmen and massive human rights abuses committed by Donbas separatists.[2] In the 2004 presidential elections, the Yanukovych

1 For a detailed discussion of US diplomatic cables and the Euromaidan, see Taras Kuzio, *Ukraine: From the Cold War to the Crimean Crisis and Euromaydan,* (forthcoming 2015).

2 "Ukraine: Mounting evidence of abduction and torture," *Amnesty International,* July 10, 2014, http://www.amnesty.ca/news/news-releases/ukraine-mounting-evidence-of-abduction-and-torture (accessed August 21, 2014). "Ukraine, Human Rights Assessment Mission: Report on the Human Rights and Minority Rights Situation, March-April 2014," *Organization for Security and Cooperation in Europe,* May 12, 2014, http://www.osce.org/odihr/118476 (accessed August 24, 2014). "Report on the Human Rights Situation in Ukraine," *Office of the United Nations High Commis-*

campaign conducted a strategy of electoral fraud and "directed chaos" that came perilously close to driving the country to civil war. A leaked strategy document from the Yanukovych election campaign outlined plans to esca- late conflict along each of the main lines of division—Galicia (west) vs. east and south; the West (USA, Europe) vs. Russia; Russian language, threat of rising extremism, and so on.[3] The Yanukovych campaign orga- nized movements in eastern Ukraine that opposed the ascendancy of Yushchenko, who was described as a reactionary, pro-American, radically oriented candidate.[4] In 2014, huge levels of violence in the Euromaidan and the Donbas were orchestrated by Yanukovych, separatists backed by the Party of Regions, local organized crime, and Russia. *The Washington Post* explained that the aggression in eastern Ukraine was the correct manner to describe what had transpired after the Euromaidan came to power when Yanukovych fled from Ukraine:

> *Aggression is the right word. Although the separatists may not be wearing Russian military insignia, no one should be under any illusions: This was a rebellion with roots in Moscow. After seizing Crimea, Mr. Putin set a wildfire ablaze in eastern Ukraine in order to meddle and control. Mr. Putin's ap- proach has been terribly sly, from the "little green men" who took over Cri- mea without noticeable military insignia, to the "uprising" in eastern Ukraine of separatist fighters who just suddenly happened to possess anti-aircraft missiles.[5]*

Xenophobia and racism are highest in Crimea among the Party of Re- gions, the Communist Party, and Russian nationalists, all of whom believe that Soviet dictator Joseph Stalin was justified in the ethnic cleansing of the Crimean Tatars. Antagonism to "Ukrainian nationalism" and Ukrainian national identity drew on a Soviet legacy of "anti-nationalist" tirades against World War II-era Ukrainian nationalists, dissidents, and émigrés. The belit- tling of the Ukrainian language and culture was traditionally undertaken

---

sioner for Human Rights, May 15, 2014, http://www.ohchr.org/Documents/Countrie
s/UA/HRMMUReport15May2014.pdf (accessed August 24, 2014).

3   Taras Kuzio, "State-Led Violence in Ukraine's 2004 Elections and Orange Revolu- tion," *Communist and Post-Communist Studies* 43, no. 4 (December 2010): 383– 395.

4   Ibid.

5   "On Ukraine, any bargain is a bad bargain," *The Washington Post*, August 21, 2014, http://www.washingtonpost.com/opinions/on-ukraine-any-bargain-is-a-bad-ba rgain/2014/08/21/90826b90-2964-11e4-958c-268a320a60ce_story.html (accessed August 25, 2014).

alongside anti-Tatar stereotypes. Crimean Prime Minister Anatolii Mohylov was particularly well known for his xenophobic attitudes. Writing in the local paper, *Krymskaya Pravda*, he penned words of support for Stalin's ethnic cleansing of the Crimean Tatars in the 1940s, subscribing to Stalin's justification that they were "Nazi collaborators."[6] These were not isolated views, but racial prejudices common in the Crimea.[7] Former Crimean Parliamentary Chair Anatolii Hrytsenko told US Ambassador William B. Taylor Jr. that Crimean Tatars "betrayed" the USSR in World War II and that "a majority of Crimea's inhabitants view Tatars as traitors."[8] Crimean Tatars fear for their future under Russian occupation and their leaders have been banned from entering the occupied region.[9]

Violence committed by Russian and Eurasian nationalists has been more prevalent in Ukraine than that committed by Ukrainian nationalists. Prior to the Euromaidan, two Ukrainian activists were murdered by Russian nationalists: composer Ihor Bilozir in Lviv on May 8, 2000 and Odesa State University student, member of the Ukrainian nationalist youth movement *Sich*, Maksym Chaika in Odesa on April 17, 2009. By contrast, no pro-Russian nationalist or activist had died at the hands of Ukrainian nationalists in post-Soviet Ukraine prior to the Euromaidan. During the Euromaidan, over 100 unarmed protesters were murdered by vigilante skinheads (the so-called *titushky* named after Vadym Titushko who attacked journalists in Kyiv in May 2013) and the security forces. Violence was common throughout Yanukovych's four-year presidency.[10] During it, he

---

6   The *Krymskaya Pravda* article is reprinted in Taras Kuzio, "Donetski ksenofoby i stalinisty [Donetsk xenophobes and Stalinists]," *Ukrainska Pravda*, December 4, 2011, http://blogs.pravda.com.ua/authors/kuzyo/4edabbffaa116/ (accessed August 24, 2014).

7   Enver Abibulla, "U Krymu Vymahayut Zaboronyty Prorosiiski Orhanizatsii [In Crimea, there is a need to ban pro-Russian organizations]," *BBC Ukraine*, January 6, 2013, http://www.bbc.co.uk/ukrainian/politics/2013/01/130106_crimea_protests_it. shtml (accessed May 9, 2014).

8   "Ukraine: Crimea Update—Less Tense than in 2006; Interethnic, Russia, Land Factors Remain Central," *US Embassy Kyiv*, June 8, 2007, http://wikileaks.org/cable/2 007/06/07KYIV1418.html (accessed May 9, 2014).

9   T. Kuzio, "Tatars Fear a Future Under Russia," *Al Jazeera America*, April 2, 2014, http://america.aljazeera.com/opinions/2014/4/ukraine-crimean-tatarsinputinsrussia. html (accessed May 9, 2014).

10 See video of Party of Regions candidate Petro Melnyk physically attacking Our Ukraine-People's Self-Defense parliamentary deputy Iryna Herashchenko at "Rehional Melnyk nakynuvsya na Herashchenko na vyborchii dilnytsi [The Party of Regions Deputy Melnyk attacks Herashchenko at the polling station]," *Ukrainska*

again "[placed] Ukraine on the verge of civil war"—as he had when he backed mass election fraud and violence during the 2004 presidential elections.[11]

Vigilante Skinhead Sportsmen

In Ukraine and the post-Soviet space, the term "skinheads" [brytoholovi] has three meanings. The first meaning refers to athletic-looking employees of security companies who are used in corporate raiding and business disputes. Corporate raiding has always been a major problem in Ukraine, but was especially prevalent under Yanukovych. Security forces often operated with sportsmen who worked in private security firms. Many of these were often tied indirectly to organized crime going back to the 1990s when Crimea, Donetsk, and Odesa were the most violent regions during Ukraine's transition to a market economy. Donetsk and Crimea were two of the major strongholds of the Party of Regions and Communist Party.[12]

The Party of Regions integrated former and current organized crime leaders. First Deputy Head of the Parliamentary Committee for the Struggle against Organized Crime and Corruption Hennadii Moskal, who has a long professional career in the Security Service and police, possessed intelligence on eighteen organized crime avtorytety [criminal leaders in the Party of Regions].[13] It is therefore not surprising that the political culture of the Party of Regions is violent, criminal, and authoritarian. When it was in power, the criminal world was free to emerge from the shadows and flex its muscles. In 2006–07, the US Embassy in Kyiv reported, "organized crime feels that there will be no follow up from the government."[14] Moskal said

---

Pravda, March 19, 2012, http://www.pravda.com.ua/news/2012/03/19/6960930/ (accessed May 9, 2014).

11 Irina Shtohrin, "Ukrainu shtovkhayut do Serbsko-Khorvatskoho Variantu Rozvytku Podii—Hrytsak [Ukraine is moving towards a Serbo-Croatian version of events]," Radio Svoboda, July 14, 2012, www.radiosvoboda.org/content/article/24644777 .html (accessed May 9, 2014).

12 Its literal meaning is "heads shaved by cut throat razors."

13 Tetyana Nikolayenko and Serhii Shcherbyna "Hennadii Moskal: Ti, na koho z administratsii Yushchenka davali komandu 'fas,' platyly miliony [Hennadii Moskal: those victims 'attacked' by the Yushchenko administration paid millions]," Ukrainska Pravda, March 21, 2013, http://www.pravda.com.ua/articles/2013/03/21/6986155/ (accessed May 9, 2014).

14 "Ukraine: Engaging Yanukovych, The Man of the Moment," November 20, 2006. US Embassy Kyiv, http://wikileaks.org/cable/2006/11/06KYIV4313.html (accessed April 16, 2014).

that organized crime gangs operated more freely under Yanukovych than they did under Presidents Kuchma and Yushchenko: "Some *oblasts* are fully controlled by crime bosses and for criminal groups today it is a complete paradise for them because they have complete freedom." Each year under Yanukovych at least one Crimean mayor was assassinated.[15]

The early biography of Donetsk oligarch, and business and political partner of Yanukovych, Rinat Akhmetov is largely unknown from the mid-1980s to the mid-1990s as it has not been made publicly available. It is as though he did not exist during that decade. What information we possess though is indicative of how former criminal leaders in the 1980s and 1990s established the Party of Regions.[16] Hans van Zon writes, "as early as 1986, Rinat and his brother Igor were involved in criminal activities" and Igor was apprehended after a robbery that led to the deaths of three people.[17] Akhmetov was questioned in 1988 for being a member of an organized crime group in the Donetsk region. These allegations seem to be supported by a 1999 Ministry of Internal Affairs Directorate on Combating Organized Crime leaked document entitled "Overview of the Most Dangerous Organized Crime Structures in Ukraine" that listed seven groups in Donetsk oblast.[18] The Akhmetov organized crime group, "dealt with money laundering and financial fraud, and controlled a large number of both real and fictitious companies. It goes by the name *Lyuksovska hrupa*." Written underneath the report: "The leader is Akhmetov Rinat Leonidovych born in 1966, and living at 16 Udarniy Street, Donetsk."[19]

---

15 Dmytro Shurkhalo, "Ne plutaite borotbu z koruptsiyeyu zi zvedennyam politychnykh rakhunkiv—Hennadii Moskal [Do not confuse the fight against corruption with the construction of political vendettas]," *Radio Svoboda*, April 14, 2012, http://www.ra diosvoboda.org/content/article/24547796.html (accessed May 9, 2014).

16 The author requested a copy of his biography for the missing decade from the mid-1980s to mid-1990s from Jock Mendoza-Wilson, Director of International and Investor Relations for System Capital Management in Kyiv, but he was unable to provide one. Kyiv, April 16, 2014.

17 Hans van Zon, "The Rise of Conglomerates in Ukraine: the Donetsk Case," in *Big Business and Economic Development. Conglomerates and Economic Groups in Developing Countries and Transition Economies under Globalization*, eds. Alex E. Fernandez Jilberto and Barbara Hogenboom (London: Routledge, 2007), 386.

18 "Ohlyad: Naibilsh Nebezpechnykh Organizovanykh Kryminalnykh Struktur, shcho diyut Ukraini [Overview: The Most Dangerous Criminal Structures that Act in Ukraine]," *MVC Ukraini*, 1999. http://reportingproject.net/new/REPORTS/Docume nt%20about%20Donetsk%20crime%20group.pdf (accessed April 16, 2014).

19 Ibid.

In the first half of the 1990s, Akhat Brahin, a well-known Donetsk entrepreneur and criminal "*avtorytet*" with the underworld nickname "Alik the Greek," became Akhmetov's "mentor."[20] Photographs and video footage of Akhmetov and Brahin at the funeral of Oleksandr Krantz, a major Donetsk organized crime boss who was murdered in 1992, and at other events, were published and leaked by the Ministry of Internal Affairs.[21] "Links between Akhmetov and Brahin were documented in the operational evidence of the Ministry of Internal Affairs" and "In the first half of the 1990s, he was probably linked to Akhat Brahin, a leader of the criminal underworld in the Donetsk Oblast, who was the president of Shakhtar Donetsk Football Club."[22] Yevhen Shcherban also had close ties to Brahin who was seen on many occasions in the Anton Corporation offices that he owned.[23]

Yurii Ivanyushchenko is a fixer for "The Family," a clan of Yanukovych loyalists from Yanukovych's home town of Yenakiyeve in Donetsk oblast. He was a Party of Regions deputy with a criminal past from the 1990s who switched his allegiance from the Dolidze organized crime brothers to Brahin.[24] "Yurii Yenakovo," as he has been nicknamed, has been dogged by

20 van Zon, "The Rise of Conglomerates in Ukraine," 382.

21 "Donetskaya Mafiya—Chast Pervaya: Prishestvie Akhmetova [The Donetsk Mafia—Part One: The Coming of Akhmetov]," http://www.youtube.com/watch?v=dA29BDRfCEA (accessed May 9, 2014).

22 Slawomir Matuszak, *The Oligarchic Democracy: The Influence of Business Groups on Ukrainian Politics, no. 42* (Warsaw: Centre for Eastern Studies, 2012), 88. http://www.osw.waw.pl/sites/default/files/prace_42_en_0.pdf (accessed May 9, 2014).

23 Maksim Kamenev, "Biznes-partner Shcherbania: U Evgeniya s Rinatom Akhmetovym byl obshchii biznes s 1990 goda [Shcherban's Business-Partner: Eugene and Rinat Akhmetov have had business ties since 1990]," *Ukraina Forbes*, March 21, 2013, http://forbes.ua/nation/1349572-biznes-partner-shcherbanya-u-evgeniya-s-rinatom-akhmetovym-byl-obshchij-biznes-s-1990-goda (accessed May 9, 2014). Maksim Kamenev, "Biznes-partner Shcherbania: S Timoshenko Evgenii ne voeval. Ego "zakazali" Kuchma i Lazarenko [Shcherban's Business Partner: Eugene did not fight with Timoshenko. Kuchma and Lazarenko 'put a hit' on Shcherban]," *Ukraina Forbes*, March 25, 2013, http://forbes.ua/nation/1349768-biznes-partner-shcherbanya-s-timoshenko-evgeniy-ne-voeval-ego-zakazali-kuchma-i-lazarenko (accessed May 9, 2014).

24 Tetyana Chornovol, "Donetska vendeta (dopovnena) [Donetsk vendetta (updated)]," *Ukrainska Pravda blogi*, January 28, 2013, http://blogs.pravda.com.ua/author s/chornovol/5106584eed6da/ (accessed May 9, 2014). "Donetska vendeta 2. Ukraina mala shans, shcho 'Yenakiivski' ta 'Donetski' perestriliayut odyn odnoho [Donetsk vendetta 2. There is a chance in Ukraine that the 'Yanekevo Family' and the 'Donetsk Family' will kill each other]," *Ukrainska Pravda blogi*, January 28, 2013,

allegations that he "had a dodgy and even criminal past" that "link[ed] him to an organized crime group allegedly involved in the assassination of Akhat Brahin" and "to the 2005 assassination of Anatolyi Bandura, head of Mariupol-based Azov Shipping Company."[25] In September 2008, a shoot-out in Kyiv between two organized crime gangs from the Caucasus was traced to Party of Regions' deputy Elbrus Tedeyev. A Mercedes-Benz car was seen driving away from the scene—where one person was killed and a second was seriously injured—with plates of Party of Regions' parliamentary deputy Tedeyev. Tedeyev initially stated that his cousin and colleagues were playing "sports" in the park where the shoot-out took place and claimed he did not have a cousin called Robert Tedeyev. Minister of Internal Affairs Yurii Lutsenko ordered the arrest of Robert and revealed documents that Party of Regions deputy Elbrus Tedeyev belonged to the Savlokhy organized crime group.[26] Tedeyev had been on an organized crime wanted list, compiled by the Ministry of Internal Affairs, but was then suspiciously removed from the list.[27] In the 2007 and 2012 parliamentary elections, he was awarded a seat as a Party of Regions deputy in the *Verkhovna Rada* under Ukraine's party-list proportional representation electoral system. He is one of eighteen organized crime leaders in the Party of Regions.[28]

---

http://blogs.pravda.com.ua/authors/chornovol/5106744265709/ (accessed May 9, 2014). "Donetska vendeta 3. Zpada Yuriya Yenakiivskoho. Abo yak Yanukovych ta Akhmetov napeshti opynylyeia v odnomu chovni [Donetsk Vendetta 3. Yurii's betrayal of Yanekevo. Or how Yanukovych and Akhmetov finally found themselves in the same boat]," *Ukrainska Pravda blogi*, January 28, 2013, http://blogs.pravda.com.ua/authors/chornovol/51069d2d85e92/ (accessed May 9, 2014). "Donetska vendeta 4. Kinets [Donetsk vendetta 4. The End]," *Ukrainska Pravda blogi*, January 30, 2014, http://blogs.pravda.com.ua/authors/chornovol/51091bb245751/ (accessed May 9, 2014).

25 Vlad Lavrov, "Ivanyushchenko works to clean up reputation," *Kyiv Post*, April 29, 2011, http://www.kyivpost.com/content/ukraine/ivaniushchenko-works-to-clean-up-reputation-103198.html (accessed May 9, 2014).

26 Anna Hryhorash, "Lutsenko vs Tedeyev. Ministr oprylyudniyeye dokumenty pro kryminalne mynule deputata," *Ukrainska Pravda*, September 25, 2009, http://www.pravda.com.ua/articles/2009/09/25/4204681/ (accessed May 9, 2014).

27 Ibid.

28 "Narodnyi deputat Ukrainy VII Sklykannya—Tedeyev Elbrus Soslanovych [National Deputy of Ukraine's Eighth Parliament—Elbrus Soslanovych Tedeyev]," *Verkhovna rada Ukraini ofitsiinyi veb-portal*, http://gapp.rada.gov.ua/mps/info/page/8701 (accessed May 9, 2014).

The Party of Regions and Yanukovych always drew on vigilante skin-head sportsmen with links to organized crime and on private security companies. The same was true of Crimean politicians. In Transcarpathia, controlled by the Social Democratic Party of Ukraine (united) [*SDPUo*] from the late 1990s until 2004, organized crime, politics, and business formed a similar nexus to that found in Donetsk, Crimea, and Odesa.[29] These *bratky*, prison slang for *bratstvo* [brotherhood], intimidated voters, supported election fraud, and abducted, tortured, and murdered journalists and opposition activists.[30] Vigilantes from organized crime joined violent separatists in the Donetsk region in spring 2014 when Akhmetov, in contrast to oligarch and governor of Dnipropetrovsk Ihor Kolomoiskyi, remained passive.[31]

The standard look of these criminal thugs—very short hair, leather jackets, athletic trousers—was common throughout the former USSR: "Intimidating physical proportions and brand-name sportswear" accompany their preference for short hair.[32] Anna Fournier describes these "bandits" as rough and aggressive who speak rarely, and when they do it is often Russian prison slang. They are immune to feelings and are fearless with no remorse. *Patsany* [guys] wear tight-fitting clothes, love to flash their fashionable jewelry (gold necklaces, expensive watches, etc.) and are sporty-looking with well-honed muscles.[33]

Like all totalitarian states, the USSR placed great emphasis on public sports activities, and Vadim Volkov writes that, "sportsmen naturally formed the core of the emerging racketeering groups."[34] Sports in the USSR were intimately linked to the Interior Ministry and military. These ties facilitated close collaboration between sportsmen and young, battle-

29 Kuzio, "State-Led Violence," 386–8.
30 Meaning brotherhood or criminal fraternity. For a video of an attack on a journalist in Kherson, see "U Khersony "bratky" pobili zhurnalistiv pid chas ziomky [In Kherson, the 'Brotherhood' beat journalists during the shooting]," *Ukrainska Pravda*, March 15, 2013, http://www.pravda.com.ua/news/2013/03/15/6985600/ (accessed May 9, 2014).
31 T. Kuzio, "Why is Akhmetov not combating separatism?" *Financial Times*, April 14, 2014, 2014, http://blogs.ft.com/beyond-brics/2014/04/14/guest-post-why-is-akhmetov-not-combating-separatism/ (accessed May 9, 2014).
32 Vadim Volkov, *Violent Entrepreneurs: the Use of Force in the Making of Russian Capitalism* (Ithaca, NY: Cornell University Press, 2002), 6.
33 A.Fournier, *Forging Rights in a New Democracy, Ukrainian Students Between Freedom and Justice* (Philadelphia: University of Pennsylvania Press, 2012), 85–8.
34 Volkov, *Violent Entrepreneurs*, 7.

scarred Afghan veterans who returned *en masse* to the Soviet Union in the late 1980s. Together they provided the "muscle" for an organized crime *brigada* [brigade] due to their fighting skills, will power, discipline, and team spirit.[35] *Afgantsy* [Soviet veterans of the Afghan War] added to these traits a contemptuous attitude to death. They resolutely supported the use of force and placed a low value on life.[36] The disintegration of the USSR in the late-1980s and the decline of state funding for sports forced sportsmen to the emerging private sector for employment. Volkov writes that, "therefore, the crisis in the state budget and in enterprise finances, combined with the corrosion of the Soviet system of values disrupted the reproduction of the institution of sports and triggered various adaptive responses on the part of sportsmen."[37]

A second meaning of the term "skinheads" is its use by the authorities to attack violently political opponents, as during the Euromaidan, and by the Party of Regions to secure desired election results.[38] Serhii Tihipko, then head of the Yanukovych election campaign, threatened Polish negotiators during the first EU-brokered round-table that he would bring 20,000 "coalminers" to Kyiv, perhaps in a similar display of authoritarian violence to that used in Romania during the 1990s against the democratic opposition.[39] Yanukovych told the Party of Regions congress, "they simply awaited the signal to defend our choice. With regret I called upon them to return

---

35 Ibid., 8.
36 Ibid., 8.
37 Ibid.
38 For examples see, T. Kuzio, "Kuchma Regime Using 'skinheads' Against Opposition," *Eurasian Daily Monitor* 1, no. 7 (May 11, 2004), http://www.jamestown.org /single/?no_cache=1&tx_ttnews[tt_news]=26486 (accessed May 9, 2014); "Ukrainian Opposition Candidate Targeted by 'Skinheads'," *Eurasian Daily Monitor* 1, no. 25 (June 7, 2004); http://www.jamestown.org/single/?no_cache=1&tx_ttnews[tt _news]=26621 (accessed May 9, 2014); "Skinhead Attacks on the Rise in Ukraine," *Eurasian Daily Monitor* 2, no. 94 (May 13, 2005), http://www.jamestown.org/single/? no_cache=1&tx_ttnews[tt_news]=30399 (accessed May 9, 2014). On the use of vigilante skinheads undertaking election fraud in the 2012 elections, see Tetyana Nikolayenko, "Yak brytoholovi 'zhurnalisty' vyrishuyut dolyu vyboryu [How skinhead 'journalists' decide the fate of elections]," *Ukrainska Pravda*, November 28, 2012, http://www.pravda.com.ua/articles/2012/11/2/6976500/ (accessed May 9, 2014).
39 Marcin Bosacki and Marcin Wojciechowski, "Behind the Scenes of the Ukrainian Revolution," *Gazeta Wyborcza*, April 3, 2005. On Romania, see Ion Bogdan Vasi, "The Fist of the Working Class: The Social Movements of Jiu Valley Miners in Post-Socialist Romania," *East European Politics and Society*, 18, no. 1 (February 2004): 132–57.

home but I told them we would soon return."[40] In the 2004 elections, the Yanukovych election campaign paid for somewhere between 20,000 and 40,000 "supporters" to travel to Kyiv to unblock government buildings, which would not have been possible without violence, and to disperse the Maidan.[41] They "looked more characteristic of the 1990s and wore sports pants and leather jackets with short cropped hair. They huddled close together and spoke quietly "as in the *zona*" [prison camp]."[42]

The authorities used police cadets to attack pro-democracy protestors during the 2000–01 "Ukraine without Kuchma" protests, and during the 2004 elections.[43] During the violence outside the Central Election Commission in October 2004, the opposition found police identity cards on *agents provocateurs*. These skinheads have often been hired by the authorities, such as during the 2004 elections, when they became "members" in the Ukrainian National Assembly (UNA), led by Eduard Kovalenko, which marched in Kyiv in SS-style uniforms and pretended to be Yushchenko supporters. In April 2013, in Cherkasy, fake *Svoboda* supporters attacked an opposition rally while holding anti-Semitic banners.[44] During the Euromaidan, *Bratstvo* led charges against the police barricades outside the Presidential Administration and used bulldozers in order to give the *Berkut* riot police an excuse to attack real protesters.

This use of vigilante skinhead sportsmen was especially pronounced during Yanukovych's presidency. Tetyana Nikolayenko therefore described

---

40 "Yanukovych rozpoviv, yak zaklykav donetskykh povertatysya [Yanukovych described how he called on Donetsk people to be returned (to office)]," *Ukrainska Pravda*, December 3, 2005, http://www.pravda.com.ua/news/2005/12/3/3026772/ (accessed May 9, 2014).

41 Andrew Wilson, *Ukraine's Orange Revolution* (New Haven, CT: Yale University Press, 2005), 134–5.

42 Pavlo Solodko, "Lyudyna, Yaka stvoryla 'Nichnu Vartu.' Chastyna tretia [The person who created 'the Night Watch'. Part Three]," *Ukrainska Pravda*, January 27, 2006, http://www.pravda.com.ua/articles/2006/01/27/3057173/ (accessed May 9, 2014). This is an interview with Oleksandr Popov who was one of the organizers of *Nichna Varta* (Night Watch) during the Orange Revolution.

43 Ihor Huzhva, Oleksiy Popov, and Oleksandr Chalenko, "Tainy Maidana [Secrets of the Maidan]," *Segodnya.ua*, November 21, 2005, http://www.segodnya.ua/oldarchi ve/c2256713004f33f5c22570c0002f88b4.html (accessed May 9, 2014).

44 See the video at, "U Cherkasakh provokatory vid imeni 'svobodivtsiv' napali na mitynh opozytsii [Svoboda-provocateurs attacked the opposition rally in Cherkasy]," *Ukrainska Pravda*, April 6, 2013, http://www.pravda.com.ua/news/2013/04/6/698757 7/ (accessed May 9, 2014).

the Yanukovych administration as "*vlada brytoholovykh*" [skinhead-led authorities].[45] In February 2013, during a nation-wide Maidan with the president in which citizens were permitted to submit queries, those who attempted to submit critical questions were threatened by "people in jogging suits and black hats, and by cadets."[46] The description continues, "one of the activists said that people in sports attire promised to break his legs because he tried to put forward a question."[47]

A third meaning of the term "skinhead" refers to Nazi and political groups that espouse an eclectic mix of Ukrainian state nationalism and pan-Slavism. Overwhelmingly, instances of racism, xenophobia, and anti-Semitism committed by Nazi, skinhead, and Russian nationalist groups occur in eastern and southern Ukraine and the Crimea. The fascist Russian National Unity party sent mercenaries to fight in the Donbas where they aligned with former supporters of the Party of Regions and organized crime figures who joined the separatists. More popular in Russia, neo-Nazi skinheads in Ukraine often receive funding from Russia; this explains their prominence in eastern Ukraine. Police statistics showed that one-third of skinheads arrested in Ukraine are actually Russian nationals.[48] A US Embassy cable reported that skinheads "are present in a number of *oblasts* including Kyiv, Kharkiv, Kherson, Sumy, Donetsk, Dnipropetrovsk, Vinnytsya, Odesa, and Zhytomyr."[49] In addition, "the Sevastopol Movement against Illegal Immigrants has a following among neo-Nazi skinheads."[50] The Ukrainian Movement against Illegal Immigrants has two wings, one pro-Russian and the other pro-Ukrainian, and the US Embassy in Kyiv re-

---

45 Tetyana Nikolayenko, "Vlada brytoholovykh [The power of skinheads]," *Ukrainska Pravda*, February 8, 2013, http://www.pravda.com.ua/articles/2013/02/8/6983115/ (accessed May 9, 2014).
46 Ibid.
47 See news report, photographs, and video film of pro-regime vigilante skinheads at, "Dialoh Yanukovycha z maidanom. Sutychky i liudy v sportyvkakh [Yanukovych's Dialogue about the Maidan," *Ukrainska Pravda*, February 22, 2013, http://www.prav da.com.ua/photo-video/2013/02/22/6984131/ (accessed May 9, 2014). "Aktyvistu, yakii priishov na dialoh z Yanukovychem, obitsialy polamaty nohy [Activists who came to speak with Yanukovych were threatened with broken legs]," *Ukrainska Pravda*, February 22, 2013, http://www.pravda.com.ua/news/2013/02/22/6984136/ (accessed May 9, 2014).
48 "Ukraine's Main Extremist Groups," *US Embassy Kyiv*, November 26, 2008, http://wikileaks.org/cable/2008/11/08KYIV2323.html (accessed May 9, 2014).
49 Ibid.
50 Ibid.

ported, "some experts allege that both wings get financing and guidance from Russia."[51] This was a product of "the nexus of Russian and Ukrainian skinhead movements to common cultural, linguistic, and historical ties. There is frequent contact between Ukrainian and Russian skinheads including attendance of demonstrations and concerts in their respective countries."[52]

Pan-Slavic groups have emerged from Ukrainian nationalist parties such as *Bratstvo*, an outgrowth from the Ukrainian National Assembly-Ukrainian People's Self Defense Forces (UNA-UNSO). *Bratstvo* joined the Highest Council of the Moscow-based International Eurasian Movement and the highest council of the Eurasian Youth Union. In the 2012 elections, the Party of Regions supported *Bratstvo* party leader Dmytro Korchynskii who ran in a Kyiv-single-mandate seat. The Eurasian Youth Union whose "ideology favors Russian imperialism," which is "extremist and anti-American," and is controlled by the Kremlin, is most active inside Ukraine in Crimea, Sumy, Donetsk, Kyiv, and Kharkiv.[53] Pan-Slavic Eurasianism has always been part of UNA's ideological arsenal, and UNSO fought with Transnistria separatist forces against the Moldovan state in 1992. Transnistria, which had been the Moldovan Autonomous Soviet Socialist Republic (ASSR) in inter-war Soviet Ukraine, has a sizeable Ukrainian population, and UNSO claimed to be fighting on the side of Ukrainians.

Patriot Ukrainy [Patriot of Ukraine], formerly the youth wing of the *Svoboda* party until 2004, cooperated with the unregistered Ukrainian National Labor Party and pro-Russian Crimean Cossack groups. In 2005, the Ministry of Justice registered it as a civic organization with branches in Kyiv, Poltava, and Chernihiv. It received public attention in August 2011 when the *Sluzhba Bezpeky Ukrainy* [Security Service of Ukraine] arrested its leaders for allegedly planning to organize a terrorist attack on August 24, Ukraine's annual holiday to commemorate the 1991 Declaration of Independence. A wing of UNA united with *Patriot Ukrainy* , and the *Vseukrainska Orhanizatsiya "Tryzub" imeni Stepana Bandery* [Stepan Bandera Sports-Patriotic Association *Tryzub* (Trident)], led by Dmytro Yarosh, during the Euromaidan to form the nationalist *Pravyi Sektor* [Right Sector].

---

51 Ibid.
52 "Ukraine's Skinhead Subculture," *US Embassy Kyiv*, December 8, 2008, http://wiki
    leaks.org/cable/2008/12/08KYIV2441.html# (accessed May 9, 2014).
53 "Ukraine's Main Extremist Groups." http://wikileaks.org/cable/2008/12/08KYIV24
    41.html#.

Members of the Ukrainian National Labor Party are primarily skinheads and neo-Nazis who operate in Crimea (Simferopol), Zaporizhzhya, Kharkiv, and Kherson, all in eastern and southern Ukraine, Kyiv, Uman, Vynnytsia, and Kirovohrad in central Ukraine, and in Galicia and Rivne in western Ukraine.[54] The National Socialist Party of Slavs has a similar regional distribution of supporters with both Russian and Ukrainian branches.[55] In Sevastopol, skinheads organized underground cells with assistance from other skinheads in Yalta, Kharkiv, and St. Petersburg, and have undertaken violent attacks, sometimes using explosives and weapons, against non-Slavic peoples. [56]

Donetsk and the Crimea: Crime, Politics, and Business

In the USSR, the Donbas was always a haven for fugitives who were attracted there because of labor shortages in industry and coalmining. Postwar reconstruction of the Donbas took place with the assistance of labor transferred from other regions of the USSR. According to Hiroaki Kuromiya, some of these included "criminals and adventurers" and "street waifs."[57] In postwar Donetsk, one in ten residents was imprisoned, and the region's penitentiaries held three times the number of inmates that these institutions were constructed to hold. The largest numbers of criminal prosecutions in Soviet Ukraine were in Stalino (Donetsk) and Voroshilovohrad (Luhansk) oblasts, which accounted for one-third of all criminal prosecutions in Soviet Ukraine. In the Donbas, "everyone was said to participate in robbery" and, "every night people were terrorized by the sound of incessant shots from automatic rifles."[58]

Twice imprisoned, Viktor Yanukovych had been a *pakhan* [don or underworld boss] whose nickname was *kham* [boor]. As a *pakhan*, his cooperation with Soviet authorities in prison facilitated his progress upon his release. Donetsk voters viewed Yanukovych's imprisonments as a *nesh-*

---

54 Ibid.
55 See the video of the National Socialist Movement at, "National Socialist Movement—The Slavic Union. Ukrainian Branch," hosted by *Liveleak*, http://www.livelea k.com/view?i=593_1224001386 (accessed May 9, 2014).
56 "Ukraine's Main Extremist Groups." http://wikileaks.org/cable/2008/12/08KYIV2441. html#.
57 Hiroaki Kuromiya, *Freedom and Terror in the Donbas* (Cambridge: Cambridge University Press, 1998), 301.
58 Ibid., 301.

chastia [misfortune] rather than something that made him morally unfit to be the Ukrainian president. In the USSR, criminals from all over the country worked in Donbas coalmines. This created a tolerant culture toward those who spent time in prison. Alexander Kupatadze writes, "as a result, the residents of Donbas region believe 'if a man has never gone to prison he is not a man.'" Indeed, a past prison sentence is not an embarrassment in Donbas but is rather considered an enrichment of experience.[59]

After World War II, criminality in the Donbas was high. This emerged openly during Soviet leader Mikhail Gorbachev's era as small business ventures were permitted and Soviet power disintegrated. Serhii Zhuk, who grew up in Dnipropetrovsk, writes that Donetsk racketeers who he describes as the "Tatar mafia" came to his city in the 1980s to extort discotheques and emerging small businesses.[60] Donbas organized crime boss Brahin controlled many discotheques that were a major source of income.[61] Donetsk has a large Tatar minority from the Republic of Tatarstan, Russia—these ethnic ties connected Brahin, Shcherban, and Akhmetov. A large Islamic school and mosque, opened in honor of Brahin in Donetsk in the late 1990s, was paid for by Akhmetov.[62]

The law of the jungle, about which Fournier's interlocutors spoke, was especially prevalent in Crimea, Donetsk, and Odesa.[63] These regions experienced the greatest degree of violence during the transition of the 1990s and *prykhvatizatsiya*, a *portmanteau* of the Ukrainian words for "privatization" and "grabbing control over."[64] The rampant violence and *dur-*

---

59 Alexander Kupatadze, "Transitions After Transitions: Coloured Revolutions and Organised Crime in Georgia, Ukraine and Kyrgyzstan" (Ph.D Diss., University of St Andrews, 2010), 141. Kupatadze quotes his November 2007 interview with Professor Alexander Kostenko, head of the Institute of Criminology, National Academy of Sciences of Ukraine.

60 Serhiy Zhuk, "The Dnipropetrovsk Clan in the Soviet Era and Why It Lost Out to Donetsk in Independent Ukraine." Paper presented at Canada-Ukraine Parliamentary Program and Oxford University Ukrainian Society's conference titled "Ukraine's Domestic and Foreign Affairs: Quo Vadis?," New College, Oxford University, Oxford, UK, April 7–8, 2011.

61 Ibid.

62 See the photograph in T. Kuzio, "Crime, Politics and Business in 1990s Ukraine," *Communist and Post-Communist Politics* 47, no. 2 (July 2014): 195–210.

63 A. Fournier, *Forging Rights in a New Democracy, Ukrainian Students Between Freedom and Justice*, 85–8.

64 On the 1990s criminal-business-political nexus in Ukraine, see T.Kuzio, "Murder and Selective Use of Justice in Ukraine (Parts One and Two)," *Eurasia Daily Monitor* 10, no. 35 & 44 (February 25 and March 8, 2013), http://www.jamestown.org/sin

dom-like [madhouse] conditions only ameliorated after Yanukovych, sent by Kuchma to become both a peacemaker and a deal maker, became governor in May 1997. Governor Yanukovych oversaw the integration of local criminal and business elites into the Donetsk clan and offered *krysha* [Russian for "roof" and widely used as a term for political and legal cover] to favored associates. Hans van Zon writes, "Yanukovych, Akhmetov and [Borys] Kolesnikov (Akhmetov's associate and close friend) put an end to uncontrolled criminal activities and restored order. Restoring order, however, did not mean restoring rule of law; in Donetsk the law of the strongest reigned."[65] The unification of local elites under Yanukovych was pursued during a period when Kyiv granted the region *de facto* autonomy in exchange for political loyalty. Yanukovych, according to Taras Chornovil, remained insecure throughout this period and kept an armored personnel carrier behind his office in which he could quickly escape to the Russian border, sixty kilometers away.[66] This fear was undoubtedly behind his rapid flight from Kyiv in February 2014 after Euromaidan activists and nationalists threatened to march on his palatial Mezhyhirya residence.

The Prosecutor-General's office assisted in protecting ties between politicians, businesspersons, and criminals. From the 1990s to the first half of the following decade, the Donetsk prosecutor's office was led by Rinat Kuzmin, ousted Prosecutor-General Viktor Pshonka, and former Prosecutors-General Hennadii Vasylyev and Oleksandr Medvedko, all of whom had strong ties to the Party of Regions. With a background in covering up gangland murders on behalf of political and business bosses, it is little wonder that rule of law did not exist in Ukraine. Perversely, Kuzmin led the criminal cases against Tymoshenko upon whom he tried to pin the Shcherban murder.

---

gle/?no_cache=1&tx_ttnews[tt_news]=40503#.UchFuW31F1w (last accessed May 9, 2014).

65 van Zon, "The Rise of Conglomerates", 383.

66 Interview with Taras Chornovil, "Tymoshenko—tse Yanukovych u spidnytsi. Ale vona—aktyvna, a vin—lezheboka," *Hazeta.ua*, January 1, 2013, http://gazeta.ua/ar ticles/politics-newspaper/_timoshenko-ce-yanukovich-u-spidnici-ale-vona-aktivna-a-vin-lezheboka/480185 (accessed May 9, 2014). See also, T. Kuzio, "Assassination Phobia Spreads in Ukraine," *Eurasia Daily Monitor* 7, no. 124 (June 28, 2010), http://www.jamestown.org/single/?no_cache=1&tx_ttnews[tt_news]=36540   (accessed May 9, 2014); and T. Kuzio, "Yanukovych's Assassination-Phobia Deepens," *Jamestown Foundation Blog*, October 28, 2010, http://jamestownfoundation.b logspot.ca/2010/10/yanukovychs-assassination-phobia.html   (accessed   May   9, 2014).

Former Deputy Prosecutor-General Kuzmin ensured Sieilem organized crime leader Oleksandr Melnyk evaded justice after the Party of Regions lobbied the prosecutor's office not to press charges. Interior Minister
Lutsenko said, "having all the evidence connecting the [Sieilem] gang to
murders," Kuzmin "releases the man who Yanukovych shelters, the head
of an organized crime gang." Lutsenko told the US Embassy in Kyiv that
the Sieilem organized crime gang had been responsible in the 1990s for
52 contract murders, including a journalist, two police officers, 30 busi-
nessmen, and 15 organized crime competitors.[67] Kuzmin "rehabilitated"
another of Ukraine's most notorious crime bosses, Gyvy Nemsadze, who
led a syndicate that committed over a hundred murders. In 2010, after
Yanukovych came to power, criminal charges against Nemsadze were
dropped. In the second half of the 1990s, when Yanukovych was governor
of Donetsk, Nemsadze's organized crime group destroyed a rival gang led
by Yevhen Kushnir who was blamed for the murders of Donetsk crime
boss Brahin and Ukraine's then wealthiest oligarch Shcherban.[68]

From 1997, when Yanukovych became Donetsk governor, to 1999,
the eve of the formation of the Party of Regions, twenty-four Kushnir gang
members were murdered and eight imprisoned. Meanwhile, none of the
Nemsadze gang were arrested. Melnyk and the Sieilem group, which included Sergey Aksionov who became the leader of Crimea after the peninsula's annexation by Russia, provided local protection for the business interests of Yanukovych and Donetsk oligarch Rinat Akhmetov. Subsequently, the Sieilem and Nemsadze gangs defeated their Kushnir and Bashmaky
rivals. In Donetsk, organized crime coalesced under the *krysha* of the Party of Regions, whereas in Crimea they established Russian nationalist parties such as Russian National Unity led by Aksyonov.

With business and organized crime competitors destroyed, Governor
Yanukovych set about uniting the warring Donetsk clans into a new political force. The Party of Regional Revival "Labor Solidarity Ukraine" was established in 2000 through the merger of five political parties: Petro Poroshenko's Party of Ukrainian Solidarity, Volodymyr Rybak's Party of Re-

---

67 "Ukraine: Land, Power, and Criminality in Crimea," US Embassy Kyiv, December
    14, 2006. http://wikileaks.org/cable/2006/12/06KYIV4558.html (accessed May 9,
    2014).
68 Nemszade was employed by Akhmetov. See Kupatadz, "Transitions After Transi-
    tions," 133.

gional Revival, Valentyn Landik's Party of Labor, Leonid Chernovetskyi's Party for a Beautiful Ukraine, and Anton Kaputsa's All-Ukrainian Party of Pensioners. A year later it changed its name to the Party of Regions and was led by Nikolay Azarov (2001 and 2010–14), Volodymyr Semynozhenko (2001–03), and Yanukovych (2003–10). The gas lobby was integrated into the Party of Regions from 2006 and received prominent positions in the Yanukovych administration and in Azarov's government.[69] The gas lobby led by Dmytro Firtash, Serhiy Leyvochkin, and Yuriy Boyko invested in democratic alternatives to Tymoshenko; for example, Arsenii Yatsenyuk in the 2010 elections and UDAR (Ukrainian Democratic Alliance for Reform) and Vitalii Klychko (Klitschko) since 2011. Firtash persuaded Klychko during a meeting in Vienna to withdraw his candidacy in favor of Poroshenko for the May 2014 presidential elections.[70]

Gas tycoon Dmytro Firtash, who was detained in Vienna at the request of the US Department of Justice on March 14, 2014, the "Family," and Akhmetov received the highest proportion of government contracts during Yanukovych's presidency.[71] In December 2008, Firtash admitted to US Ambassador Taylor that he received assistance from FBI-wanted mafia don Semen Mogylevych in order to enter the energy business.[72] Mogylev-

---

69 See, T. Kuzio, "Gas Lobby Takes Control of Ukraine's Security Service," *Eurasia Daily Monitor* 7, no. 53 (March 18, 2010), http://www.jamestown.org/single/?tx_tt news%5Btt_news%5D=36172&no_cache=1#.U1ZvQF6qwVs (accessed May 9, 2014). T. Kuzio, "Gas lobby runs Yanukovych administration," *Kyiv Post*, 19 July 2010, http://www.kyivpost.com/opinion/op-ed/gas-lobby-runs-yanukovych-administr ation-74233.html (accessed May 9, 2014).

70 T. Kuzio, "UDAR—Our Ukraine Pragmatists in a Radical Opposition Era," *Eurasia Daily Monitor* 9, no. 197 (October 29, 2012), http://www.jamestown.org/single/?tx _ttnews%5Btt_news%5D=40030&no_cache=1#.U1Z17V6qwVs (accessed May 9, 2014). On the ties between Firtash, Poroshenko, and Firtash, see Serhii Leshchenko, "Poroshenko-Klychko. Videnskyi alyans pid patronatom Firtasha [Poroshenko-Klychko. Vienna under the auspices of the Firtash alliance]," *Ukrainska Pravda,* April 2, 2014, http://www.pravda.com.ua/articles/2014/04/2/7021142/ (accessed May 9, 2014).

71 The charges are outlined here, "Six Defendants Indicted in Alleged Conspiracy to Bribe Government Officials in India to Mine Titanium Minerals," *United States Department of Justice—Office of Public Affairs*, April 2, 2014, http://www.justice.gov /opa/pr/2014/April/14-crm-333.html (accessed May 9, 2014). On Firtash's background, see Michael Weiss, "Married to the Ukrainian Mob," *Foreign Policy*, March 19, 2014, http://www.foreignpolicy.com/articles/2014/03/19/dmytro_firtash_ukrain e_billionaire_corruption_arrest (accessed May 9, 2014).

72 "Ukraine: Firtash Makes His Case to the USG," *US Embassy Kyiv*, December 10, 2008, http://wikileaks.org/cable/2008/12/08KYIV2414.html (accessed May 9, 2014).

ych protected the energy market and worked with Russian leaders until 2008, just ahead of *RosUkrEnergo*'s, an opaque gas intermediary 45 percent owned by Firtash, removal from the January 2009 gas contract that was negotiated by Prime Ministers Vladimir Putin and Tymoshenko. In his capacity as prime minister and president, Yanukovych strengthened the already close ties between crime and energy. The 2006–07 Yanukovych government signed an oil deal with the four owners of *Vanco Prykerchenska Ltd.* These included Akhmetov's *Donbaska Palyvno-Energetychna Kompaniya* [DTEK (Donbas Fuel-Energy Company)], Party of Regions Deputy Vasyl Khmelnytskyi's Austrian-registered Integrum Technologies, and Russian oligarch Yevgeniy Novitskiy's Shadowlight Investments. A US cable from Moscow and other sources described Novitsky as the leader of the *Solntsevskaya* criminal gang that provided protection to gas intermediaries such as the Itera Oil and Gas Company that had been operated in the 1990s by Gazprom.[73]

Ties between Crimean and Donetsk business and criminal groups have always been strong, and these were cemented in 2006 when the Party of Regions and Crimean Russian nationalists allied in the regional parliamentary and local elections. In March 2014, when Russia invaded and annexed Crimea, the Party of Regions and its Russian nationalist allies controlled 82 of 100 seats in the Crimean Parliament, and they supported Russia's annexation. Many candidates in the "For Yanukovych!" bloc, like Aksionov, whose criminal nickname was "Goblin," and Oleksandr Melnyk, were members of the Sieilem organized crime gang. Yanukovych reportedly told a Party of Regions deputy who criticized this alliance with organized crime that, "I take responsibility for him [Melnyk]."[74] He also asked police chief Lutsenko not to touch "my Sasha" [Melnyk].[75]

---

73 "The Luzhkov Dilemma," *US Embassy Moscow*, February 12, 2010, http://wiki leaks.org/cable/2010/02/10MOSCOW317.html (accessed May 9, 2014). For a more detailed discussion, see Chapter Eight on "Organized Crime" in David Satter, *Darkness at Dawn: the Rise of the Russian Criminal State* (New Haven: Yale University Press, 2003).127–55; and Myroslav Demydenko, "Ukraine, Vanco Energy, and the Russian Mob," *Eurasia Daily Monitor* 5, no. 177, September 16, 2008, http://www.jamestown.org/single/?no_cache=1&tx_ttnews[swords]=8fd58939 41d69d0be3f378576261ae3e&tx_ttnews[any_of_the_words]=PKK&tx_ttnews[point er]=3&tx_ttnews[tt_news]=33941&tx_ttnews[backPid]=381&cHash=ae9e19184c#.U gJ5lqxvCSq (accessed August 25, 2014).

74 "Tyurma—tsina neprodazhnoho perebuvannya u vladi i nezminnosti pohlyadiv v opozytsii. Politychna zayava Yuriya Lutsenka [Prison—the price of an incorruptible period in power and immutable views in opposition. The political statement of Yuryi

From the late-1990s onwards, Donetsk and Crimean organized crime *avtorytety—vory v zakone* [thieves in law]—were integrated into the Party of Regions and Crimean Russian nationalists.[76] Donetsk and Crimean organized crime have cooperated in business since the 1990s and in politics since 2006.[77] The Party of Economic Revival, previously known as the Party of Economic Revival of Crimea, was closely linked to organized crime since the early 1990s, even though its leaders included senior and former Crimean Communists such as Mykola Bahrov.[78] The Christian-Liberal Party of Crimea was a "straightforward mafia front" where "only the words 'of Crimea' bore any relation to reality."[79] Organized crime warfare in the first half of the 1990s destroyed the PEVC and Christian-Liberal parties. The end of political *krysha* for Crimean organized crime only took place when Moskal headed the Crimean Autonomous Republic's police department (1997–2000) and when Lutsenko was Minister of Internal Affairs (2005–06 and 2007–10).

Yanukovych is the only Ukrainian president, and the Party of Regions the main political force, to have drawn on vigilante skinhead sportsmen. This relationship can be traced to the 1980s and 1990s when Crimea and Donetsk experienced high levels of violence, and when a nexus was established between organized crime, politics, and business. Violence by vigilantes was facilitated by the integration of organized crime leaders into the Party of Regions and Crimean Russian nationalist groups and parties. The more authoritarian political culture that exists in eastern and southern Ukraine and Crimea also aided this process. The willingness of vigilantes to use extreme forms of violence resulted in over 100 deaths and more than 1,000 wounded in the Euromaidan, and gave rise to Russian-backed

Lutsenko]," *Ukrainskyi Tyzhden*, February 16, 2012, http://tyzhden.ua/Politics/42 449 (accessed August 24, 2014).

75 Ibid.

76 See Borys Penchuk and Serhiy Kuzyn, eds., *Donetska Mafiya. Antolohiya* (Kyiv: Fund Antikoruputsiya, 2006). B.Penchuk, Serhiy Pantyk, Yevhen Zolotaryov, Andriy Yusov, and Vitaliy Zahaynyy eds., *Donetska Mafiya. Perezavantazhennya* (Kyiv: Fund Antikoruptsiya, 2007).

77 T. Kuzio, "Crime, Politics and Business in 1990s Ukraine."

78 On Crimean *avtorytety* integration into the Party of Regions, see T. Kuzio, "Yanukovych Provides a Krysha for Organized Crime," *Eurasia Daily Monitor* 9, no. 34 (February 17, 2012), http://www.jamestown.org/single/?no_cache=1&tx_ttnews[tt_n ews]=39024 (accessed May 9, 2014).

79 Andrew Wilson, *Virtual Politics. Faking Democracy in the Post-Soviet World* (New Haven, CT: Yale University Press, 2005), 69 and 247.

violent separatism in the Crimea and eastern Ukraine that led to at least 2,500 civilian deaths, and the deaths of 600 Ukrainian soldiers with another 2,000 wounded. Former President Yanukovych will be remembered in Ukrainian history for provoking two revolutions (Orange and Euromaidan), for committing mass murder, and for supporting Russia's military intervention in Crimea and Donbas.

Mass Media Framing, Representations, and Impact on Public Opinion

Marta Dyczok

Introduction

Information is used as a weapon in any confrontation or conflict. The newly appointed Director General of the National Television Company of Ukraine, Zurab Alasania, went so far as to say, "Russia showed us that media can be not only a tool, but a nuclear weapon."[1] It is widely believed that media shape public opinion, which is why elites everywhere use mass media to try to control or spin information.

Ukraine's Euromaidan protests and the Russian invasion that followed are good illustrations of how media is used, yet the media's effects are often ambiguous. The regime of former President Victor Yanukovych went to great lengths to control mass media, frame the news, set the agenda for public debates, and was prepared to use various tactics, including violence. This did not prevent massive public protests from erupting and growing, which ended with him fleeing the country. Yet, not all Ukrainians either protested or supported the protesters. Despite having access to a wide range of media, including live streams of events, some chose to watch Russian television that depicted the protesters as a small group of radical, unemployed, rabble-rousing nationalists, fascists, and anti-Semites.

After Yanukovych fled the country, the media's situation changed. Censorship in Ukraine largely ended. Mainstream media began promoting a message of unity and openness. But Russia's invasion of Crimea, then incursion into Donetsk and Luhansk, brought new forms of violence: kidnappings, beatings, the shutting down of Ukrainian media outlets, and Russia's labeling of Ukraine's interim government as illegitimate. While some in Ukraine and the world saw through these media untruths and distortions, others were persuaded by Russian media.

Numerous scholars have revealed confirmation biases in how people select media sources and interpret media messages. Individuals seek me-

---

1 Interview with Zurab Alasania in Kyiv, June 4, 2014. On March 25, 2014, he was appointed Director of the National Television Company of Ukraine.

dia sources that are already aligned with their values, beliefs, and life experiences, and usually seek out sources that confirm, rather than challenge pre-existing views.[2] Media are one of the factors that shape beliefs, but values change slowly. Thus, the long-term effect of media messages, framing, and agenda setting during the Euromaidan protests and the Russian invasion are likely to become visible over time.

Journalists and media managers play an important part in this process. Their normative role is to provide objective information and analysis for society, to act as watchdogs. Yet, they are often used as instruments in information wars and become adjuncts of political authorities. In Ukraine, some complied with political and economic pressures; others blurred the line between journalism and activism. A few continued to maintain high standards, at times risking their safety and even lives, and refused to be used as instruments in information wars.

The Media Landscape

The Euromaidan protests erupted amidst rather intense censorship. After coming to power in 2010, Viktor Yanukovych curtailed media freedom to the point that analyst Nataliya Ligachova, head of Telekritika, a media watchdog website and magazine, noted that things were worse than during the dark days of President Kuchma's restrictions of 1999–2003, when journalist Heorhii Gongadze was killed in 2000, for example.

Throughout the Yanukovych presidency, Ukraine's mainstream media largely towed the official line. Most of the media system is privately owned, and similar to most countries, composed of large media corporations. The three big players are U.A. Inter Media Group, whose ownership is kept in the hands of individuals loyal to the state and thus changes regularly, StarLightMedia Group, owned by former President Leonid Kuchma's son-in-law Viktor Pinchuk, and 1+1 Media Group, purchased in 2007 by one of Ukraine's richest men, Ihor Kolomoiskyi.[3] Rinat Akhmetov, who used to fi-

---

2   See Marta Dyczok, "Was Kuchma's Censorship Effective? Mass media in Ukraine before 2004," *Europe-Asia Studies*, 58, no. 2 (March 2006): 215–38; Stuart Hall, "Encoding/Decoding," in S. Hall, D. Hobson, A. Lowe and P. Willis, eds., *Culture, Media, Language* (London: Hutchinson, 1980), 128–38; Maxwell E. McCombs, *Setting The Agenda: The Mass Media And Public Opinion* (New York: Polity, 2004); and John Street, *Mass Media, Politics, and Democracy*, second edition (New York: Palgrave Macmillan, 2011).

3   U.A. Inter Media Group includes the channel INTER, Ukraine's most watched station. StarLightMedia Group includes the ICTV, STB, and Novyi Kanal, which to-

nance Yanukovych's election campaigns and is reportedly Ukraine's richest executive, owns the also influential Ukraine Media Group.[4] Like corporations everywhere, owners are primarily interested in profits, and that requires maintaining good relations with the state. In Ukraine, this relationship is more intense than in other countries in large part because of the way media privatization occurred in the 1990s. State assets were transferred into private hands in a non-transparent way, and this made media owners dependent on the state.[5] Furthermore, media owners are also the largest corporate actors in Ukraine, and use their media assets as a political tool to curry favour with the state to protect their other business interests where they make their main profits. The state continues to own part of the media system (television, radio, and print) and they were used as mouthpieces of the government during the Yanukovych presidency.

Outside the control of the state were digital and social media, which grew steadily and in tandem with internet usage in Ukraine over the previous ten years. Roughly half of Ukraine's adult population regularly used the internet by September 2013, a 16% increase from February 2012.[6] This grew considerably during the months of the Euromaidan protests, and by January 2014, around 17.8 million Ukrainians were online.[7] Fortunately, a few months before the protests erupted, a number of new, independent, online media outlets appeared. Public Television (Hromadske.TV), Public Radio (Hromadske Radio), Spilno.TV, and Espresso.TV, were all well placed to report on events as they unfolded. Audiences to social media networks and online news media increased even more in Ukraine during the Euromaidan protests.[8] In February 2014, the independent online publi-

---

gether constitute the largest percentage of audience share. The 1+1 Media Group includes the channel 1+1.

4 Ukraine Media Group includes the channel Ukraina.
5 For a discussion on the privatization process, see Marta Dyczok, "Threats to Free Speech in Ukraine: The Bigger Picture," in Giovanna Brogi, Marta Dyczok, and Oxana Pachlovska, eds., *Ukraine Twenty Years After Independence: Assessments, Perspectives, Challenges* (Berne: Peter Lang, forthcoming).
6 See "Dynamika vykorystannya internet v Ukraini [Dynamics of Internet Usage in Ukraine]," *Kyiv International Insitute of Sociology*, November 28, 2013, http://www.kiis.com.ua/?lang=ukr&cat=reports&id=199&page=7 (accessed August 20, 2014).
7 Roman Kaspirovych, "Auditoriya internet Ukraina Yanvar 2014 g. [Ukraine's Internet Users—January 2014]," *gemiusAudience*, http://www.slideshare.net/rkaspirovych/2 01401-gemius-audienceoverview (accessed August 20, 2014).
8 Kyrylo Galushko and Natalia Zorba, "Ukrainian Facebook-Revolution? Social Networks Against a Background of Euromaidan Social Research (November-

cation *Ukrainska Pravda* became one of the most commonly visited news sites, with 1.5 to 2.5 million visitors daily. By March, the number had climbed to 4.5 million.[9] U-stream, a high definition video streaming platform, allowed anyone with a smartphone to broadcast live footage online, and many ordinary people used this technology to share live video with anyone interested. This type of content also began appearing in mainstream media because of what scholars have called media convergence, whereby barriers between "traditional" and "new" forms of media disappear. Media convergence is also characterized by the inclusion of user-generated social media content in traditional media platforms.[10] This is important since although the internet has become the second highest source of news for Ukrainians, and some even feel, "We do not really need television anymore," statistics show that 96.8% of the population watches television news at least once a week.[11]

Mainstream Media Reporting, Silencing, Framing

Mainstream media's reportage of the early days of Euromaidan protests were by all accounts fair and objective.[12] This is likely due to the small number of and disunity among the protesters. Originally, there were two sites of protest. Activists and students gathered in Independence Square

---

December 2013)," *Contemporary Ukrainian Research Forum*, April 28, 2014, http://euromaidan-researchforum.ca/2014/04/28/ukrainian-facebook-revolution-soc ial-networks-against-a-background-of-euromaidan-social-research-november-december-2013/#more-1017 (accessed August 21, 2014).

9 Maksym Savanevskyi, "Za ostanni 5 misyatsiv perekhody z sotsialnykh merezh na saity ZMI zrosly u 8–10 raziv," *watcher:*, March 17, 2014, http://watcher.com.ua/201 4/04/07/4-5-mln-korystuvachiv-vidvidaly-ukrayinsku-pravdu-protyahom-odnoho-dn ya/; http://watcher.com.ua/2014/03/17/za-ostanni-5-misyatsiv-perehody-z-sotsialnyh -merezh-na-sayty-zmi-zrosly-u-8-10-raziv/ (accessed August 23, 2014).

10 Tim Dwyer, *Media Convergence* (New York: McGraw Hill, 2010).

11 Interview with Yevhen Fedchenko, Kyiv, May 28, 2014. Fedchenko is the Director of Kyiv Mohyla Academy's School of Journalism. "Contemporary Media Use in Ukraine," *Broadcasting Board of Governors—Gallup*, June 3, 2014, http://www.bbg. gov/wp-content/media/2014/06/Ukraine-research-brief.pdf (accessed August 20, 2014).

12 See commentary by Diana Dutsyk and Andriy Kulykov on Radio Free Europe/Radio Liberty, Dmytro Shurkhalo, "Peredvyborchi kampanii vplyvayut ne duzhe pozytyvno na ZMI—Dutsyk [The pre-election campaign's influence on the media is not very positive]," *Radiosvoboda.ua*, January 3, 2014, http://www.radiosvoboda.org/conten t/article/25219932.html (accessed August 21, 2014).

[*Maidan Nezalezhnosti*], while political parties and politicians met on European Square, close to the Khreshchatyk. Since protests had occurred throughout Yanukovych's presidency, these at first did not appear to pose any real threat. In fact, the top lapdog government-mouthpiece television channel, INTER, broadcast what many analysts say was the best account of the first assault against protesters on the night of November 30, 2013. The report clearly showed how police violently beat unarmed students in the dead of night and chased them out of the Maidan.

Things changed, however, after huge crowds gathered in the Maidan the next morning to express their horror. Less information about the protests appeared in the mainstream media, fewer talking heads appeared on television, many incidents were not reported, protesters' comments were not aired directly, and criticisms of the Yanukovych government were softened, or not aired. International condemnation of the regime's use of violence was also ignored in mainstream reports.[13]

As the protesters refused to disperse and their demands grew, the media started to frame the protests negatively. The size of the Euromaidan was downplayed and the image of the protesters was distorted. They were portrayed as a small group of radical and unemployed rabble-rousers who had nothing better to do than to make trouble. Gradually, the small but vocal far right segment of the protest movement dominated headlines. Increasingly, according to media reports, the protests were caused by an unruly mass of violent radical nationalists, extremists, fascists, and anti-Semites. Incidents such as the toppling of the Lenin Statue, the World War II nationalist leader Stepan Bandera's portrait appearing next to the main stage in the Maidan, and the use of the slogan, *Slava Ukraini—Heroyam Slava* [Glory to Ukraine, Glory to the Heroes] were all widely reported. Although right wing extremists did protest, for most who were present on the Square the nationalist slogans were not about ideology or history but were, rather, empowering and easy to chant.[14] Yet the media commentary increasingly focused on the alleged fascist-nationalist-Banderite character of the Maidan. This narrative resonated with certain parts of society, as it was the continuation of the negative Soviet portrayal of Second World War-era

---

13 Interview with Diana Dutsyk, Kyiv, May 30, 2014. Dutsyk is an editor for the website MediaSapiens.com and is the Deputy Director of Kyiv Mohyla Academy's School of Journalism.

14 Interview with Tetiana Pastushenko, Kyiv, June 10, 2014. Pastushenko is a historian based at the National Academy of Sciences Institute of History.

Ukrainian nationalists, and the more recent discourse used against the right-wing nationalist *Svoboda* Party by Yanukovych's Party of Regions.

The administration's aim was to try to demoralize the protesters, to prevent others from coming out in support, so that the movement would gradually abate, as had happened with other previous protests, such as those against tax and language legislation. The greatest number of silencings and distortions were on the state television channel, *Pershyi Natsionalnyi*, and on many regional media outlets. As violence and uncertainty grew, some media outlets began to take sides, and this led to a further distortion of the overall reportage.

Table 1. Number of news reports that may show evidence of censorship

Channel	October 2013	November 2013	December 2013	January 2014	March 2014	May 2014
INTER	16	24	29	53	19	14
ICTV	21	27	13	27	10	14
Ukraina	11	24	20	29	11	9
Novyi Kanal	5	13	10	13	3	8
5 Kanal	8	9	8	12	7	6
Pershyi Natsionalnyi	38	39	46	66	18	5
1+1	13	23	27	31	9	2
TVi	0	5	7	7	5	2
STB	8	13	15	6	4	2

Table adapted from "Pro shcho movchaly novyny u travni-2014 [What news was silenced in May 2014]," *MediaSapiens*, June 11, 2014, http://osvita.mediasapiens.ua /material/31551 (accessed August 21, 2014).

Table 2. Number of news reports that showed government authorities and the president in an unbalanced manner

Channel	October 2013	November 2013	December 2013	January 2014	March 2014	May 2014
INTER	14	21	29	49	7	0
ICTV	20	25	13	27	6	3
Ukraina	11	23	19	28	9	1
Novyi Kanal	3	13	9	13	3	2
5 Kanal	8	8	8	12	4	2
Pershyi Natsionalnyi	36	37	44	63	15	4
1+1	13	22	27	29	7	1
TVi	0	21	29	49	7	0
STB	8	12	15	6	4	0

Table adapted from "Pro shcho movchaly novyny u travni-2014 [What news was silenced in May 2014]," *MediaSapiens*, June 11, 2014, http://osvita.mediasapiens.ua/material/31551_(accessed August 21, 2014).

Table 3. Number of news reports that silenced various aspects of protests

Channel	October 2013	November 2013	December 2013	January 2014	March 2014	May 2014
INTER	6	9	71	64	32	3
ICTV	7	10	72	48	36	2
Ukraina	7	8	78	65	41	3
Novyi Kanal	4	10	83	68	35	3
5 Kanal	6	9	86	73	40	2
Pershyi Natsionalnyi	8	9	82	75	32	2
1+1	5	5	60	46	33	1
TVi	2	8	82	63	30	2
STB	5	10	72	48	36	2

Table adapted from "Pro shcho movchaly novyny u travni-2014 [What news was silenced in May 2014]," *MediaSapiens*, June 11, 2014, http://osvita.mediasapiens.ua/material/31551 (accessed August 21, 2014).

Things changed again after Yanukovych fled for Russia in the wake of the February 18–20 violence. Censorship largely ended, media reporting became more objective and balanced, and most mainstream media began broadcasting messages of unity. Major television channels added logos that permanently appeared on the screen, the national blue and yellow flag with the words "A United Ukraine" flashed in both Ukrainian and Russian. The former director of the state national television channel was replaced with Zurab Alasania, one of the founders of the online Hromadske.TV. Soon afterward, the online initiative was given a few hours airtime on the state broadcaster, and the grassroots online Hromadske Radio was given a daily two-hour broadcast spot on the state radio station.

After Russia annexed Crimea on March 1, 2014, and began sending arms and fighters into Donetsk and Luhansk, it intensified its information war against Ukraine. To gain control over information flows, Ukrainian television and radio channels were taken off the air in areas that Russia came to control, and anti-Kyiv propaganda increased. In response, some Ukrainians advocated blocking transmissions of Russian television on Ukrainian territory, while others like ICTV political talk show host and Public Radio founder Andrii Kulykov suggested that the best way to fight against propaganda is to dispel it.[15] Channel 1+1 decided to discontinue purchasing and airing Russian entertainment programming that glorified their military forces, and instead focused on developing quality Ukrainian programming.[16]

Russian and International Media Framing

Ukraine's Euromaidan protests were widely reported in international and Russian media. Russian media depicted the protesters in a negative light from the beginning, downplaying the size of the crowds, labeling the protesters as an unruly mass of violent radical nationalists, extremists, fascists, and anti-Semites. The standard themes of Russian media representations were the same as those used by Yanukovych's spin doctors, which suggests the earlier framing in Ukraine's media came from the Kremlin.

Russian diplomats, such as Foreign Minister Sergey Lavrov and UN Ambassador Vitaliy Churkin, regularly commented on the situation in

---

15 "Kruhlyi stil: Informatsiyna bezpeka Ukrainy v umovakh neoholoshenoi viiny [Information security in Ukraine during an undeclared war]," *Ukrinform*, May 13, 2014, http://www.ukrinform.ua/ukr/news/krugliy_stil_1938013 (accessed August 21, 2014).

16 "Ukrainski kanaly pochaly znimaty z pokasu zakupleni rosiiski serialy pro viiskovykh i spetsnaz—Oleksandr Tkachenko [Ukrainian channels start to cancel the broadcasting of Russian shows about military and special forces]," *Telekritika*, June 6, 2014, http://www.telekritika.ua/rinok/2014-06-06/94515 (accessed August 20, 2014).

Ukraine, and these statements were widely reported by international media outlets. The Russian information infrastructure was well developed and effective in communicating Russia's views on Ukrainian events, much more so than Ukraine's. Despite evidence that Russia was distorting information, including Russia Today anchor Liz Wahl's dramatic March 5, 2014, on air resignation, in which she announced, "I can't be part of [a] network that whitewashes Putin's actions," to a degree Russian statements shaped the international presentation of events in Ukraine, most notably by portraying the protesters, and later the interim government, as extremists.[17] In large part, this was because Ukrainian officials were far less active and effective in communicating their messages.

Many Western media outlets regularly labeled the situation "Crisis in Ukraine." The focus often shifted away from the causes and creativity of the protests, and government-sanctioned violence, to issues of anti-Semitism in Ukraine, its historic roots, and fears of its resurgence. Many reported that Bandera's portrait was displayed on the Maidan. Few noted, however, that the portrait of the national bard Taras Shevchenko was more prominently displayed, or that the images of Jesus, and Soviet era dissident-turned politician Vyacheslav Chornovil were equally prominently displayed. This trend intensified after Yanukovych fled, and an interim President was chosen until an election could be held. Russian media constantly reported their government's statements that a "fascist coup" had occurred in Kyiv, that the acting president was illegitimate, and that anti-Semitism was on the rise in Ukraine.

This message was picked up and repeated by Western media outlets and politicians. When US Vice President Joseph Biden visited Kyiv on April 22, 2014 he offered American support to Ukraine's interim government, called on Russia to pull back it troops, but also said, "just as corruption can have no place in a new Ukraine, neither can anti-Semitism or bigotry. Let me say that again. Neither can anti-Semitism [n]or bigotry. No place. None. Zero."[18] A few days later American National Public Radio devoted an entire show to the topic, "Is Anti-Semitism a Real Threat in Ukraine?" where

---

17 Greg Botelho, "Anchor Quits: I can't be part of network that whitewashes Putin's actions," *CNN*, March 6, 2014, http://www.cnn.com/2014/03/05/world/europe/rus sia-news-anchor-resigns/index.html (accessed August 21, 2014).

18 "Remarks to the Press by Vice President Joe Biden and Ukrainian Prime Minister Arseniy Yatsenyuk," *The White House: Office of the Vice President*, April 22, 2014, http://www.whitehouse.gov/the-press-office/2014/04/22/remarks-press-vice-preside nt-joe-biden-and-ukrainian-prime-minister-arse (accessed August 22, 2014).

guest Richard Brodsky said, "[anti-Semitism] is real and it's real not just in Ukraine but in Russia itself and of course, Europe. There is a growing resurgent set of Nazi and neo-Nazi movements."[19] This discourse has also been voiced in academic circles.[20] It largely disappeared from the media discourse after the nationalist candidates for president gained less than 1% of the vote in the May 25, 2014 election, the same week that far right parties won roughly a quarter of the vote in some West European countries in EU parliamentary elections. Russia quickly changed its message on Ukraine to condemnations of the intensified Anti-Terrorist Operation aimed at ending the violence in Donetsk and Luhansk. It began falsely reporting that the Ukrainian government was bombing its own civilians and that thousands were fleeing to Russia.

A number of grassroots initiatives arose from Ukraine's civil society during the Euromaidan protests to counter the Yanukovych and Russian governments' disinformation campaign, and later the interim Ukrainian government's ineffectiveness in spreading its message. The Civil Sector of the Maidan began publishing a weekly online newsletter that was widely distributed, spreading information about their activities and what was really going on.[21] A group of experts in the field of international relations, communications, and public relations set up a Ukraine Media Crisis Center on the third floor of the Ukraina Hotel, located on the Maidan. They provided free services "in order to help Ukraine get a strong voice in the global dialogue about the latest happenings" and insisted that the center remain a non-partisan project. It quickly became a clearinghouse where Ukrainian and international figures made statements and issued press releases.[22] Small initiatives, such as the growth of *samizdat* like "Teritoriya Voli" on the

---

19 "Is Anti-Semitism in Ukraine a Real Threat," *NPR*, April 25, 2014, http://www.npr.org/2014/04/25/306832654/is-anti-semitism-in-ukraine-a-real-threat (accessed August 20, 2014).
20 Tarik Cyril Amar, Omer Bartov, and Per Anders Rudling, "Supporting Ukraine Means Opposing Anti-Semitic Nationalism Now, Not Later," *Tablet—A New Read on Jewish Life*, March 24, 2014, http://www.tabletmag.com/jewish-news-and-politics/166945/no-time-to-waste-in-ukraine (accessed August 21, 2014).
21 For past issues of the newsletter, see: http://issuu.com/karabashi/stacks/07fe697da3a349c0b4bbb21136ffc5bd.
22 For further information about the Ukraine Media Crisis Centre and to access their holdings, please see: http://uacrisis.org/.

Maidan, also became common.[23] After Russia annexed Crimea and began instigating violence in Donetsk, the Journalism School at the National University of the Kyiv Mohyla Academy launched a site called "Stop Fake," wherein it systematically tracked and posted examples of blatant untruths in Russian media, and countered them with facts.

Journalists Targeted

One of the most worrying aspects of the media situation during the protests and the Russian invasion that followed was that journalists were deliberately targeted as part of the effort to control information. Although the Yanukovych regime had an established record of suppressing free speech by pressuring journalists in various ways, including hiring thugs to beat them up, the level of violence intensified dramatically as protests grew.

Not only were journalists censored, their editorial offices were raided, they were slapped with legal charges, and they faced cyber-attacks. Members of the press were threatened, arrested, assaulted, beaten, and had their equipment destroyed. A Radio Free Europe/Radio Liberty camera operator captured a chilling moment on video when on the night of December 11, 2013, he filmed *militsiya* shooting at protesters. The armed man spotted him, turned the rifle on him, and fired. The video ends abruptly as the camera lens shatters.[24] Reports also claim that four cinematographers were deliberately shot in their eyes and were permanently disabled.[25]

Early in the morning on Christmas Day, 2013, journalist-activist Tetyana Chornovol was involved in a run-off-the-road collision as she was on her way home from the Square. She was dragged from the car, severely beaten, and left in a snowy ditch. Fortunately, she was rescued and survived; but this was not an isolated incident. Eighty-two journalists were assaulted in January 2014, and seventeen survived gunshot wounds. On

---

23 For a discussion of *samizdat*, see the Facebook group "Vilnyi prostir na Maidani [Free Space on the Maidan]," https://www.facebook.com/groups/1375730606018763/?fref=ts (accessed August 22, 2014).

24 "Militsiya tsilyt u zhurnalista [Militsiya points gun at journalist]," *Radiosvoboda.ua*, January 20, 2014, http://www.radiosvoboda.org/media/video/25235296.html (accessed August 22, 2014).

25 Marichka Naboka," Zatrymannya zhurnalistiv Radio Svoboda—tse 'vzyattya v zaruchnyky'—yuryst [Detention of Radio Svoboda journalists is a "hostage taking", says lawyer]," *Radiosvoboda.ua*, January 20, 2014, http://www.radiosvoboda.org/content/article/25236411.html (accessed August 22, 2014).

February 18, 2014, Vyacheslav Veremyi was killed by a group of thugs as he was photographing them perpetrating violence. Much of this was not widely reported at the time.

After Russia invaded Crimea, and began moving into Donetsk and Luhansk, journalists in those areas faced even greater threats. Some from Crimea fled after repeated persecution. In Donetsk and Luhansk, heavily armed men began attacking editorial offices, and kidnapping, and beating independent journalists. Serhii Harmash, founding editor of Donetsk's online OstroV Information Agency told his editorial staff to stop coming to work after their office was attacked by unknown gunmen. He relocated his family to Kyiv and continued to produce the publication by communicating with his staff via Skype. "I still go back to Donetsk from time to time," he said in Kyiv, "but I have to wear a baseball cap and dark glasses so as not to be recognized."[26]

Forty-six journalists, including Western ones, were reportedly kidnapped in May 2014 in eastern Ukraine. Italian journalist Andrea Rocchelli and his translator and fixer Andrei Mironov were killed. Ukraine's Institute of Mass Information introduced a new category of free press violations, "journalists forced to go into hiding, or flee."

---

26 Interview with Serhiy Harmash, Kyiv, June 21, 2014, Harmash is the editor-in-chief of OsrtoV Information Agency.

Table 4. Journalists Targeted: Incidents Reported to Ukraine's Institute of Mass Information

	Nov 2013	Dec 2013	Jan 2014	Feb 2014	Mar 2014	Apr 2014	May 2014 (most violations in Crimea, Donetsk, Luhansk)
Access to information denied	1			1	1		
Arrests, detentions		2	8				7
Attacks, assaults	9	49	82 (17 gunshot victims, two cameramen targeted by *militsiya*)	70	44 (30 in Crimea, 14 in Ukraine)	22	87
Censorship	11	12	5	5	16 (14 in Crimea, 2 in Ukraine)	21	88
Cyber attacks	3	20	13	5	18 (4 in Crimea, 14 in Ukraine)	1	25
Economic pressures		1		1			
Foreign journalists denied access		2		1			
Hindering in performing professional	5	11	11	18	34 (25 in Crimea,	6	66

duties					9 in Ukraine)		
Journalists forced to go into hiding or flee the country (category introduced Jan 2014)			3				
Journalists internally displaced (category introduced Mar 2014)					1 (from Crimea)	1 (10 unconfirmed)	7 (6 from eastern Ukraine, 1 from Crimea)
Kidnappings					11 (all in Crimea)	20 (all in eastern Ukraine)	46
Killings		1					1
Legal charges	3					2	7
Offices raided		2		4	12	13	43
Political pressures	4	1	2		3 (in Ukraine)		2
Searches		1					
Threats, intimidation		8	13	7	9 (5 in Crimea, 4 in Ukraine)	11	27

Adapted from "Barometr svobody slova za gruden 2013 roku [Freedom of Speech Barometer for December 2013]," Institute *of Mass Information* January 15, 2014, http://imi.org.ua/barametr/42710-barometr-svobodi-slova-za-gruden-2013-roku.html (accessed August 21, 2014).

Impact on Public Opinion

What impact did media reports and violence have on public opinion? Before protests and war began, polls showed that most Ukrainians were dissatisfied with their government and not interested in uniting with Russia. During the course of the protests and following Russia's invasion, this did not fundamentally change. Thus, it seems that the media did not alter but perhaps strengthened people's views.

While he was president, Viktor Yanukovych used the media to present himself and his government positively. However, his corruption and use of state-sanctioned violence against society were evident to most Ukrainians. A public opinion poll conducted a few weeks before the November protests erupted showed that 87% of the population were dissatisfied with the state of the economy, and 79% were unhappy with the political state of affairs. [27] Yet not everyone took to the streets, even after reports of police beating unarmed student protesters aired. Ukrainian journalist Andrii Kulykov explained:

> The extensive, if not always fair, media coverage of the Euromaidan events had a different impact on different people. For those who sympathized with the protesters it further strengthened their resolve. For those who supported the Yanukovych government, were more or less indifferent, or not used to this kind of protest, it was scary, it reinforced their fears. [28]

Increased internet and social media usage facilitated the flow of information among activists and those who supported the protests. But, the question remains whether it led to increased mobilization nationwide. Perhaps the most curious findings are that despite quantitative evidence collected by media monitoring organizations that news was distorted, many Ukrainians felt that television coverage during the Euromaidan protests was objective, [29] and that there was an increase in viewership of Russian

---

27 "Ukraine 2013 Public Opinion Poll Shows Dissastisfaction [sic] with Socio-Political Conditions," International Foundation for Electoral System, December 5, 2013, http://www.ifes.org/Content/Publications/Press-Release/2013/2013-Public-Opinion-Survey-in-Ukraine.aspx (accessed August 22, 2014).

28 Interview with Andriy Kulykov in Kyiv, June 7, 2014. Kulykov is a journalist for the Ukrainian International Commercial Television (ICTV). He also founded Hromadske Radio.

29 "KMIS Doslidyv, yak hlyadachi spryimaly yakist naibilsh vplyvovykh telenovyn pro podii 'Yevromaidanu' [KMIS researched on how viewers assessed the quality of news on the most influential news broadcasts about the 'Euromaidan']," MediaSa-

TV channels from November 2013 to January 2014, although it declined in February.[30]

Stereotypes and fear mongering about fascists, Banderites, and the Right Sector continued to be broadcast on Russian television and repeated by some politicians. Some believed it, yet others rejected it once it proved false. Donetsk Union leader Mykola Volynko explained on the live political talk show Svoboda Slova on April 22, 2014:

> In February, towards the end of the month, the [Donetsk] city council secretary Bohachev announced that 700, then 800 Banderites are headed here to kill and rape. Everyone began to look for these Banderites. Kramatorsk businessmen offered a reward of 500 hryvni [Ukrainian currency] for a live Banderite. Everyone started searching for Banderites—they did not find any.[31]

Dislike of the Yanukovych regime became clearly evident in the May 2014 presidential election when Party of Regions candidate Mykhailo Dobkin received only 3.3% of the vote.[32] Yet attitudes towards political participation or the EU did not radically change after Yanukovych's ouster. Despite the lifting of censorship and fair coverage of the election campaign, voter turnout for the presidential election was relatively low at 60.3%.[33] Petro Poroshenko won in the first round; however, the 54.7% of the vote he received corresponds to pro-EU attitudes nationally. Despite Poroshenko's repeated media statements on his intention to fight corruption, responses from Euromaidan activists and other civil society groups were cautious. Euromaidan Civil Sector newsletter editor Anastasiya Bezverkha said about the new President:

piens, March 24, 2014, http://osvita.mediasapiens.ua/material/28929 (accessed August 21, 2014).

30 "How Ukrainians Watch Russian TV Channels," "Yak ukraintsi dyvliatsya rossiski kanaly [How Ukrainians Watch Russian TV Channels]," Telekritika, March 14, 2014, http://www.telekritika.ua/rinok/2014-03-14/91503 (accessed August 21, 2014).

31 "Na 'Skhidnomu Fronti' bez zmin [No change on the 'Eastern Front']," Svobodaslova, April 22, 2014, http://svobodaslova.ictv.ua/ukr/catalog/2014-04-22/text699.html (accessed August 20, 2014).

32 For full election results, see Central Electoral Commission of Ukraine's website at, http://www.cvk.gov.ua/pls/vp2014/wp001.

33 The cited percentage excludes turnout in areas not controlled by the Ukrainian government.

His task is not to ruin the trust of the Ukrainians. From the very start he has to establish and maintain these relations of trust—be open to critical questions from journalists, reveal all his assets and profits, get rid of everything that will create conflicts of interest, and get a team of professionals to conduct reforms in cooperation with civil society, and engage more actively in relations with the EU.[34]

Attitudes towards Russia and the separatists also did not significantly change in the immediate aftermath of the Euromaidan protests or the Russian invasion. During the Yanukovych era, media often framed political and historical issues in a pro-Russian fashion. Yet in mid-February 2014, just before the Russian invasion, a survey showed that only 12% of Ukrainians wanted to unite politically with Russia, although there were regional variations, with the figure being 41% in Crimea, 33% in Donetsk, and 24% in both Luhansk and Odesa.[35]

After Russia's annexation of Crimea and while the Donetsk and Luhansk Peoples' Republics were proclaimed by small groups of heavily armed men, public attitudes on the issues changed only slightly. Russia continued its powerful information campaign aimed at discrediting the Ukrainian state, yet a Pew Research Centre poll conducted in April 2014 showed that Ukrainians who felt regions should be allowed to secede had increased only slightly to 14% nationwide. In the east it was 18% overall, 27% among Russian speakers, and 54% in Crimea.[36]

Conclusion

An independent media is considered crucial for democracy, since citizens need accurate, objective news to make informed decisions. Though this ideal does not truly exist anywhere, Ukrainians have enjoyed little press freedom in their first few decades of independence. During the Euromaidan protests, and the Russian military invasion that followed, the media

---

34 Interview with Anastasiya Bezverkha in Kyiv, May 28, 2014. Bezverkha is an activist and a member of the media team for the Civic Sector of Euromaidan.

35 See, "Dynamika ctavlennya naselennya Ukrainy do Rosii ta naselennya Rosii do Ukrainy [Dynamics of Attitudes of Ukrainians towards Russia and Russians Towards Ukraine]," *International Institute of Sociology*, March 4, 2014, http://www.kiis.com.ua/?lang=ukr&cat=reports&id=236&page=3&t=3 (accessed August 21, 2014).

36 "Despite Concerns about Governance, Ukrainians Want to Remain One Country," *PewResearch on Global Attitudes*, May 8, 2014, http://www.pewglobal.org/2014/05/08/despite-concerns-about-governance-ukrainians-want-to-remain-one-country/ (accessed August 21, 2014).

were a battleground in Ukraine. All sides tried to use and control information, and frame the story in a way favorable to themselves. Some journalists towed the official line or sat on the fence, while others tried to show things as they actually were. Many were targeted, kidnapped, beaten, and even killed.

The key question is: what impact did the media have on public opinion during these events? Available evidence suggests that it was mixed. A wide range of media sources was available in Ukraine and internationally, and people sought out and used the ones that corresponded to their value systems and life experiences. Although mainstream media set the agenda about what audiences thought, that did not necessarily mean that it determined how people reacted to the information made available to them. Media messages can play an important role in shaping societal opinions, albeit in a variety of ways. As Alasania noted, "People can find the truth, but some choose to listen to lies." Yet he ended our interview on a positive note, explaining his vision of how to create a public broadcaster that would promote democracy, he said, "The relationship between values and media needs to be nurtured."[37]

---

37 Interview with Alasania, June 4, 2014.

A Ukrainian Thesaurus in Russian

Tanya Zaharchenko[*]

Much has been written about Ukraine lately, as commentators continue to offer competing interpretations of the recent complex and grueling events in this diverse and dynamic Eastern European country. Rather than recount the chronology of these events, this chapter discusses a new voice that has emerged in the country in response to its current realities, but has not yet received much international recognition. This manifold presence springs from a set of semantic changes to the thesaurus of the nation, which—over the course of several months—has expanded to encompass Russophone Ukrainians. In Ukraine's new semantic landscape, speakers of the Russian language have assumed an important position: one at the forefront of the nation's response to international discord.

This is not a role Russophone Ukrainians are used to. For years after the Soviet Union collapsed, they were regarded as "the other" by some of the population of their own country, particularly by those who positioned themselves as the national intellectual elite.[1] Likewise, some western commentators have consistently cast them as "something akin to the fifth column in Ukraine."[2] Now among the main players in the region's political arena, Ukraine's Russian-speakers are suddenly at the forefront of defining and voicing their country's interaction with Russia—and they are doing so with an assertiveness quite unexpected by less perceptive observers. In the process, they challenge stereotype after stereotype: of Ukraine as a divided country; of equating language and geopolitical orientation; of a homogeneous Russophile "south-east"; and of a weak or nonexistent national identity as a diagnostically functional concept, among others.

Across the border, in the Russian Federation, it has not been uncommon to describe Russian-speaking residents of nearby east Ukraine as

---

[*] Unless otherwise noted, all Ukrainian-language and Russian-language sources are cited in this piece in my translation. I am thus responsible for any imperfections. This article, written in April 2014, was originally commissioned as a reflections-based essay, thus its more personal tone compared to other chapters.

[1] Volodymyr Kulyk, "Shchyri ukraintsi ta ikhnii 'othering' [True Ukrainians and their 'othering']," *Krytyka* 12 (2000): 28–31.

[2] Paul S. Pirie, "National Identity and Politics in Southern and Eastern Ukraine," *Europe-Asia Studies* 48 (1996): 1080.

"our own other."[3] This view was mutual for a fair number of east Ukrainians, until the moment troops entered their country in Crimea. In an intriguing turn of events, those closest to Russia—by virtue of language, culture, or both—now stood at the vanguard of formulating a response to its policies. Many of the Russophone voices that began to appear in the mass media and on personal websites turned out to be fiercely protective of Ukraine's independence.

As a reaction to—or perhaps as a part of—these profound changes to the nation's sense of itself, as well as to the voices rising on its behalf, one of Ukraine's top TV channels, Channel 5, diversified its usual Ukrainophone broadcasting by introducing a daily news hour in Russian. In early March 2014, it also joined the wider mass media trend of displaying a banner that rotated between Russian and Ukrainian words for "One Country" (other participating TV channels include Inter Media Group, Starlight Media, 1+1 Media, and Media Grupa Ukraina). In a classic case of silver lining, Ukraine is stubbornly pulling together at a time when centrifugal forces try to pull it apart.

Interestingly, some analysts pointed to the country's diversity, including linguistic diversity, as a mediating and positive factor years before the current information war erupted. Historian Andrii Portnov, for instance, wrote in 2010 in response to commentators who called and continue to call Ukraine's cultural heterogeneity "feckless": "The challenge facing Ukrainian society and elites nowadays is how to perceive regional diversity not in confrontational and mutually exclusive terms, but as a wealth of differences; how to recognize "the other" not as a threat, but as an opportunity."[4] It appears that now, such voices are finally beginning to be heard. And with good reason: throughout recent developments, the feelings of many Russophone residents of Ukraine towards their home nation have been revealed to be nothing short of powerful.

Something important is happening in Ukraine in this regard. Or perhaps it took shape a long time ago, and is now revealing its voice. We are witnessing a phenomenon whose layers analysts have yet to address fully. When Russian writers from east Ukraine spread their call to keep Russia's

---

3   Mykhailo Karasikov, "Slobozhanska mentalnist: mif chy realnist? [The Sloboda mentality: myth or reality?]," *Kultura ta etnoetika* 3 (1994): 19-20.

4   Andrei Portnov, *Uprazhneniya s istoriyei po-ukrainski* [Exercises with history in Ukrainian] (Moscow: Memorial, 2010), p. 103.

troops out of the country, their strong wording was unsurprising.[5] Contrary to much of the recent media coverage, winter 2013–14's Ukrainian uprising was not an either-or struggle between European and Russian allegiances. Rather, for the majority of participants the demonstrations had to do with people's growing sense of dignity—and its violation. A wide spectrum of society took part, and about a quarter of those on the Maidan identified Russian as the primary language they speak at home.[6] This nuance appears to have surprised some observers (those wary of the perils of multiculturalism) more than it did others (those who have celebrated, and continue to celebrate, the complexity of Ukraine's diverse population). It is becoming increasingly clear that there is no longer such thing as a Russophile south-east [iugo-vostok] of Ukraine. And thoughtful observers know that, in its imagined monochrome form, it never existed in the first place.

All these events hit close to home, both literally and figuratively speaking. I hail from east Ukraine, from the culturally vibrant city of Kharkiv/Kharkov, which became the centerpiece of my academic work as well. While finalizing a doctoral dissertation on the topics of literature, memory, and identity in the eastern borderlands of Ukraine, I sought ways to process the developments at home and to separate these two challengingly different perspectives: that of a scholar and that of a local.[7] Meanwhile, continually emerging analytic texts of various calibers proved helpful in pondering the changes Ukraine was undergoing. Nevertheless, for a while, pinpointing the force behind these changes was not an easy task.

A column by political scientist Olga Mikhailova helped piece the puzzle together. Discussing the emergence of a group she calls "the Ukrainian Russians" in *Ukrainska Pravda*, Mikhailova used a key word to explain why many in this cohort are standing up for Ukraine's territorial and cultural unity. That word was "betrayal." A new animal in the existing thesaurus of analytical media coverage, it is key to much of the emotional reaction observable in the country today. Mikhailova's suggestion that "in the historical

5   "Message from Kharkiv's Russian Writers", *Of Memory and Identity*, March 2, 2014 http://memoryidentity.wordpress.com/2014/03/02/message-from-kharkiv (accessed March 23, 2014).

6   "Maidan-dekabri Maidan-fevral: chto izmenilos? [December-Maidan and February-Maidan: what has changed?]," *Kievskii Mezhdunarodnyi Institut Sotsiologii*, February 6, 2014 http://www.kiis.com.ua/?lang=rus&cat=reports&id=226 (accessed March 1, 2014).

7   Tanya Zaharchenko, "Where the Currents Meet: Frontiers of Memory in the Post-Soviet Fiction of East Ukraine," University of Cambridge, 2014.

narrative of the Ukrainian Russians, [supporting] an empire is [...] a betrayal they refuse to commit" illuminates the origin of the force sustaining
Ukrainian society at this time: a sense of responsibility and loyalty.[8] It is a
community in the making—or, more precisely, in the awakening.

Scholars and journalists may continue to discuss recent events in the
languages of nation, post-colonialism, politics, patriotism, or cultural
memory. But it is the vocabulary of sentiment that hits closest to explaining
developments in Ukraine today. Russian and Russophone Ukrainians alike
(the former are ethnic Russians living in Ukraine, the latter are Ukrainians
whose native language is Russian) are vocal in refusing military protection
from the Russian Federation. This issue has adopted, and is now framed
by, the discourse of dignity. In fact, a number of commentators have highlighted the term "dignity" as central to the lexicon of the Maidan uprising.

In an apt illustration of Leonard Cohen's lyric, "I love the country but I
can't stand the scene," many (though, at this point, not all) Russophone
Ukrainians continue to appreciate Russia's language and culture. Most of
them, however, have little tolerance for the Russian Federation's current
politics. To such people, supporting these politics would mean turning their
backs on those with whom for years they have shared streets, cities, and a
nation—even if they did not always share the same language, literally or
figuratively. This conscious loyalty is what stands behind the country's
coming together at this time of crisis: a refusal to betray, no matter how
sentimental it may sound, can be observed among much of the Russian-
speaking community today.

Meanwhile, some of those who used to condemn the Russian language in Ukraine as undesirable —a contaminating remnant to be rectified
for the sake of nation-building—are seeing these processes, and are responding to them as well. As a result, things appear to be changing on all
sides. Initiatives in spring 2014, such as a group of Lviv residents choosing
to speak Russian for a day in February and a group of Donetsk residents
responding by speaking Ukrainian, have shown that many Ukrainians have
processed their revolution on terms different from the divisive rhetoric imposed on them by some international opinion. [9]

---

8 Olga Mikhailova, "Ukrainskie russkie [Ukrainian Russians]," *Ukrainska Pravda*,
   March 26, 2014, http://life.pravda.com.ua/columns/2014/03/26/160035 (accessed
   April 20, 2014).
9 "Lvov zagovorit po-russki, a Donetsk i Odessa—na ukrainskom [Lvov will speak
   Russian; Donetsk and Odessa will speak Ukrainian]," *Ukrainska Pravda*, February

This is not to paint a pastoral landscape where none exists. Shredding forces continue to test uniting ones on a daily basis. They draw their strength not only from grievances and hostility in the streets, but also from commentators who still present Ukraine as a fatally divided nation, maintaining the outdated and prejudiced myth of the "Two Ukraines." This fairly popular misconception, which portrays the country as a synthetic and flammable combination of irreconcilable halves, relies in part on the notion of "mentality"—a vague and useless concept applied to a subset of the population in order to shrink-wrap its motivations, feelings, and perceptions into one general standardized psychological condition. If this sounds inaccurate and irresponsible, that's because it is. Recent battles have, unfortunately, revived the "Two Ukraines" framework as the most accessible explanation for events taking place in the region. In line with this approach, for instance, international media has often wrongly painted the Maidan as two parts of the nation pulling in two directions.[10] What could be easier? The western part is "fascist" or "nationalist" (also known as pro-European); the eastern part is "contaminated" or "zombified" by its Soviet past (also known as pro-Russian or pro-multicultural, depending on whom one asks). Who needs to know more?

Refreshingly, many do. A number of respected historians and commentators, both inside and outside of Ukraine, have done much to counter this inept interpretation of multi-layered social processes that unequivocally lack homogeneity. Nevertheless, heavy-handed and uncompromising verdicts continue to appear in media coverage of the Ukrainian situation. They are fairly easy to recognize: a nationally framed argument that relies on variations of the notion of mentality is limited in both content and utility, because it explicitly lacks nuance. Among these rigid judgments, one that continues to hit hard is that of *bydlo*, a curious word derived from the Polish term for cattle [*bydło*].

Having travelled from the West Slavic languages to Ukrainian to Russian, *bydlo* gained a heavily pejorative meaning and is currently used to describe those who are purportedly cattle-like—backward and unrefined—in terms of their mental and spiritual development. In recent discussions,

---

26, 2014, http://www.pravda.com.ua/rus/news/2014/02/26/7016309 (accessed April 1, 2014).

10 For one of numerous examples, see "Press says Ukraine torn between EU and Russia," *BBC News Europe*, November 14, 2013, http://www.bbc.co.uk/news/world-europe-24941697 (accessed December 13, 2013).

this word has been revitalized and repurposed to refer to a certain type of east Ukrainian, particularly those hailing from the country's easternmost region, the long-suffering Donbas (Donets Basin). On the map of stereotypes, this area is renowned for its coal mining, its industry and, thus, its blue-collar workers. This setting has attracted uncompromising and unkind generalizations about its inhabitants. Even in a recent attempt to illuminate the genuine hardship that shaped these lands over the past century, a Donbas-born commentator portrayed its residents as "a quivering biomass." Some of the so-called intellectual elite have also fallen victim to this judgmental stance, which Portnov described recently as a dangerous kind of "reductionism":

> Let us get rid of the country's 'far east' (where the people are 'completely different', meaning: worse) and have us a nice life in European Ukraine... And such arrogant, generalizing, isolationist, orientalist and narcissistic ideas come from those who are so impressed with 'multicultural Austria' and 'lost diversity'. Of course, inventing a nice past while impersonating an enlightened and tolerant intellectual is much easier than to put at least some effort into comprehending and accepting the heterogeneity and complexity of contemporary Ukraine.[11]

Indeed, it is easier. A well-known Ukrainian historian and an equally well-known writer have both recently come up with offensive texts reducing their eastern neighbors to brainless *homo sovieticus*. This unfortunate and myopic cycle of self-perpetuating discrimination involves similarly uncompromising verdicts on 'pro-Ukrainian' activists as neo-Nazis—a technique particularly favored by Vladimir Putin's information war machinery.

The reductive approach maintains, among other things, that those who stand to protect Lenin monuments are standing up for Putin's Russia. However, the gap between these two causes may be wider than usually acknowledged. The alternate view is that such persons are trying to defend a sense of self and a narrative of their past that, they feel, is being wrenched from them without adequate replacement. A closer look at video footage of such demonstrations suggests that the majority of participants are elderly. For them, the gap created by the collapse of the country they knew as home was never quite filled by anything else. In response, they may be defending old monuments to Lenin as a symbol of their youth—which they now perceive as negated, re-narrated as nothing but meaning-

---

11 Translated from Portnov's Facebook account with permission.

less existence under an oppressive regime—rather than a genuinely political symbol of any kind, much less a Putin-related one. Serhii Zhadan, a brilliant Ukrainophone writer who lives and works in Kharkiv (and who hails, incidentally, from Donbas), describes their ordeal as follows:

> Stonemasons of the new world [...] returned as heroes and victors, and all they could do in that bizarre situation was to erect their plaster Holy Grail in a park of culture and leisure, hoping for the ultimate victory of communist ideas and for the good memory of their offspring, who instead will stone you to death, toppling all your monuments, having no faith in your past, having no past of their own.[12]

As I have previously argued, there is a fine line between denouncing a regime and denouncing human lives that coincided with it.[13] Some people may misperceive this line as warped or absent. The resulting anxiety, erroneous or not, provides prime grounds for abuse and misuse by a whole slew of political forces and players, and such manipulation is happening on a daily basis. Yet there is another way to see the troubles gripping Donbas: some of its people, who have become targets of both condescension from within the country and manipulation from without, were simply not as fortunate as those of us whose parents kept collections of Ukrainian poetry in our Russophone households, and made sure we could recite Ukrainian poet Oleksandr Oles (1878–1944) as soon as we started reciting his contemporary—Russian poet Anna Akhmatova (1889–1966). They were possibly also less fortunate in encountering approachable language tutors who were enthusiastic about Ukrainian and interested in helping people speak it with confidence. What they know of the rest of Ukraine instead, and face on a daily basis, is precisely the "reductionism" that says the country would be better off without them—the zombified *bydlo* incapable of anything other than having ridiculous feelings about obsolete monuments. In this light,

---

12 Serhii Zhadan, *Anarchy in the UKR* (Kharkiv: Folio, 2011), p. 26. Other Donbas Ukrainians who topple the Ukrainian west/Russian east stereotype include Volodymyr Sosyura, Vasyl Stus, and Ivan Dzyuba. In the nearby region of Sloboda, also known as the east, the city of Kharkiv is one of the country's key cultural hubs. With its university as the centre of the Romantic Movement in the nineteenth century, Kharkiv gave birth to the modern Ukrainian national idea, and was decisive for its future. These examples, which do not fit the stereotypical delineation, are just some of many—in both eastern and western regions of the country.

13 Tanya Zaharchenko, "While the Ox is Still Alive: Memory and Emptiness in Serhiy Zhadan's *Voroshylovhrad*," *Canadian Slavonic Papers/Revue Canadienne des Slavistes*, 55 (2013): 45–70.

their frustration appears far less surprising and the politicians' willingness to manipulate this frustration—even more despicable.

In one of his works Zhadan describes the ageing post-Soviet generation as "exhausted and seasoned, who carry within themselves, like an ailing heart, the entire experience of their country, of their infinite daily struggle that eventually ends, yet brings them no solace."[14] For this part of Ukraine's population, the need today is rooted in what Tamara Hundorova identifies as "an alternative paradigm to parting with the totalitarian past, rather than rupture and oblivion."[15] In my attempts at addressing this topic, I have referred to a "recalibrated architecture of separation" in hopes of emphasizing that it is not the separation from the Soviet Union with which some people continue to struggle; it is the totality of the negation that comes with its commonly imposed framework.

The complexity of the post-catastrophic ordeal, in fact, is one of the key reasons behind Zhadan's overwhelming success as a writer (and one of the key reasons why working with Ukrainian literature is such a fruitful approach to studying the country). Using Ukrainian, a language not easily accused of imperialism, he breaks through the simple dichotomy of imperial Russia and colonial Ukraine with captivating characters whose feelings about the fallen empire are anything but simple. This yields compelling imagery. "Will they be able to tell their own children and grandchildren how in their peaceful sky, right above their heads, one could still behold the majestic fading flashes of history?; this history was distant and inaccessible and had a bloodred hue—like tulips, like blood, like Coca-Cola."[16]

What will "they"—literature's first-hand witnesses to imperial collapse—be able to tell their children? Perhaps even more importantly, what will we be able to tell ours? As revolution and aggression exploded and shook our lives, did we cope by turning against "the other" in our own nation—be it the Westerner we have dubbed "Banderite" or the Easterner we have dubbed "*bydlo*" (or, in fact, vice versa)? In his thoughtful piece on Odesa/Odessa, Blair Ruble maintains: "The port city represents a Russia that always has been open to the world, with a wry smile that scoffs at the sort of ruffians and thugs dispatched by President Vladimir Putin to 'liber-

14 Zhadan, *Anarchy*, p. 65.
15 Tamara Hundorova, "Voroshylovhrad i porozhnecha [Voroshylovhrad and emptiness]," *LitAktsent*, February 8, 2011 http://litakcent.com/2011/02/08/voroshylovhrad-i-porozhnecha (accessed July 1, 2012).
16 Zhadan, *Anarchy*, p. 76.

ate' the city."[17] Ruble identifies an important tendency among Russophone Ukrainians: that of habitual subversion of official narratives, coupled with strong local loyalties. Now that Odesa, known for its humorous and relaxed disposition, has become a site of violence and death, amplifying resentment and anguish on all sides, these loyalties will require courage. And now that a portion of the population of Donbas has declared independence and warfare has begun, the people of Ukraine face another fundamental challenge: not giving up on the entirety of the region's inhabitants—and refraining from sweeping them all under the rug of the clichéd image of the east as a "nature reserve of all things foreign."[18]

Like in the south, many of the Russophone residents of east Ukraine have nurtured a distinctive regional identity that provides "an alternative to the ethnically and linguistically determined 'national idea'."[19] Now this regional identity is decisive to Ukraine's next steps as a country. A writer from Donetsk, the largest city in Donbas, articulated it eloquently on April 22, 2014, in Moscow, where she travelled to receive an award for her Russian prose. At the microphone, Elena (Olena) Stiazhkina recited her piece called "About Love": "I want to talk about love, a realization that was a surprise for me. There was once a country; then it turned out to be motherland." She continued:

> There is a problem of hearing in our countries these days. But to those who do hear I'd like to say this: the only language of love I know is Russian, and it certainly does not need military protection. [...] The Russian language does not need blood. [...] You cannot kill Ukraine in the south and the east, because killing Ukraine would mean murdering me, a Russian, and others, also Russians.[20]

---

17 Blair A. Ruble, "Odessa: Ukrainian port that inspired big dreams", *Reuters Blogs*, April 15, 2014 http://blogs.reuters.com/great-debate/2014/04/15/odessa-ukrainian-port-that-inspired-big-dreams (accessed April 20, 2014).

18 Hundorova, "Voroshylovhrad".

19 Tatiana Zhurzhenko, "Cross-border Cooperation and Transformation of Regional Identities in the Ukrainian-Russian Borderlands: Towards a Euroregion 'Slobozhanshschyna'? Part 2," *Nationalities Papers* 32 (2004): 508.

20 "Russkoyazychnaya pisatelnitsa iz Donetska zayavila v Moskve: Ubit Ukrainu nelzya. Video [Russophone writer from Donetsk stated in Moscow: One cannot kill Ukraine. Video]," *Argument UA*, April 24, 2014 http://argumentua.com/novosti/russkoyazychnaya-pisatelnitsa-iz-donetska-zayavila-v-moskve-ubit-ukrainu-nelzya-video (accessed April 25, 2014).

When in 1996 Paul Pirie took issue with "an unfortunate tendency to assume the national consciousness and homogeneity of the Russian minority and the Ukrainian majority," and argued that "the national orientation of individuals officially classified as Russians in different parts of the country is often only tenuously so," he hit the nail on the head, as such voices have made exceedingly clear.[21] Today, the intricate relationship between Russia and Ukraine is, as ever, decisive for the future of this part of the world. And, as ever, it remains largely simplified as either antagonistic or fraternal. Russian-speakers in Ukraine effectively topple this dichotomy. They are akin to soldiers of sentiment in a war of calculation. Whether they refer to the motherland as *rodina* (in Russian) or as *batkivshchyna* (in Ukrainian) is secondary. And, importantly, there are also people who do not use any version of the term "motherland" for any nation—for a wide array of reasons—but still choose to support those who do.

Viewed outside of an academic framework, Ukraine these days is a conglomeration of hands, stretching towards each other from all its centers and peripheries. Beneath the hands, dirty stones fly in all directions, swung from every center and periphery as well. Some of these stones hit hard, or hit a wound (Ukraine comes with many), and the hand above it trembles. The pendulum of deleterious mutual diagnoses that underlies the processes of othering is in full swing here at the moment. It is aided in part by history—the Ukrainian language, for instance, was "othered" in these lands for many years—and in part by the harrowing tension and fervor of armed conflict. One thing academic observers can do at this time is to support those in Ukraine who are still reaching out to each other: to ensure they have a place for which to write, and a platform from which to speak.

In the commentary on Ukraine these days, it seems, if no one is offended, you have not been heard. A gifted Russian rock-bard, Aleksandr Bashlachev (1960–88), sang on the verge of the Soviet Union's collapse: "I am most ashamed when you cannot see that I have heard what I listened to." Ukrainians are currently making a choice: in a large country with a mosaic of histories, there is much to mutually resent; there is also much to admire. This choice and its aftermaths generate a crucial set of sociocultural and political processes. It remains to be seen whether the centrifugal forces surrounding these processes can be countered, and at what cost. At the moment, this much is clear: despite adversity, despite a sustained assault on the very possibility of a whole Ukraine, Ukrainians of all

---

21 Pirie, "National Identity," 1080.

kinds (and there are, indeed, many kinds) continue to demonstrate, to each other and to external observers, that all their ways of invoking "one country"—be it *yedyna kraina* or y*edinaya strana*—are worth listening to.

EuroRevolution:
A Historian's Street-Side Observations

William Risch

In late November 2013, I had no idea I would write a paper like this. My sights were set on anything but Ukrainian politics. On November 22, I was in Boston giving a paper on youth cultures in the Soviet western borderlands during the "Era of Stagnation." Before the panel on which I presented started, fellow panelist Serhii Zhuk stood up and told the audience about protests happening in Kyiv that involved his friends from Dnipropetrovsk, some of whom were mentioned in his presentation. He also said that there was a danger that President Viktor Yanukovych would send forces to disperse the protests. Frankly, I had no idea what was going on. The details only became clear over the rest of the convention, when fellow scholars of Ukraine spoke of "mass demonstrations" in Kyiv that were unbelievably historic. Over the next few days, I began following, mostly on Facebook, what seemed like a revolution—the assaults on student demonstrators on November 30, the million-man march that followed, and the toppling of the Lenin Monument on December 8. I decided to go to Kyiv from December 14-23. That trip led to another, from January 6-20. A third trip followed, from March 15-23. This paper will focus on my first two trips, when the EuroRevolution, as it is sometimes called, was in its "peaceful" phase.

When I arrived in Kyiv on December 14, 2013, I was convinced that the Yanukovych regime's days might be numbered. Just a few days before, an attempt by *Berkut*, the special police of the Ukrainian *militsiya*, to clear Independence Square failed. Hundreds of thousands of people were demonstrating on Kyiv's main avenue, the Khreshchatyk. Yet as I soon discovered, it seemed more like a peaceful standoff than a revolution midstride. The Square was full of barricades, evoking Europe's revolutions of 1848 and Cossack forts from the 1600s. While students and academics set up several tents at the protest site, other tents were inhabited mostly by farmers, workers, and ordinary people, predominately from western Ukraine, but some from Ukraine's other regions, too. When I took part in an all-night vigil at the Maidan on December 17–18, I was struck by the Ukrainian flags gathered near the stage where pop singer Ruslana was singing, reading people's messages, introducing speakers, and broadcasting phone calls from the Ukrainian Diaspora from Chicago to Moscow. The demonstrators came from western Ukrainian towns and it seemed like most of the people on stage were also from western Ukraine as well. It felt like the Lviv Region came to visit me in the center of Kyiv. Still, heartbreaking stories were read from the stage, written by people bussed in from eastern Ukraine for the anti-Maidan rally taking place in Mariinskiy Park near the Supreme *Rada* that week. Some had been misled into thinking they were going to the Maidan. Others complained of being ordered around and were given almost nothing on which to live during their time in Kyiv. One teenager, a Russian speaker, addressed the crowd with an account of how he escaped a group of anti-Maidan youth sent to Kyiv.

I spent another night at the Maidan on December 19–20, serving in what was then called the "Night Watch." A historian from Lviv, Ihor, invited me to patrol the barricades with a group of men who were mostly from western Ukraine, but also included people from central Ukraine, southern Ukraine, and even Crimea. It was damp and freezing. We stayed up all night huddled near a fire, wearing plastic helmets. At one point, someone in green camouflage, presumably belonging to a self-defense unit, came by to check on us and to complain that I was not wearing a helmet. We took turns watching the barricades near the McDonalds and the Crimean Tatar restaurant at a far end of the Maidan.

As we discussed politics, one of the guards, Serhiy, was eager to know what the US was going to do about the situation in Ukraine. His suggestion, though, was couched in irony: "Send in the troops now!" he laughed. Unemployed, 38-years old, Serhii came to Kyiv from Poltava. He found work here as a welder [*svarshchyk*]. "That's good!" said Ihor. "What do you mean, good!?" exclaimed Serhii. "The boss fucking laid us all off after two weeks, because he took off somewhere!" Before Yanukovych became president, Serhii owned a small store near Poltava, a medium-sized city located on the Vorskala River in central Ukraine. As the economy deteriorated, he quickly went into debt to as many as three banks. Within three months of the new presidency, he said, he lost 150,000 *hryvnias*, the whole store.[1] His wife left him. ("It means she did not love you," said one of the older men with a smile.) He was left with an eight-year old son. As Serhii talked about his problems, I could hear some sniffling. At first, I

---

1   On May 1, 2010, three months after Yanukovych came to power, the hryvnya traded at 8.1246 to the American dollar. Thus 150,000 hryvnyas was roughly $18,500.

thought he was cold from the weather, but it turned out he was crying. Ihor tried to console him: "Get some lawyers! They can get you out of this mess!" Serhii said he saw a lawyer, who took a lot of money for nothing. "Go to America!" Ihor said.

Serhii exploded: "Why the fuck do I need to go to America!? Why can't I stay here? I am almost forty, no job, why the fuck must I leave? What job could I get?" Ihor then said, "Look, it's tough everywhere!" We then debated the merits of going to America for work, the job market in Ukraine, and what Serhii could do to get legal help. Arguments flew back and forth, between Serhii and Ihor, between Serhii and others, between others and Ihor. And, then the Ukrainian national anthem began to play from the stage.

Suddenly everyone around the fire went silent. They stood up and took off their hats. Some had their hands on their hearts. Others from a group nearby also rose and joined us.

I was used to singing the Ukrainian national anthem collectively every hour. But as we stared at the lit screen on the Trade Unions Building [Budynok Profspilok], looking on as priests and musicians led us in song, I thought that this was the Maidan. Serhii could tell us about his dilemmas; we were there to listen. Despite arguments, we were there for each other. The Ukrainian opposition leaders did not represent us. The foreign officials occasionally touring the Maidan did not represent us. We had only ourselves to speak for us.

While mass rallies on Sunday, December 22, filled the Maidan and the Khreshchatyk, on both Sundays when I was in Kyiv, in mid-December, it seemed like the Maidan's days were numbered. While the Maidan's night vigils seemed dominated by western Ukrainians, national themes tended to dominate the stage during the day. What I thought would be a revolution by students on behalf of Ukraine's "European Dream" seemed overshadowed by patriotic rallies against the Yanukovych regime. Still, there were suggestions that this was about more than protest against the regime. There was an "Open University" stage on the Maidan featuring speakers who talked about things like British local government. Amid readings in Ukrainian history and recitations of Ukrainian poetry, one of the afternoon speakers on the main stage gave a brief lecture on the importance of nonviolent resistance and how the actions of individuals can make a difference. On one afternoon, an activist from Belarus spoke to the audience in Russian about the political problems in Belarus and how it was important for Ukraine to fight Yanukovych's authoritarian regime. The crowd unfurled a huge Belarusian nationalist flag during the man's speech. I interviewed one of the organizers of the tent for the Stryi District, located in Lviv Oblast. He spoke of the Maidan's long-term importance. The protests sought to change Ukraine's system of government—these protests were just the beginning. By the end of the week, I had interviewed activists from the *Studentska Koordynatsiyna Rada* [Student Coordinating Council] and the *Hromadskyi Sektor Yevromaidanu* [Civil Sector of the Euromaidan]. They, too, suggested that this revolution was about the long-term change of values, practices, and institutions. SKR activists talked about forming an independent students' union, similar to those found in Chile, which would become a nationwide voice for students.[2] They talked about introducing new laws in the Supreme *Rada* that supported greater transparency in policing. They relayed plans to open up a dialogue between civil society, political opposition, and the regime, as well as forming a temporary government of professionals —those not affiliated with political parties—to resolve Ukraine's pressing financial problems. Activists from the Civil Sector of the Maidan discussed similar measures aimed at systemic change, not just regime change. As I interviewed one activist, I was struck by the role that this organization played in mediating conflict in the early days of the protests. They were on the streets on November 30 and December 1 trying to calm down Kyivans who were throwing rocks and assaulting anyone who resembled a policeman. In other words, they and probably other civic organizations may have kept Kyiv from erupting into a bloodbath after *Berkut* attacked students.

When I left Kyiv on December 23, I knew that the Euromaidan protests would not end the Yanukovych regime any time soon. The standoff was relatively peaceful; not a single armed policeman was in view near the Maidan. (At best, armed *Berkut* forces were on Hrushevskyi Street blocking access to the Supreme *Rada*.) For me, it was important to come back in early January, this time to understand those who did not support the Maidan protests or who were actively against them. I had a hunch that this would prove interesting. On December 19, St. Mykola Day in Ukraine, a Kyiv sociologist and I decided to go visit the anti-Maidan camp in Kyiv's

---

2   The activists were referencing the Federation of Catholic University Students (Federación de Estudiantes de la Universidad Católica de Chile—FEUC) and the University of Chile Student Federation (Federación de Estudiantes de la Universidad de Chile—FECH).

Mariinskyi Park. Unlike the Maidan, the anti-Maidan seemed dark, gloomy, and regimented. We saw entire groups of people being marched in and out of the park, with supervisors doing head counts of everyone in each group, making sure no one had strayed. Then we started talking with so-called "*titushky*" who were camped out at the anti-Maidan.[3] Frightening at first (our conversation started when they asked us why we were taking photos of them, and I had a Euromaidan protest ribbon on my backpack), our conversation turned into a debate about the merits of the Maidan protests. We were speaking with men in their teens and early twenties from the Poltava Region, athletes clearly brought in to cause trouble if necessary. They tended to repeat familiar stereotypes about the Maidan movement: that it was led by crazy "Banderites" from western Ukraine (more exactly, Lviv) who dared to topple Kyiv's Lenin Monument in order to erect one to Bandera. One of the young men said that if Ukraine joined the EU, then Ukraine would enter NATO. "Then my children will have to fight for NATO, and they were against the Soviet Union in the Cold War!" he exclaimed. He said that his family was part Polish, and that they remember what happened in World War II when the Germans were the occupiers and the Ukrainians helped them. He said that recently, when he was in Lviv for a kick boxing tournament, he went to a store, asked for something in Russian, and the store clerk rudely told him to leave. He added that his family suffered in "1933," an indication that they were victims of the "Holodomor."

My friend tried to debunk certain myths they had about the Maidan, like the responsibility of Maidaners for the attempted storming of the Presidential Administration on Bankovyi Street, or that the Maidan protestors all supported Bandera, noting her own grandmother's trouble with Banderites in western Ukraine during World War II. We started talking about economic problems facing Ukraine. We asked these young men if they knew about the twelve newly minted Ukrainian billionaires. They did not know. We asked them if they knew about Andriy Klyuyev and Mykola Azarov's assets and homes in EU countries, or if they knew that the Party of Regions had supported integration with the EU as a matter of policy. They did not know. Eventually we came to a consensus that the system produced great social inequality, that oligarchs exploited people, and that things needed to change. "That is what people on the Maidan are saying, too," stressed my friend.

---

3   Titushky is a term for mercenaries, mostly hooligans, who supported the Ukrainian police during Yanukovych's presidency.

We had to leave these young men because it looked like we were attracting unwanted attention from their supervisors. But, I decided soon after that I needed to understand eastern Ukraine if I was to get a better idea of where this protest movement was going. So I came back to Ukraine on January 6, and I spent about two weeks in Donetsk and Kharkiv, trying to see how people understood the protest movements there.

In Donetsk, I stayed with a fellow historian and writer who, despite his strong sense of Ukrainian patriotism, had many friends who were opposed to the Euromaidan movement. In fact, his wife, an ethnic Russian, went to a birthday party and reported to me what her friends thought of the EU. Here is the list of objections and concerns they raised about an Association Agreement with the EU:

i) An Association Agreement with the EU would not raise people's standards of living.
ii) How would Ukrainians earn the wages of their western neighbors? What would happen to Ukrainian manufactured goods?
iii) What would happen to Ukrainians' jobs?
iv) The EU promises aid, but these are just vague promises.
v) An Association Agreement would lead to the EU dumping cheap, low-quality goods into Ukrainian markets, undermining Ukrainian firms.
vi) The Association Agreement would lead to a loss of people's sense of identity [identichnost].

People at the birthday party talked negatively about a German story concerning a divorce between a man and his wife; their daughter found out that her father was not with another woman, but with a man. This may sound odd to Western ears, but same-sex marriages are very controversial in a traditional Orthodox society like this one. This dissonance is also evident in the educational system. If more closely integrated with the European Union, Ukraine's education standards would fall. Students would do as they wished, and the authority of educators would be undermined.

Later, my friend's wife circulated a questionnaire I made that asked people about their attitudes toward the Maidan protest, the EU, the Customs Union, and Russia, and what they thought of the country's political crisis. I also interviewed four people in their twenties and early thirties from Donetsk and from the neighboring coal-mining city of Makiivka. While a few questionnaires were sympathetic to the Maidan protestors, most saw them as clueless, unemployed people paid by politicians who were being manipulated by extreme nationalists. Two women in their late twenties and early thirties voiced similar understandings. Yet almost all of them said that the "division" between eastern and western Ukraine was artificial, exploited by politicians. While criticizing some of the slogans made by Maidan demonstrators and associating these with the political far-right, they seemed more concerned about the protesters' lack of plans for fixing Ukraine's serious economic problems. While a woman in her late 20s saw Yanukovych as having been more effective than his predecessor, Leonid Kuchma, she stressed that Ukraine lacked leaders fit to be president, and that it was unrealistic to remove Yanukovych from power. This woman also suggested that the Donetsk Region's skepticism about the EU did not mean a greater affinity for Russia. She said that Ukraine faced a false dichotomy between being pro-Russia or pro-EU, and that it should look after its own interests.

Finally, there were suggestions that there were people in Donetsk who viewed the protests positively. Activists I interviewed talked about the "European Dream," and the need to conduct a non-violent struggle to make life better for Ukrainians. Though their Euromaidan was very small—a few dozen people nightly near the Shevchenko monument downtown—it was a community-turned-family for them.

After three days in Donetsk, I went to Kharkiv, a city where Euromaidan protest leaders were planning the First All-Ukrainian Euromaidan Forum on January 11–12. Already I heard from friends that there was to be trouble. Someone said that the forum's organizers had been denied building space for their meetings, that there was talk of provocations underway, and that Vitalii Klychko was supposedly going to show up.

On the first day, January 11, Yevhen and I went to see an anti-Maidan rally that met for both days of the Forum. About 500 people lined Kharkiv's main street and they had Ukrainian and Party of Regions flags. Generally, they looked to be over the age of fifty, and were either public service employees [*pratsivnyky iz budzhetnoi sfery*] or municipal workers [*komunalnyky*]. A few were in their teens or early twenties; most likely, these were students of vocational schools [*peteushnyky*]. As we discovered, this column of demonstrators stretched all the way to the Shevchenko Monument and Constitution Square. They held posters with a variety of pro-government slogans about supporting President Yanukovych and his plans for economic development. A common refrain claimed that it was better to deal with the government's budget than to support the protests, and that peace and order were better than the chaos of the Euromaidan. Placards told Euromaidan activists to stop loafing and go back to work. Many signs said, "Fascism will not pass!" There was one slogan, though, directed specifically at Kharkiv Euromaidan activists: "Whoever is with the Euromaidan should leave Okruzhnaya!"[4]

The Euromaidan Forum was held in conspiratorial fashion. As they were denied a central meeting place, the Euromaidan activists were set to meet in five separate sections. Yevhen knew that events were being coordinated at a café called "India." We went up the street to the café. I first saw people waving a Ukrainian flag and a red and black OUN flag on the street. To our right, an alley led to the café. About twenty people were gathered in the alley's environs, smoking, on cell phones, or talking with one another. A woman with long dark hair was constantly on a cell phone, consulting her papers and people nearby now and then. She was apparently directing people where to go. Others were inside the café itself. Yevhen introduced me to Olha, a woman in her 50s or 60s who was a veteran activist in Kharkiv. She told me that Ukraine belonged in Europe, that her travels to Prague, Budapest, and other cities convinced her that Ukraine needs to develop closer ties with the EU. She expressed outrage over the beating of protesters, and she said that the protest needed to do much more than assemble at Kyiv's Maidan, stand, and listen to music. Tactics needed to change, as the regime had not changed at all—not one resignation, not one concession to the protestors. The international community was not helpful—neither the EU nor the USA. Discussions about sanctions were empty. She suggested that the virtues of nonviolent protest were exhausted. Something else needed to be done—working in groups, planning greater events, anything other than what was going on now. She introduced me to someone from Ternopil, a man in his 60s who was attacked during one protest.

It was strange to be in an alley discussing the Forum. It was even stranger that people in the alley did not really know what was going on, either. People were not sure the locations of the alternative meeting sites. As I found out later from other Kharkiv residents who observed the anti-Maidan, it sounded like some journalists were denied accreditation.

---

4   Okruzhnaya refers to the highway around Kharkiv, suggesting that these people should leave town.

Yevhen and I decided to continue to the Shevchenko Monument. Indeed, the anti-Maidan forces had taken over the entire square. Anti-Maidan speakers were broadcasting speeches from the stage; hundreds had assembled when we first arrived around noon. Even at 4pm, we saw people gathering in what was cold and windy weather. Unless people took turns warming up, it must have been an unbearable experience. Later, Yevhen said that two things could be going on in the minds of these demonstrators: they were either upset at the Yanukovych regime and the local government for making them stand out here, or they were upset at the Euromaidan demonstrators for forcing them to counter protest.

Yevhen asked if I wanted to talk to any of the people at the anti-Maidan demonstration. At first, I hesitated because I feared someone would blame the Euromaidan movement on the Americans. Then I realized that Yevhen would be there in case any trouble happened, so I agreed. We spoke with a woman in her 50s or 60s. I explained that I was a historian who wanted to know what people in Ukraine thought of "recent events." "You mean the Euromaidan?" she asked. The woman said that she worked in the "budgetary sphere," meaning that she was a state worker, and that state finances paid her salary. The Euromaidan movement caused liquidity problems for the government, and people like her relied on the state for work. The Euromaidan protests thus were preventing people like her from working. She added that a lot of money was being spent on the protests. "That money," she said, "could have been used to help sick children, disabled children." When I asked her about what Ukraine would do about its debt problems, she evaded a direct answer, preferring instead to talk about how a house not repaired in time falls apart.[5] She added that Ukrainians needed to ensure that problems are solved before they become worse. When I asked what solution she foresaw for Ukraine's political crisis, she said that the Euromaidan protesters should wait until the 2015 elections, and if they did not want Yanukovych they should vote for someone else. The woman seemed very nice, very polite, and consistently smiled and said, "It is true, no?" after every argument she presented. I thanked her for her responses, and I wished her luck. When Yevhen asked her if she would be photographed with me, she smiled and said no.

The next day, January 12, Yevhen returned to take pictures early in the morning on what became the second day for the anti-Maidan. This

---

5   As of 2013, Ukraine's national debt stood at just under $73 billion, or about 41% of its annual GDP.

same woman was there checking lists and making sure protesters were in line. She was clearly one of the organizers.

Once we were across the street from the main stage at the Shevchenko Monument, we stopped to listen to the speakers. The two speeches we heard said little. The first stressed that Yanukovych's government should not sign the Association Agreement and it praised the people of Kharkiv, while the second speech laid bare the "fascist evils" practiced by people on the Maidan. Both speeches were in Russian. Yevhen knew one of the speakers because he worked with him at a television studio.

One of the speakers asked that everyone observe a moment of silence in memory of those killed in a fire in Kharkiv that week. The speakers boomed the sound of a ticking clock, to ensure everyone was aware of it being a minute of silence. All I saw were people socializing with each other or walking in different directions. No one took off his/her hat, no one stood in silence—no one, except for Yevhen and me. We were the only ones who showed respect and paused to remember the dead.

After I saw people insulting the dead, the rest of the anti-Maidan lost any thread of sincerity for me. We spoke to a group of teenaged boys gathered together in one corner of the square. I told them that I was a historian and a cultural studies scholar, and that I wanted to find out what the youth thought of the Euromaidan protest movement. "We are not interested in politics," said one of them. "We are into soccer." A few minutes later, we tried to speak with a woman in her early twenties. Yevhen asked her if she wanted to talk with us about the Euromaidan protests. She said no.

It became quite clear that the whole event was staged. Besides ignoring elementary rituals of decency, the demonstrators were following the commands of organizers who walked around with typed lists of names, gathered together in clear plastic sheet covers. They were going from one group of people to another, taking attendance, and seeing who would hold placards or flags. I noticed that each placard had a number on the reverse side. The numbers ran in succession along the street. Everything was planned. As Yevhen noted, it was a repeat of an old Soviet ritual for state holidays, like May Day, where every factory had to offer workers for state demonstrations. People went to warm up, to socialize, to joke, and to gossip, but the actual protest held no enthusiasm for the "protesters." The same could be seen here.

Yevhen and I walked to Constitution Square, the original site of the Euromaidan protests, now decorated for Orthodox Christmas. As we talked about prominent buildings in the vicinity, a middle-aged woman, eating a chocolate bar, came to us and asked where the Maidan was going to meet. Yevhen said that they would meet later at 6pm, but not at Shevchenko, the location of the anti-Maidan forces. Yevhen asked if I wanted to ask her some questions. So I told her about my book plans, and I asked her what she thought of the Euromaidan movement. Unlike all the others with whom we spoke and to whom we listened at the "anti-Maidan," this woman spoke to us in Ukrainian. Most importantly, though, were her responses. She said that the Euromaidan was meaningful to her. She was not a regular attendee at protests because of her job, but she went to the Maidan in Kyiv with her pregnant sister. She erroneously said that the protests started over Ukraine not joining the EU, but that they became directed against the regime after students were brutally beaten. She said that these anti-regime protests were good as they were making people like her aware that they were citizens with rights, and that the government was supposed to work for them. She said that she started to feel a sense of dignity as a person, as a citizen, and that people like her mattered. And while there would always be people with opposite views, it was important for each of us to take a stand and to act. That was the essence of democracy. It was so refreshing to hear this woman's speech after the strange and vague rhetoric from the anti-Maidan organizer. They really were something. As we went to look for a place to warm up, Yevhen said, "And you know, those people [the anti-Maidan people] would call her a fascist."

While warming up with some coffee, Yevhen and I saw on Facebook that one of the sections had met in a church, and that *titushky* had broken in and thrown a tear gas canister at the attendees. As far as Yevhen could tell, no one remained at the church, so we went to another meeting. The section met at an institute that promoted local democracy in Kharkiv, run by Olha, the woman whom I had met near café India. The office was maybe on the seventh floor of a building not far away from the city council's offices. When we arrived, Olha and a man were alone. They were waiting for section members dedicated to culture and education. She was worried about provocateurs. When I asked if either hooligans or police had assaulted her, she mentioned something similar near the café, she said that she was roughed up at her office. There was a break-in. She was well aware of provocations going on that day, including the one involving activists at the church. While watching the news, including that of Ariel Sharon's death, we saw a real time, livestream of one section's meeting. The Internet linked various parts of this "conspiracy" together.

I was naive enough to bring Estonian-language flash cards to pass the time, but soon I drifted into a conversation with Olha about her institute. Established roughly ten years ago, the institute tries to promote better local government in Kharkiv. The problem is not that the institute is oppressed by the state, but that the local government in Kharkiv has registered a number of "loyal" organizations so that it can say that it promotes the growth of civil society. In fact, it does not. These officially sponsored organizations end up better at writing grant proposals, so they get more financial assistance. As for her organization, it has not been so fortunate; it is in danger of losing its office space.

At about 4 pm, members of the section arrived. As activists got coffee and tea, Yevhen and I introduced ourselves as "observers" at the section's meeting. There I met a very kind university professor who talked about her efforts to organize the students in Kharkiv in the early days of the Euromaidan protest movement. She showed me a white ribbon that they had made for wearing around their heads, which said, "Government resign!" [*Uryad u vidstavku!*]. They also set up a "Hyde Park," where students could speak their mind about the regime's problems, write those problems on pieces of paper, and then place them symbolically in an old suitcase, a symbol underscoring the need for change. When all the complaints were collected, someone read them to the audience. The woman who read also happened to be a co-chair of this section with one of the Kapranov brothers, Vitaliy, the well-known newspaper publisher who had moved to Ukraine from Moscow in 1998.

We all entered a room where the section officially convened. Kapranov chaired it. He went through the agenda and reviewed points to be considered by the final plenary session. Some of the discussion was interesting. Groups from small towns in western Ukraine, like Kalush, talked about the fundraising they accomplished, as well as local initiatives to establish "Open Universities" for the wider community. Kapranov stressed that this was going to be part of an organization that would be organized horizontally rather than vertically, to support the efforts of various Euromaidans to educate Ukrainians. But, as the section began deliberating over the wording of their resolution, it increasingly started to resemble a university department's faculty meeting. Speakers quickly went off course and onto tangents like human rights violations, with one person noting the

Tetyana Chornovol case (she was beaten by a group of men near Boryspil Airport on December 25, 2013). I was starting to fall asleep.

But then one of the section's members, after looking at a text message on his phone, announced that another section meeting in a bookstore had been attacked, that a tear gas can had been thrown into the bookstore, and that one guard had been injured. I started to wonder if we were going to have unwelcome visitors. Luckily, we were high above the street, and the stairwell was locked. But when Olha told people that the section that evacuated the bookstore was coming to our location, I became a little nervous.

Around 6 pm, a commotion occurred at the main door. Olha rushed out to meet a couple dozen people, mostly young men, as they filed into the hallway. They seemed fine physically, but they looked solemn, subdued, and scared. A cameraman from UNIAN [*Ukrainske Nezalezhne Informatsiine Agentstvo*] was there to take photos. Eventually writer Serhii Zhadan, leader of the section, entered with his chart tablet that he used to conduct the meeting. He set up the section right in the hallway, calling out, "Is everyone ready to start?" And so their section resumed its work.

The hallway, thus, was extremely crowded. Yevhen and I had to force our way gently through it as we left. I was a little nervous about what would happen outside. Olha had us wait and proceed accompanied by men who ensured that unwelcome guests would not enter. As we went out onto the street, everything was calm. Only the usual pedestrians were walking past the building.

On January 12, Yevhen and I went to see the First All-Ukrainian Euromaidan Forum release an official statement to the press outside the Kharkiv Human Rights Protection Group building on Ivanova Street. It was as if we were witnessing the birth of something akin to the Solidarity Movement. A businessman at the subsequent rally referred to "people power" taking place, similar to 1917 during the February/March Russian Revolution. The rally that marked the end of the Forum took a very dramatic turn when police and anti-Maidan forces surrounded it. Sound machines drowned out our speeches with loud Russian and Ukrainian pop music, and some street toughs threw incendiaries that exploded near us. I nearly panicked, but the crowd formed a cordon of men around the rally, the police kept separate anti-Maidan and Maidan forces, and Euromaidan activists used speakers loud enough to rise above the noise broadcast by the police.

As my second trip ended in January, it seemed like this nonviolent struggle might go on for some time, but it was starting to lose momentum. In Donetsk and Kharkiv, I heard people say that two months of demonstrations and vigilance in Kyiv had produced no results. The same people were in office. No one faced justice for the November 30, 2013, beatings of demonstrators. The same could be said about those who had assaulted journalists and activists across Ukraine since December. Yet things started to change rapidly after the Supreme *Rada* hastily passed the so-called Dictatorship Laws of January 16, which threatened Maidan protesters, and participants in the Automaidan protest movement, with considerable prison terms. On January 18, I helped some activists spread literature that condemned the laws. Stressing that the constitution had been overthrown, we called on people to attend the assembly on Sunday, January 19, at the Maidan, which was to protest political authoritarianism and to restore constitutionalism.

A friend and I went to that assembly. We heard the crowd jeer opposition politicians. We saw crowds march to the Supreme *Rada*. We walked by barricades, maintained by riot police, that surrounded government offices. Here, we saw people of all ages taunting the police. When questioned by my friend, two of these people, students, complained that two months of protesting had been fruitless, and that something else needed to be done. My friend and I went to the police cordon in Mariinskyi Park, where the police were putting on gas masks. We were afraid that something terrible was about to happen. Luckily, except for a small group that came by with Ukrainian flags and that taunted police, it quieted down. My friend decided to debate politics with two riot police patrolling the park who were from Zaporizhzhya, a city in southeastern Ukraine. After debating the stereotypes they shared about the Maidan protests, we came to a consensus that the whole system radically needed to be changed. We learned a lot about the riot police—their low pay, their disgust with claims that they served a 'crook' [*zek*] ("I serve the law, not some *zek*!" one cop said), and their own frustrations with the political system. My friend even managed to pass some protest literature to one of them for distribution to his colleagues.

It was absolutely freezing that night in Mariinskyi Park. Still, it was peaceful, with hardly a soul around. In the distance, I heard some roaring and a couple of loud booms, which I thought could have been a vehicle backfiring. Only upon returning to my hotel later that night did I realize that this was the start of a battle between protesters and police on Hrushevskyi

Street, which was down the hill from the park where my friend and I had been. The nonviolent phase of Ukraine's revolution had ended. In the following months, about 100 Maidan protesters died in Kyiv. War broke out in eastern Ukraine killing thousands and sending tens of thousands into exile, including my hosts in Donetsk. The tranquil phase of the Euromaidan Revolution now looks alien, one where peaceful, evolutionary change still seemed possible. Alas, such change did not come in 2014.

Gender and Nationalism on the Maidan

Olesya Khromeychuk

In an article on the public voice of women, Mary Beard informs that the earliest "example of a man telling a woman to 'shut up,' telling her that her voice was not to be heard in public," is recorded in one of the foundational texts of Western culture, the *Odyssey*.[1] In Book I, Telemachus, the son of Odysseus and Penelope, rebukes his mother when she publicly asks a bard to stop singing about Greek heroes and sing something more cheerful. In front of the roomful of men, Telemachus instructs Penelope: "Mother, [...] go to your quarters now, and attend to your own duties at loom and spindle, and order your maids about their tasks: let men worry about such things, and I especially, since I hold the authority in this house."[2] Fast-forward several millennia and switch from the epic poem to a street information poster, and we find a similarly archaic division of labor: "Men are needed for the night guard on the barricades. Women are needed to keep watch by the mobilization tent, to keep order, to make tea and food for the guards and to spread information, leaflets and perform other mobilization work."[3]

The poster could be found on and around Independence Square in Kyiv, the space that has come to be known as the Maidan. Another poster

---

*   I would like to express my gratitude to all interviewees who contributed to this research. I would also like to thank Olha Papash, Anna Dovgopol, and Uilleam Blacker for commenting on an early draft of this text.

1   Mary Beard, "On the Voice of Women," *London Review of Books*, 36, no. 6, March 20, 2014, 11–14 (11). Mary Beard is Professor of Classics at the University of Cambridge. In 2013, she spoke out in support of having the image of a woman on a British banknote, after which she received a large quantity of considerable misogynistic abuse via social media.

2   Homer, *The Odyssey*, Book I: 325–64, translated by A. S. Kline, http://www.poetryintranslation.com/PITBR/Greek/Odyssey1.htm (accessed August 22, 2014).

3   This is from an information poster seen on the Maidan in Kyiv in April 2014. The poster was put up in early 2014 by the sixteenth self-defense unit "*Vidsich*" [Rebuff]. The unit grew out of an existing organization, which describes itself as a "civic [...] nonviolent social movement created in 2010 as a reaction to the policies of Viktor Yanukovych and "pro-Russian"tendencies connected with his presidential administration. *Vidsich* focuses on a proactive defense of human rights, civil liberties, and constitutional freedoms." See *Vidsich* Wikipedia page http://en.wikipedia.org/wik i/Vidsich, accessed August 8, 2014.

found near the Square addressed women who happened to pass by it in an even more unambiguous way: "Dear women! If you notice any mess, tidy it up. It will be nice for the revolutionaries."[4]

Homer's depiction of space, where men inhabit the public sphere while women are relegated to their private "quarters," seems to be still relevant to much of today's world. The Maidan is no exception. The physical presence of women at the protests in Kyiv was undeniable. At the start of the Maidan protests, they comprised 42.8% of the protesters.[5] When the demonstrations got more violent, women were physically squeezed out of the Maidan and the public discourse. "Women were artificially separated from the 'true' revolutionaries," explains Anastasiya Melnychenko in her analysis of the female presence on the Maidan. "The message coming from the Maidan stage and from the activists pointed to perhaps the only place for potential female volunteers: the kitchen."[6] In spite of the limiting roles allocated to women, female protesters continued to "fight for their right to be on the Maidan."[7] To my knowledge, no data exists for the male-female ratio of the protesters for mid-February 2014, but at the height of the demonstrations, the number of female protesters was undoubtedly high:

Women received and sorted donated clothes, food, medication; delivered the food and medical supplies to the barricades and to the frontline; worked in medical stations, kept watch in hospitals, preventing abductions of the wounded patients; responded to the Automaidan calls; organized hotlines,

---

4   The word "revolutionaries" is used in its masculine form. See Nadiya Parfan, "Vita-yu Zhinochu sotnyu [Welcome, *Zhinocha Sotnya*]," *Maidan*, February 2, 2014, https://maidanua.org/2014/02/nadiya-parfan-vitayu-zhinochu-sotnyu/ (accessed August 12, 2014). See also "Zhenskaya polovina Maidana [The Female Half of the Maidan]," *The Insider,* February 5, 2014, http://www.theinsider.ua/lifestyle/zhens kaya-polovina-maidana (accessed August 12, 2014). Unless otherwise indicated, all translations from Ukrainian and Russian are mine.

5   See "Maidan-2013: khto stoit, chomu i za shcho? [The Maidan-2013: who is stand-ing, why and what are their aims?]," a survey conducted by the *Fond 'Demo-kratychni Initsiatyvy imeni Ilka Kucheriva'* on December 7–8, 2013 in Kyiv on the Maidan, www.dif.org.ua/ua/polls/2013-year/mogjorjghoeoj.htm (accessed August 24, 2014).

6   See Anastasiya Melnychenko, "Navishcho Ukraini Zhinocha Sotnia? [Why does Ukraine Need a Female Unit,]" *Heinrich Böll Stiftung*, March, 25, 2014, http://ua .boell.org/uk/2014/03/25/navishcho-ukrayini-zhinocha-sotnya (accessed August 24, 2014).

7   Ibid.

and coordinated the transportation of the wounded for treatment abroad, etc.[8]

Women's contributions, however, continued to be largely invisible, and their voices were silent or silenced.

Analyzing the act of silencing women, Beard argues that in the classical world women were allowed to speak out only in certain capacities, for example as "victims and as martyrs—usually to preface their own death."[9] They can also "legitimately rise up to speak—to defend their homes, their children, their husbands or the interests of other women."[10] The depiction of Ukraine as a young woman in a beautiful wreath, victimized by the occupier was omnipresent on the Maidan. Ukraine, often referred to as mother-Ukraine, was presented as a victim and a martyr in many speeches delivered from the Maidan stage. Many women who spoke used the rhetoric of sacrifice, and indicated a readiness to die for their children (usually sons) who were dying for their motherland. On January 21, 2014, following the shootings on Hrushevskyi Street, one woman told an interviewer, on behalf of other women present nearby: "we will cover these children with our bodies and will die here together with them, and let it be the shame of the whole country and this government."[11] Another woman interjected saying that those who were fighting on Hrushevskyi Street "are the best sons of Ukraine, the blossom of the nation."[12] She hurried to explain her own presence on Hrushevskyi Street. Addressing the fighters, she stated, "we have come here not to be stars or something like that, not because we want to say something, but to bow in front of you."[13] During the protests,

---

8   Ibid.

9   Beard, "On the Voice of Women," 11.

10   Ibid. The depiction of women exclusively in relation to men (sons, husbands, partners) was evident in a documentary film "Zhinochi oblychchya revolyutsii [The Female Faces of Revolution]," aired on 1+1 channel in May 2014. The description of the film states that "[e]verything that a woman does, she does out of love. For her son, husband, Fatherland..." See 1+1 for a 45-second teaser trailer, http://www.1plus1.ua/video/zhinochi-oblichchya-revolyuciyi-na-1-1.html, (accessed August 25, 2014).

11   See raw footage for a documentary film titled "Zhinochi oblychchya Maidanu [The Female Faces of the Maidan]," by Olia Onyshko and Petro Didula, https://www.youtube.com/watch?v=LP1BAOiUMXs (accessed June 25, 2014). At the time of writing, this documentary was incomplete and only preliminary footage was available.

12   Ibid.

13   Ibid.

most women who spoke out did so as mothers, protecting their children, or as wives, standing by their husbands; just like in the classical world, where women can "publicly defend their own sectional interests, but not speak for men or the community as a whole."[14]

One might wonder what relevance the discussion of this ancient Greek epic has to the subject of this text. The relevance lies in the existence of a certain tradition of the perception of the public sphere and the role gender plays in it. Almost from its very emergence, the Maidan has been "a battle stage as well as a theatrical stage," turning quickly into "a museum, a form of post-memory."[15] A major city square, it became a space for a public performance of revolutionary activity, patriotism, and heroism. Its actors often performed differently, depending on their gender, and the public perception of the protesters was mostly formed bearing gender expectations in mind. Even the mottos of the protests did not escape gendered language. One of the slogans, most commonly used during the protests, consisted of two parts: one glorified Ukraine and the other its male heroes.[16] The history of the Maidan, referring not just to the space, but also to a lengthy protest movement involving hundreds of thousands of participants, has already gained a firm place as a significant milestone in the history of Ukraine. The myth of the Maidan, however, is still in the making, and there is a chance that, unlike the numerous other historical myths, this one will include the stories of roughly half of its participants. It is worth remembering that *muthos* [authoritative speech, a narrative], as Beard informs us through Telemachus, is traditionally seen as "men's business."[17]

---

14 Beard, "On the Voice of Women," 11.
15 Tamara Hundorova, "Maidan as a Symptom: Trauma, Wound, and Crypt," *Krytyka*, April 16, 2014, http://krytyka.com/ua/community/blogs/maydan-yak-symptom-travm a-rana-i-krypta#sthash.ocbdKnWh.dpuf (accessed August 25, 2014).
16 Here I refer to "*Slava Ukraini!—Heroyam Slava!* [Glory to Ukraine!—Glory to the heroes!]," a slogan with a very contested history. It gained popularity among Ukrainian nationalists during the Second World War and thus has negative connotations for many both inside and outside of Ukraine. Arguably, at the Maidan, the slogan adopted a different, positive meaning; and its second part evolved to signify something much closer to Ukraine's contemporary reality: the current heroes of the Maidan rather than members of the Organization of Ukrainian Nationalists, active in the 1930s-50s. The word "heroes" in the second part of the slogan—*Heroyam Slava*—is in its masculine form, assuming no place for women within the category of heroes.
17 Beard, "On the Voice of Women," 11.

Helping Make the Revolution, or Making the Revolution?

Much of the rhetoric of the Maidan, in spite of its overwhelming civilian composition, centered around the militarized symbolism of the "national liberation movement," a concept firmly connected to the state-building attempts of Ukrainians in the first half of the twentieth century. The structure that ran the day-to-day business of the Maidan called itself the *samooborona maidanu* [the self-defense units of the Maidan]; its leader was known as the commandant and the units comprising the *samooborona* were referred to as *sotnyas*.[18] Many organized groups of activists, including those who had no formal connection to the forty-two units of the *samooborona*, adopted the designation of a *sotnya*: among them were an artistic *sotnya* and a cyber *sotnya*. There were also three all-female *sotnyas*; one of them was the Olha Kobylyanska *Zhinocha Sotnya* [women's unit]:

> We decided to call ourselves the Olha Kobylyanska Zhinocha Sotnya in order to distinguish ourselves from the others. We thought long and hard about our name. We even considered naming ourselves after Simone de Beauvoir. We also thought about Natalia Kobrynska, but no one knows her. Lesya Ukrainka already gets used by everyone. So we chose Olha Kobylyanska's name primarily because she was a feminist.[19]

Anna Dovgopol, an activist of the Olha Kobylyanska *Zhinocha Sotnya*, is a Gender Democracy program coordinator at the Kyiv branch of the

---

18 *Sotnya* is a military designation of a unit of a hundred persons, equivalent to company. The term is not used in Ukraine's contemporary Armed Forces and has the connotation of a military structure not tainted by the Soviet rule. Its earliest record use is by the Zaporizhzhyan Cossacks in the sixteenth century. It has since been used by the Sich Riflemen [*Sichovi Striltsi*], the Army of the Ukrainian People's Republic, and the Ukrainian Insurgent Army (UPA). This study focuses on the *sotnyas* and/or individuals who were active on the Maidan in Kyiv. However, it is important to note that there were a number of regional *sotnyas* (including several all-female regional units) active all over Ukraine; the analysis of these groups merits a separate study.

19 Interview with Anna Dovgopol in Kyiv, April 7, 2014. Dovgopol is an activist of the Olha Kobylyanska *Zinocha Sotnya* and Gender Democracy program coordinator at the Kyiv branch of the Heinrich Böll Foundation. The interviews cited in this text were collected in Ukrainian and/or Russian and all translations are mine. Olha Kobylyanska (1863–1942) was a Ukrainian modernist feminist writer. Simone de Beauvoir (1908–1986) was a French feminist writer, intellectual, activist, and philosopher. Natalia Kobrynska (1855–1920) was a Ukrainian writer and a women's movement activist. Lesya Ukrainka (1871–1913) is the best-known Ukrainian female poet and writer; she was also a political activist.

Heinrich Böll Foundation. Although during the protests the *sotnya* was run by activists who, like Dovgopol, self-identified as feminists, the group did not position itself as feminist for strategic reasons. "In Ukraine the term 'feminism' still scares away both men and women. Even those women who articulate clearly feminist ideas will say that feminism is not for them, that feminism is the hatred of men," said Dovgopol.[20] She explained that the initiative had started as a joke: a few of her friends wrote a Facebook post that an all-female unit was being organized. The reaction was very telling: the information was reposted and many contacted activists to find out more about the newly formed *sotnya*. "It became clear that this sort of structure was necessary," explained Dovgopol, because "women felt marginalized in the public space, in which their only opportunity was to go to the kitchen to make sandwiches."[21] Prior to the unit's formation, its future activists were engaged in the protests in different capacities, each trying to find a task in which she would be most useful:

> Some of our women stood on the barricades, some sat in the office sending out information, some participated in the "Euromaidan SOS," or helped with medication supply, others organized public discussions. We all took part in the protests as individuals one way or another. But after a while we all got fed up with the popularized discourse that women should go to the kitchen and that they should not go to the barricades, because it is dangerous; and that women should smile because it will be nice for other people (as was suggested by a guard of the Ukrainian House, who checked men's documents, but not those of women, provided they smiled nicely).[22]

Once formed, the Olha Kobylyanska *Zhinocha Sotnya* was not officially registered as part of the *samooborona*, as its activists were happy to stay outside of the highly patriarchal structure in control of the Maidan. As part of their activities, the *sotnya* organized self-defense sessions. The training attracted many women of different ages and backgrounds. The purpose of the training was not to persuade women that they must take an active part in violence, but to help them understand that they could do the

---

20 Ibid.
21 Ibid.
22 Ibid. Euromaidan SOS is a group of lawyers, activists, and journalists who collect information about missing people and those who require legal help. The Ukrainian House [*Ukrainskyi Dim*] is a conference and exhibition center located in Kyiv; it was used by the protesters during the Maidan.

same things as men.[23] Dovgopol recognized the precariousness of the *sotnya*'s situation with regard to its view on violence:

> On the one hand we all supported non-violent methods of protests, but on the other, through such a position we seemed to reinforce the discourse that women were always against war, that they were soft and non-violent. Thus, while supporting the non-violent methods of protests the unit also included women who stood on the barricades, and maintained the standpoint that an adult woman can make her own choice.[24]

The main task the *Zhinocha Sotnya* set for itself was to reveal publicly the contributions of women to the Maidan: "we want to emphasize that the making of the sandwiches does not mean supporting the revolution, it means making the revolution happen."[25]

The reason that women were seen as not making but helping make the revolution is partly due to the performativity of gender, in which "[t]he anticipation of an authoritative discourse of meaning is the means by which that authority is attributed and installed."[26] In other words, by expecting and accepting the performance of traditionally feminine gender roles on the Maidan women were reinforcing the gendered structure in which they participated. To put it in Judith Butler's words, "the anticipation conjures its object."[27] One of the protesters who came to the Maidan from Lviv said that having arrived in the center of Kyiv she and her female friend immediately headed towards the women who were serving coffee and tea to inquire whether they could be of help. When asked whether she considered other tasks apart from kitchen duties, for instance the work on the barricades, Olha Solomina asserted: "that is men's work!"[28] Her definition of what constituted men's and women's work was based on her assessment of the physical strain that a certain task involved. Yet, having described her day in the Maidan kitchen, which consisted of ten hours of preparing and serv-

---

23 Interview with Dovgopol. See also Natalia Trach, "EuroMaidan women warriors eager to fight injustice, sex discrimination," *KyivPost*, February 13, 2014, http://www.kyivpost.com/guide/people/euromaidan-women-warriors-eager-to-fight-injustice-sex-discrimination-336806.html (accessed April 25, 2014).
24 Interview with Dovgopol.
25 Ibid.
26 Judith Butler, *Gender Trouble: Feminism and the Subversion of Identity*, (New York: Routledge, 2006), xv.
27 Ibid.
28 Interview with Olha Solomina in Lviv, April 13, 2014. Solomina is a manager at a travel agency.

ing hot drinks and food, carrying five-liter water bottles up and down the three-storied Kyiv City State Administration [KMDA] building, washing-up, and other tasks, she reflected that maybe building the barricades, carrying tires or mixing the Molotov cocktails might not have been any more strenuous.[29] Solomina also recollected seeing women of all ages, many of them, she remarked, well-dressed and wearing high heels, picking out paving stones with their manicured nails and passing them to the people on the barricades.[30] Yet gender performativity, as Butler argues, is "a repetition and a ritual, which achieves its effects through its naturalization in the context of a body," and is thus not so easily challenged.[31] Solomina said that she was proud of her humble contribution to the protests because the Maidan "was made of such individual contributions."[32] Yet, in spite of her reflections of her own equally valuable and no less demanding involvement, she maintained that "a man is a man; he will be pleased if a woman supports him while he defends the fatherland."[33]

Silent and Silenced

An important thought raised by Mary Beard in her analysis of the ancient Western tradition of silencing women is that in the classical world "an integral part of growing up, as a man, is learning to take control of public utterance and to silence the female of the species," in other words, making a woman invisible and inaudible in the public space, even if she is physically present there.[34] There has been much talk of the fact that the Maidan revolution produced a new league of Ukrainian heroes (almost always used in its masculine form). According to the logic outlined by Beard, these men would only have been able to become "real heroes" (or "real men") through silencing their fellow revolutionaries of a different gender. Judith Butler offers a theoretical framing to the traditional perception of the voiceless feminine "nature" that is "in need of subordination by culture that is invariably figured as male, active, and abstract."[35] "As in the existential dialectic of misogyny, this is yet another instance in which reason and mind are asso-

---

29 Ibid.
30 Ibid.
31 Butler, *Gender Trouble*, xv.
32 Interview with Solomina.
33 Ibid.
34 Beard, "On the Voice of Women." 11.
35 Butler, "Gender Trouble," 50.

ciated with masculinity and agency, while the body and nature are considered the mute facticity of the feminine, awaiting signification from an opposing masculine subject."[36] The general attitude of men on the Maidan entailed a silencing of female protesters, treating their voicelessness as "natural." A specific signification, based on the traditional perception of femininity, was applied by men to the women of the Maidan and, by default, women more generally.

Ruslana Panukhnyk, a human rights activist and a co-organizer of the Olha Kobylyanska *Zhinocha Sotnya*, spoke of her and her colleagues' experience of being prevented from defining their own roles in the protests:

> We were all very upset when we were forbidden from entering Hrushevskyi Street during the most heated days of the protests. Women were simply not allowed there, just because they were women. At the same time, young boys of sixteen or seventeen could freely pass the checkpoint, as no document to check the age or the emotional or physical preparedness of the individuals who participated in the Hrushevskyi Street events was required.[37]

Mariya Berlinska, a student of a Master's course in Jewish Studies who was at the epicenter of violence for the whole duration of the active phase of the clashes, confessed that the desire of men to "protect her" simply "drove her insane."[38] She was often prevented from going through the barricades during ceasefires.

> I would be standing for the umpteenth time at a checkpoint, knowing full well that beyond that very barricade, I took my first rubber bullet but now, when it is completely peaceful, I have to explain my basic rights to yet another stump at the checkpoint who is preventing me from going through. At that moment one of the guys would call out from the barricades: "Masha! Come over here! Let her through, she's been with us all this time!" And suddenly I would get "permission."[39]

Berlinska called this a "banal injustice."[40] She also tried another approach to raise the issue of women's discrimination on the Maidan: the pro-

---

36 Ibid.
37 Interview with Ruslana Panukhnyk in Kyiv, April 8, 2014. Panukhnyk is a "No Borders" project worker at the Social Action Center. She is also an activist of the Olha Kobylyanska *Zhinocha Sotnya*.
38 Interview with Mariya Berlinska, Kyiv, April 8, 2014. Berlinska is a student of a Master's course in Jewish Studies.
39 Ibid.
40 Ibid.

tester approached Ruslana Lyzhychko, a Ukrainian pop singer and an icon of the Maidan, who in March 2014 received the Women of Courage award for her role in the protests, and asked her to speak about gender discrimination publicly.[41] According to Berlinska, Ruslana, as the singer is widely known in Ukraine, recognized the validity of the complaint and suggested that Berlinska herself should voice her concerns from the Maidan stage. When the protester finally got the chance to deliver the speech, which was already late at night, Berlinska was asked to show her speech to the man in charge of the stage. His verdict was that this concern was not timely, and that such a speech could encourage women to risk their lives; "a woman is delicate and she has different functions," remembers Berlinska.[42] Eventually, she was surrounded by a number of men whose arguments against the delivering of the speech ranged from the patronizing to the primitive: "what I have between my legs and what you have between yours are two different things," "women have a lower pain threshold," "you should do that which you do well: borscht, sewing, etc."[43] Her speech on gender equality was eventually delivered but it seems to have been ignored.

This sort of "protection" affected all women, including those who were performing their professional duties. Berlinska remembers: "Once when I was stopped at the checkpoint, two journalists who were streaming the events were also trying to pass: a man and a woman. The man got the permission to go through while the woman was stopped."[44] The irony of these situations lies in the fact that the "defenders" usually turned up not during the actual clashes, while the women were performing a great variety of duties on par with the men, but at moments when violence stopped. During the actual clashes, Berlinska's fellow protesters did not even notice her gender, only occasionally exclaiming in astonishment "wait: you are a woman!"[45] She remembers that after a night of violent conflict, at daybreak, Berlinska and another protester, beside whom she stood throughout the

---

41 See Masuma Ahuja, "Why did Michelle Obama give a Ukrainian pop star the Women of Courage award," March 4, 2014, *Washington Post*, http://www.washingtonpos t.com/blogs/post-politics/wp/2014/03/04/why-did-michelle-obama-give-a-ukrainian-pop-star-the-women-of-courage-award/ (accessed August 24, 2014).
42 Interview with Berlinska.
43 Ibid.
44 Ibid.
45 Ibid.

night, sat down for a cigarette. They finally asked each other's age. Berlinska's companion turned out to be a young man of sixteen.[46]

While there were occasions when gender differences were invisible, often, female participation in violence was recognized only in order to shame the men into action.[47] The conventional position of many men was to dismiss a woman's capacity to participate in a revolution. A man who identified himself only as a "*sotnyk*" (a leader of a *sotnya*), continued to live on the Maidan even some months after Viktor Yanukovych fled the country, claiming to have lived there "since day one."[48] At the suggestion that women could participate in the protests in the same capacity as men he simply burst into laughter. Having spent his full arsenal of arguments such as "women are naturally peaceful," "women are future mothers," "that is not the job for women," the "*sotnyk*" revealed his main argument: he picked up a metal bar from the side of the tent and handed it over to me. The weapon turned out to be predictably heavy, and seeing me struggle with it, he triumphantly exclaimed: "See! Women cannot even hold the weapon, let alone fight with it."[49] The "*sotnyk*," however, admitted that women regularly visited the unit: "one needs to change the picture sometimes; it is nice to look at something pretty for a change."[50] At the same time, the man insisted that their *sotnya* would never recruit women other than to cook and clean. The "*sotnyk*'s" rhetoric, behavior, and appearance were similar to those of many other men in military-style outfits who, as described by Tamara Hundorova, "mill about the barricades" and "bustle around busily, although, it seems, there is no reason to rush" on the still smoldering but essentially derelict Maidan.[51] Their behavior was also an example of gender performativity, where "acts and gestures, articulated and enacted desires create the illusion of an interior and organizing gender core."[52] They gave the impression of trying to live up to the image of Maidan heroes that had been constructed by the media and endorsed by the

---

46 Ibid.

47 See Mariya Dmytriyeva, "Zhinky na maidani—stari mikhy, nove vyno? [Women on the Maidan—old wineskins, new wine?]," *Odyn z nás* [One of Us], May 16, 2014, http://maryxmas.livejournal.com/3961386.html (accessed August 24, 2014).

48 I was unable to verify the actual position of the man, but it would seem that he was one of the *sotnya* members rather than its leader.

49 Interview with a "*sotnyk*" in Kyiv, April 8, 2014.

50 Ibid.

51 Hundorova, "Maidan as a Symptom."

52 Butler, *Gender Trouble*, 188.

public. Many were eager to tell bitter-heroic stories of "participating in action" during the protests. Their gender and its freighted expectations left men little choice: men had to be known to have fought; they could hardly be expected to tell of their heroic contribution to the making of sandwiches.

Gender performativity, therefore, can be part of a conscious decision to act as a man or as a woman. Sometimes this act is performed in order to achieve a certain aim. Anna Zayachkivska is primarily known for her looks: in 2013 she won the title of Miss Ukraine. She was also a student of Iconography in Ivano-Frankivsk, but left her native city to support the protests. Having arrived in Kyiv, like most other women, she headed to the Maidan kitchen to "help the volunteers who had had no sleep for three days."[53] She then helped at the Maidan free "university," worked with an independent television crew, and hosted New Year's Eve celebrations on the Maidan stage. During the most violent protests, Zayachkivska worked in a makeshift hospital, assisting professional doctors, nursing the wounded, and sometimes simply talking to those who were in pain, exhausted, and depressed. "Sometimes I had nowhere to sleep or I was cold, but I always had to be strong. I had no right to be weak. If a man came with a fractured skull and I showed my weakness, this person would feel even worse. So, I tried to hold myself together all the time."[54]

While performing these various duties Zayachkivska realized that a number of men were offering assistance because they found her attractive. She decided that being a woman could be used in a constructive way: "maybe it was not right to use the fact that the men were trying to win my affection, but to me what mattered at that moment was that they could help. I did not ask for personal help but I thought that it would be okay to ask them to bring wood or food, or whatever the kitchen needed at the time," explained Zayachkivska, blushing and revealing a degree of discomfort.[55] She also encountered men who were less cooperative: "When I spoke to some members of *Pravyi Sektor* [Right Sector], they stressed the fact that I am *a girl*, and I do not know what I am getting myself into. To

---

53 Interview with Anna Zayachkivska in Kyiv, April 9, 2014. She was "Miss Ukraine 2013," an actress, a singer-song-writer, and is a student of Iconography. During the protests, Zayachkivska set up and coordinated an interactive map of the needs of the Maidan protesters, http://maydanneeds.com.
54 Ibid.
55 Ibid.

which I answered that I knew exactly what I was doing. We were all equally involved in that war. It did not matter to me that I was a girl."[56]

Publicly, however, *Pravyi Sektor* claimed that it fully supported gender equality and did not see any reason to exclude women from the public sphere in general and their organization-*cum*-political party in particular. "We are prepared to welcome people of all ages, genders, nationalities, and religious views, as long as they are prepared to fight together with us for the united and independent Ukrainian state," argued Artem Skoropadskyi, *Pravyi Sektor's* press officer and a former journalist. [57] The radical nationalists of *Pravyi Sektor* claim to continue the tradition of Ukrainian integral nationalism and hail Stepan Bandera and the Organization of Ukrainian Nationalists (OUN) as their heroes.[58] The OUN's own position on gender roles was crystal clear: the functions they allocated for women in times of political disturbances ranged from "intelligence gathering behind enemy lines" and performing nursing duties and the tasks of couriers, typists, and stenographers to the "organization of celebratory events."[59] But *Pravyi Sektor's* press officer argued that times change and that nationalists change with them.[60] When asked how many women belong to the organization, Skoropadskyi had no clear answer. He said that his secretary was a female and that the deputy coordinator of regional work was a woman.[61] Another woman, singled out by Skoropadskyi to highlight the female presence in the organization, was a leader of *Pravyi Sektor's* international department: "she is a young woman [*devushka*] and her deputy is a young man," clarified the press officer.[62] Sensing my skepticism, Skoropadskyi returned to a more realistic portrayal of *Pravyi Sektor's* gender politics: "We have many activists whose attitude to the role of women is traditional:

---

56 Ibid. Right Sector] is an organization that united a number of radical nationalist groups during the protests in 2013–14. On March 22, 2014 they registered as a political party. See *Pravyi Sektor's* official webpage, http://pravyysektor.i nfo/organization/ (accessed May 9, 2014).
57 Interview with Artem Skoropadskyi, Kyiv, April 9, 2014.
58 Stepan Bandera (1909–59) was the leader of one of the branches of the Organization of Ukrainian Nationalists (OUN). For a discussion of Ukrainian integral nationalism, see Oleksandr Zaitsev, *Ukrainskyi integralnyi natsionalizm* [Ukrainian Integral Nationalism] (Kyiv: Krytyka, 2013).
59 Ia. Rak, *Do pytannya pryznachennya ukrainskoi zhinky,* [On the question of the role of a Ukrainian woman], HDA SBU, F. 13.—Spr. 376.—T. 48.—Ark.—9–13.
60 Interview with Skoropadskyi.
61 Ibid.
62 Ibid.

kitchen, children, and church. We have no women in the *provid* [leadership], but there are females in some managerial posts in the election headquarters."[63] Skoropadskyi also confirmed that as a party, should they win seats in the parliament, they would campaign for laws such as the abolition of abortion. He explained that they did not support the "*demoliberalizm*" supposedly practiced in the West: "we campaign against abortion, against same-sex marriages. We are traditionalists and consider such things to be overtly Satanic and unacceptable."[64]

There is, in fact, no need to speculate on the potential activity of the nationalists if they gain seats in the parliament. The existing nationalist members of parliament who belong to the nationalist *Svoboda* party, *Pravyi Sektor's* rival for the nationalist vote, have a clear position on gender roles.[65] A current member of the Ukrainian parliament from *Svoboda*, Yurii Mykhalchyshyn, published a manual on 'Social-Nationalism' in which he upholds the following view of an ideal woman: "The girlfriend of a Social-Nationalist is a smart, beautiful, humble, and educated girl, looking at whom inspires him to create perfection and protect the world from the plague of the politically correct world of *demoliberalizm*."[66]

The rest of the party seems to share Mykhalchyshyn's views on gender roles. In April 2013, it registered a bill that would have banned abortion in Ukraine.[67] According to the proposed bill, abortion would only be allowed in exceptional circumstances, among them if pregnancy could be proven to have resulted from rape. When asked what a woman should do if she falls pregnant as a result of rape but is unable to prove it, Oleksandr Sych, one of the bill's authors stated the following: "I do not work in the law enforcement and do not know how a woman can or cannot prove this... But, first of all, one should lead such a lifestyle as to not be exposed to the risk of

---

63 Ibid.

64 Ibid.

65 *Vseukrainske obyednannya "Svoboda"* [the All-Ukrainian Union "Svoboda"], a nationalist political party.

66 See Taras Voznyak, "Neonatsyzm i VO Svoboda" [Neo-Nazism and the All-Ukrainian Union Svoboda], *Ukrainska Pravda*, October 27, 2011, www.pravda. com.ua/articles/2011/10/27/6708115/ (accessed August 24, 2014).

67 See "Svoboda faction proposes legislatively banning abortions in Ukraine," *KyivPost* , April 8, 2013, http://www.kyivpost.com/content/ukraine/svoboda-faction-pr oposes-legislatively-banning-abortions-in-ukraine-322930.html (accessed August 24, 2014). The bill was not passed.

rape. That includes drinking alcoholic beverages in questionable company."[68]

Following the Maidan protests on February 27, 2014, Oleksandr Sych was appointed Deputy Prime Minister.[69] If one of the objectives of the protesters of the Maidan was to reboot the political system of Ukraine, appointments like this leave much doubt as to the success of this rebooting. A hijacking of the protest movement by the conservative nationalist right could lead to a devastating consolidation of the exclusion of women from the public sphere that has been evident, but also challenged, during the Maidan protests.

Sisters in Arms

One woman who confronted the gender politics of the Maidan, if not ideologically then through her experience of participating in the protests on an equal footing with the male protesters, is Anna Kovalenko. She formed the official thirty-ninth all-female *sotnya*. Following the Maidan protests, she became an adviser to the new acting defense minister. The 22-year-old is a theater critic by training and has already worked as a radio journalist for several years; she also works for the *Antykvar* [Antiquarian] publishing house, organizes antique auctions, and has a particular passion for battle reconstructions. She initially came to the Maidan as a journalist, reporting for Radio Era. As the protests intensified, Kovalenko became more and more involved in the events. At one point, she advised the protesters on methods of resistance, knowledge she claimed to have gained through her battle reconstruction hobby. Eventually Kovalenko joined the eleventh *sotnya*, led by her father, Anatolii, known by his nickname *Vedmid* [bear]. She became her father's deputy. "There were men and women in the *sotnya*. Some women came and said that they did not want to make sandwiches. We even had female karate masters," explained Kovalenko.[70]

68 Oleksandr Sych in Mariya Vasylieva, "Svobodivtsyu-avtoru zaborony abortiv baiduzhe na zhinok, shcho zavahitnily pislya zgvaltuvannya [The Svoboda member, and author of the abortion ban does not care about women who got pregnant as a result of rape]," *TSN*, April 11, 2013, http://tsn.ua/article/print/ukrayina/svobodivcyu-avtoru-zaboroni-abortiv-bayduzhe-na-zhinok-scho-zavagitnili-pislya-zgvaltuvannya-290019.html (accessed May 23, 2014).

69 Government of Ukraine, *Government Portal*, http://www.kmu.gov.ua/control/en/publish/officialcategory?cat_id=247077618 (accessed August 25, 2014).

70 Interview with Anna Kovalenko, Kyiv, April 8, 2014.

However, the apparent need for an all-female *sotnya,* she said, became evident when an all-female platoon of the sixteenth *sotnya* took part in one of the marches in January 2014: "This caused a certain splash in the media. Mothers would bring their daughters and say that they want their child to join the *sotnya*. At the same time, there were woman-provocateurs, who declared themselves *sotnyks* and organized some kind of activities. So a real all-female *sotnya* had to be organized and I was given this task."[71]

Although very certain of her own potential, Kovalenko questioned that of her female subordinates: "Women who joined wanted to take part in the protests on par with men. But as their desire differed from their capabilities, we immediately started martial arts, first aid, and gas mask training, as well as legal and psychology briefings, to inform them how to react in certain situations."[72]

Kovalenko claimed that the other forty-one (male) *sotnyks* considered her their sister-in-arms [*boiova podruha*] and were always ready to support her at any sign of discrimination.[73] Of her own experience of being a leader of a *sotnya*, Kovalenko said that "essentially you do the same thing as the male *sotnyks*, but you happen to be a woman."[74] She argued that her experience of working with women and men differed significantly: "It is really easy to work with men: you give them a task and they do it. In an all-female *sotnya*, you give them a task and they think about it for a while before they get going."[75]

The *sotnya* accepted women of all ages, provided they were over eighteen: "I had a woman who was sixty, but she was more vigorous than the eighteen-year olds," said Kovalenko.[76] In three days, the *sotnya* recruited more than 150 women. It took part in the violent clashes on Hrushevskyi Street, resisted the police, and continued to have a strong presence on the Maidan even after its active phase was over.[77] When

---

71 Ibid. The provocateurs to which Kovalenko refers include the journalist and activist Irma Krat, who at one point claimed to have organized the so-called First Independent All-female Unit. See "Zhinocha sotnya vidmovylasya rozbyraty barykady [The female unit refused to dismantle the barricades]," *Den*, February 16, 2014, http://www.day.kiev.ua/uk/news/160214-zhinocha-sotnya-vidmovilasya-rozbirati-barikadi (accessed August 25, 2014).
72 Interview with Kovalenko.
73 Ibid.
74 Ibid.
75 Ibid.
76 Ibid.
77 Ibid.

asked why, in her opinion, willing women could not simply join existing units, as she had when she joined her father's *sotnya*, Kovalenko explained:

> It is a question of discipline. If there are one hundred persons in the sotnya and fifty of them are women, you can forget about discipline. Men react to women: they show off, they fall in love. In our circumstances, we had to even live together. By the end of the revolution, I had two pregnant women. Men want to defend women. Even on the battlefield, men's first instinct is to defend that girl that is running there, which is distracting.[78]

Kovalenko seemed to identify less with "her girls" and more as "one of the boys." Nevertheless, the *sotnya* leader had similar experiences to those identified by Mariya Berlinska, and had to ask male colleagues to vouch for her right to take an active part in the protests. "Even when I told them 'I am a *sotnyk*', they would tell me to go home."[79] Occasionally Kovalenko resolved such situations in a conventionally masculine way: "I knocked one to the ground and there were no more problems like that."[80]

Throughout the interview, Kovalenko used the traditional, "default" masculine form of self-reference. When asked whether she considered herself a *sotnyk* or *sotnytsya* she hesitated and said that she was not sure: "men call me '*sotnytsya*' or '*trydtsyat-devyatenka*'.[81] But on my badge it says that I am the thirty-ninth *sotnyk*."[82] That same badge of the *samooborona* portrays a uniformed man holding a shield. Kovalenko said that she was not happy with that image. For her own *sotnya*'s Facebook page, she did a photoshoot where the unit's members held large rolling pins (traditionally used to depict a feisty woman, who stands up to her husband). Kovalenko hinted that this kind of image could easily replace the man with the shield.

Unsurprisingly, the *sotnytsya* argued that the militarization of Ukrainian society was not a bad thing and suggested the Israeli model of the conscription of males and females as the most appropriate for Ukraine. Of her personal experiences of combat, Kovalenko admitted that following her time "with the boys" her gait started to resemble that of a man, she started

---

78 Ibid.
79 Ibid.
80 Ibid.
81 *Sotnytsya* is the feminine form of the word *sotnyk*. *Trydtsyat-devyatenka* is a diminutive feminine form of "thirty-ninth," the numerical designation of Kovalenko's *sotnya*.
82 Interview with Kovalenko.

to curse more, and adopted some of the manners traditionally associated with men. It could thus be argued that in her role as a *sotnyk* she resorted to certain performativity of gender, in this case masculine. Feeling comfortable in the men's world of the *samooborona* and the patriarchal society more generally, Kovalenko firmly said that she was not a feminist: "I think that women run the world. Women run the men. A woman is allowed everything. And that is so cool. So why would you want to stand equal with men and prove something to someone? [...] The strength is in the weakness."[83]

Kovalenko, however, was not the only one who ran an official group of women as part of the *samooborona*. Kateryna Chepura, an activist of the *Vidsich* organization and a professional theater director, led the already mentioned all-female platoon of the sixteenth *sotnya*. She gave her reasons for the formation of the group, not dissimilar to those of Dovgopol or Kovalenko:

> The all-female platoon was created because of the gender politics of the Maidan. When the protests started, our organization, Vidsich, became the sixteenth sotnya of the Maidan's samooborona. Women comprise over a half of our organization, but our girls who were active in the protests always had problems with people, including the samooborona, telling them: "you are women, what are you doing here?" So we created this all-female platoon to formalize our presence on the Maidan and so we could show our samooborona ID and say "look, buddy, I am a part of the self-defense, just as you are, and I have the right to be here." Although, even this did not remove all problems.[84]

Chepura's organization supported non-violent methods of resistance. As part of its resistance, it believed that unarmed women should march in the first echelons in front of the troops, "as that would soften the behavior of the opponent."[85] "We realized that we could be killed or injured, but we knew that such a sacrifice would not be wasted, because the society would see that peaceful, unarmed people were killed. But we did not want to march next to people armed with sticks."[86] Chepura explained that on the first day of the Hrushevskyi Street conflicts, before the clashes started, the

83 Ibid.
84 Interview with Kateryna Chepura in Kyiv, April 10, 2014. Chepura is an activist of the *Vidsich* organisation and a theater director.
85 Ibid.
86 Ibid.

women of the sixteenth *sotnya* got through to the Internal Troops of Ukraine [*Vnutrishni Viiska*] and started talking to them. As a result, some of them started tying blue and yellow ribbons to their uniforms and engaged in a much-desired dialogue. "But the *samooborona* shouted: 'Are you crazy? Women, get out of there! You are ordered to leave!' And, being part of the *samooborona*, we had to obey the order. And that is when the violence started," said Chepura.[87]

As the women of the sixteenth *sotnya* lived and worked together with men, Chepura's experience of this coexistence differed entirely from that of Kovalenko:

When women and men exist within the same structure, there is an element of flirtation, but it is minuscule. What happened in reality was that women and men became more cultured in each other's presence. I entered one of the barracks of an all-male sotnya and was hit with cigarette smoke and a lot of cursing. [...] Men smoked less around us, and behaved in a more cultured way and that attracted more people to our sotnya.[88]

When first asked for an interview, Chepura rushed to explain that she took no part in violence, assuming that that was the primary interest of my research. She explained the reason behind her assumption: "Many journalists seek out a delicate girl who threw stones or took part in violence. Because when a delicate girl makes sandwiches and does her work in the middle of explosions that is not interesting."[89] Perhaps the heightened interest of the media in females who do not conform to the prevalent gender stereotype could be explained not by their wish to challenge the tradition of gender performativity, but to seek out an exception that would prove the rule.

Maidan as a State of Mind

Those interviewed for the purposes of this text differed in their participation in and perception of the Maidan. They, however, all agreed that the revolution had changed them profoundly. Some spoke of the feeling of hatred that they felt for the first time, of their desire for justice or, at least, revenge for the many lost lives. Some spoke of learning compassion and caring for the common good more than one's own comfort. Many spoke of fear. All

---

87 Ibid.
88 Ibid.
89 Ibid.

agreed that the Maidan would stay with them forever, and that it had altered them for good. The protests that started in November 2013, and especially those that unfolded in early 2014, altered not only the participants
of the events but the country as a whole. The question remains what this
alteration means for the country and its population. The Maidan originally
rose up to defend Ukraine's right to choose "European values" but it grew
into a "revolution of dignity" for Ukrainians themselves.[90] The defense of
dignity and freedom of expression, movement, association, as well as other values often seen as European must, no doubt, include the right to self-
determination of the 53.8% of Ukraine's population that are women.[91] It is,
nonetheless, questionable whether the Maidan revolution signified a transition from the anachronistic "protection" of women through the restriction of
their basic rights or a strengthening of the patriarchal tendencies already
dominant in the society.

"The Maidan has activated the nationalist movement," said Anna Dovgopol.[92] "*Pravyi Sektor* usurped the public space. People use their slogans
such as "Glory to Ukraine!," "Glory to the Nation!," and "Death to the Enemies!"[93] The ideas that the nation has the highest value and that nationalist principles come before the rights and freedoms of individuals are being
propagated by the radical nationalist groups whose place in the actual protests as well as in Ukrainian politics more generally is relatively marginal,
but nevertheless undeniably visible.[94] The fact that this sort of rhetoric
goes against the much-supported European values does not seem to raise

90 See Kateryna Kruk, "In Ukraine, we are protesting to preserve our dignity," *The
    Guardian*, December 17, 2013, http://www.theguardian.com/commentisfree/2013/
    dec/17/ukraine-protesting-euromaidan (accessed August 24, 2014).
91 "Statistics of the population of Ukraine," *The State Service of the Statistics of
    Ukraine*, http://database.ukrcensus.gov.ua/MULT/Dialog/statfile_c.asp (accessed
    August 25, 2014).
92 Interview with Dovgopol.
93 Ibid. These slogans are associated with the Organization of Ukrainian Nationalists,
    active in the 1930s-1950s. The repeated use of these mottos and the nationalist
    symbolism during the Maidan by the *Pravyi Sektor* and other nationalists spread the
    use of the slogans more widely to people who did not associate themselves with
    radical nationalist ideology. It has thus been argued that their use on the Maidan did
    not necessarily endorse the radical nationalist ideology propagated by the *Pravyi
    Sektor*.
94 See Andreas Umland, Anton Shekhovtsov, "Ukrainskie pravye radikaly, yevrointe-
    gratsya i neofashistskaya zahroza [Ukrainian far-right radicals, Euro-integration,
    and the Neo-Fascist Threat]," *Polit.ru*, May 21, 2014, http://www.polit.ru/article/20
    14/05/21/ukraine/ (accessed August 25, 2014).

much concern for the nationalists themselves. *Pravyi Sektor's* press officer makes their position clear:

> *Europe is versatile. In some parts of Europe, like in Denmark, they allow all sorts of things, even female priesthood, which we would find impermissible. Or in France they have gay pride marches, which are attended by thousands of people. But there are also countries like Poland, where the influence of the Catholic Church is strongly felt and abortions are banned. This kind of Europe is closer to us, no doubt.* [95]

While finding it perturbing, many in Ukraine doubt the longevity of the nationalists' rhetoric; the Maidan served as both the space for the creation of this hodgepodge organization of nationalists as well as the space for its unmaking. "*Pravyi Sektor* received an ambiguous reception, thanks to its involvement in a number of conflicts," argued Dovgopol.[96] "Many still consider them to be the heroes without whom there would be no events on Hrushevskyi Street, but others say that they were not even present there, and that all they get involved in are provocations."[97] Whether a real political player or a convenient media tool, the Ukrainian far right speaks to some of the very real fears of the population as a whole. A regularly threatened national identity creates fertile ground for the growth of nationalism. Whether radical, as propagated by *Pravyi Sektor* or the *Svoboda* party, or popular nationalism, with which most current political parties in Ukraine are happy to flirt, this sort of ideology issues fixed definitions of masculinity and femininity. "We are revitalizing the nation, right? And for the purposes of this revitalization, we use Ukraine of the eighteenth and nineteenth century as a standard: the Cossacks, a traditional family that serves as an ideal; this image is actively cultivated," said Dovgopol, adding, "on the other hand, it conflicts with the desire of Ukraine to integrate into Europe."[98] Thus, despite, or, possibly, because of the Maidan, the Ukrainian population faces a choice: to follow the well-trodden route of traditionalism together with its strictly prescribed roles for men and women or to reboot truly the whole system.

At an exhibition of photographs dedicated to the women who took part in the Maidan protests Olha Vesnianka, a human rights activist, journalist and a co-organizer of the Olha Kobylyanska *Zhinocha Sotnya*, said that

95 Interview with Skoropadskyi.
96 Interview with Dovgopol.
97 Ibid.
98 Ibid.

she wished to witness the day when there would be no need to announce that women managed to prove something to someone. "Why should we, women, girls, have to justify ourselves? We are absolutely equal participants of all events in Ukraine; good or bad."[99] Present at the exhibition, Mariya Berlinska remarked that "when exhibitions open, that is when a page of history opens. That is when textbooks start to get written; when people start to remember and re-evaluate."[100] Perhaps this sort of re-evaluation could consider the advice of Mary Beard, whose thoughts opened this text:

> We should [...] try to bring to the surface the kinds of question we tend to shelve about how we speak in public, why and whose voice fits. What we need is some old fashioned consciousness-raising about what we mean by the voice of authority and how we've come to construct it. We need to work that out before we figure out how we modern Penelopes might answer back to our own Telemachuses [...].[101]

This text does not for a moment assume that all Ukrainian "Penelopes" need or desire to answer back to their Ukrainian "Telemachuses." The concept of women as a group, and the existence of some assumed "commonality among women" is one that has troubled feminists of all times and countries.[102] In the case of the Maidan, it is not the commonality, but the diversity of female protesters, in terms of background, age, and ethnicity, that is striking. No less striking is the fact that most of these women were equally voiceless. There is no doubt that women are capable of participating in political violence or revolutions. There are sufficient examples of female combatants, revolutionaries, bomb-makers, and assassins. Even on the territory of contemporary Ukraine alone, women partook in the anti-Tsarist campaigns of the late nineteenth and early twentieth centuries, the civil wars, the Red Army, the Second World War partisan groups, and the

---

99 Olha Vesnyanka, at the "Women of the Maidan" exhibition, Fulbright Program headquarters, Kyiv, April 4, 2014. This exhibition was organized by the Fulbright Program in Ukraine, the International Charitable Fund "Ukrainian Women's Fund," and the Olha Kobylyanska *Zhinocha Sotnya*. See "*Fotovystavka: 'Zhinky* Maidanu' [A Photo-Exhibition: the Women of the Maidan]," April 4, 2014, http://www.fulbright .org.ua/uk/events/126/photo-exhibit.html (accessed August 25, 2014).

100 Mariya Berlinska in "Fotovystavka 'Zhinky Maidanu' [Photo Exhibition: the Women of the Maidan]," https://www.youtube.com/watch?v=uE-6tC5vWSg (accessed August 25, 2014).

101 Beard, "On the Voice of Women," 14.

102 See Butler, *Gender Trouble*, 5.

Ukrainian nationalist underground. It is also undeniable that historically as well as in present-day Ukraine many women will identify political violence or revolutionary resistance as belonging to the masculine sphere. Whether their choice is between the "front" or the "home front," at present, the majority of Ukrainian women find it difficult to make it on their own rather than having it made on their behalf. On International Women's Day, not long after the hostilities ended, an initiative was held at the Maidan involving several hundred women. One of them sent the following message: "We know that women need freedom and free societies. Life for women is much better in societies where we can speak out, where the men are not running the military and then trying to run us, and that we really need a free life, because in the twenty-first century that is our right."[103]

---

103 This project was organized by the Olha Kobylyanska *Zhinocha Sotnya* and carried out on March 8, 2014 in Kyiv. It collected over 200 postcard messages from women in Kyiv to women of Crimea, and recorded numerous video messages. See "Zhenshchiny Maidana-zhenshchinam Kryma. Videoobrashchenie [Women of the Maidan to women of Crimea. A video address]," March 8, 2014, https://www. youtube.com/watch?v=PbfFR-hKnGk (accessed August 25, 2014).

The Regions of Ukraine

A demonstration on Kyiv's Independence Square, November 27, 2014

A Euromaidan rally in Luhansk

Berkut blocking access to Independence Square

'A United Country' under construction, Khreshchatyk, Kyiv, May 23, 2014
(© Marta Dyczok)

'Protest and Indifference' on European Square, Kyiv, May 20, 2014
(© Marta Dyczok)

Bullet hole in Ukraina Hotel window, Kyiv, July 25, 2014

Beyond the Square: The Real and Symbolic Landscapes of the Euromaidan

Natalia Otrishchenko

*Finally, the Maidan of Independence became **the** Maidan of Independence.*
From an interview with a 32-year-old man, Kyiv, February 7, 2014

For three winter months in 2013–14, the central square of Kyiv became a focal point for politicians, journalists, academics, and ordinary citizens in both Ukraine and beyond. Concerning the scale of civil mobilization and urban violence, these events were without parallel in Ukraine's contemporary history. Actions, which from their very beginning were named Euromaidan, transformed urban space and brought new meanings to Kyiv.[1] The word "maidan," in a Ukrainian context, became synonymous with protest. However, a maidan, protest, is first a maidan, public square, and thus it is part of an urban landscape localized in the physical space of a concrete city. The identity and sense of "maidan" has changed dramatically, from a celebratory center of apolitical activity for students who stood for European integration to a melting pot of Ukrainian self-consciousness and a paramilitary fortress that was forced to defend itself against armed forces. Finally, it became a place where more than 100 people died. Such rapid transformation in the polarity, the attitudes, and the general atmosphere of the Euromaidan created unique circumstances, which need to be conceptualized.

The tendency to view the Euromaidan as a colossal social movement has led to myriad reflections and studies intended to understand, explain, and perhaps even predict future developments in the current Ukrainian situation. In early December the Center for Urban History in Lviv launched a research project called "Voices of Resistance and Hope: Kyiv-Lviv-Kharkiv" that aimed to document personal stories, emotions, and expectations of the participants of Euromaidan. The project endeavored to capture first-hand perspectives and experiences so that they may be used for further reflection in the academic and public spheres. The "first wave" of the study was conducted in December 2013. In connection with the further deterioration of Ukraine's sociopolitical situation, the "second wave" was un-

---

1　The use of the term is analogous to previous protests such as Language Maidan and Tax Maidan, which opposed language reform and the new tax codex respectively.

dertaken in February 2014. In total, around 140 in-depth interviews were collected in Kyiv, Lviv, and Kharkiv. There were also five interviews with leaders and participants of the Euromaidan in Warsaw and Lublin.

The methodology of the research was based on qualitative, in-depth, semi-structured interviews that emphasized the personal experience of the interviewee. Questions were dedicated to the motivations, practices, forms of participation, feelings, expectations, perceptions of space, and thoughts on European integration and European values. As interviews were conducted mainly at the locations where protests occurred, the total length of interviews was quite short, ranging from ten to ninety minutes. In some cases, the interview was conducted in a nearby café, inside one of the tents on Independence Square, or outside the main squares in Kyiv, Lviv, or Kharkiv. The questionnaire was slightly modified for the second wave; questions were added that probed personal identity, changes in perception of the Ukrainian state and society, and heroes and antiheroes of Euromaidan and Ukraine in general. Furthermore, interviewees in Kyiv during the second wave of the survey were asked to draw their perspectives of the space of the Euromaidan, thereby adding a visual dimension to their responses. This approach provides mental maps of the space in which protests occurred during the winter of 2013–14.

This article intends to answer two questions: How are "protest spaces" perceived, and how were these perceptions changed by Euromaidan? Space, generally, is used as a category of social geography. Andrzej Mayer identifies the following approaches to the study of space: the idealistic view, space as a product of cognitive activity; the materialistic view, space that exists independently of human perception; and the sociological view, space that exists because of human activities.[2] Space, as well as a more specific concept of landscape, "is defined by our vision and interpreted by our minds."[3] A place is a concrete and distinct space with the characteristics of geographic location, material form, and an investment of meaning and value.[4] A symbolic landscape is conceptualized in two ways: as the physical, which is visible, and as the ideal, which is the mental part of the

2 Andrzej Majer, *Socjologia i Przestrzeń Miejska* [Sociology and Urban Space] (Warszawa: Wydawnictwo Naukowe PWN, 2010), 20.

3 Donald W. Meinig, "Introduction" to *The Interpretation of Ordinary Landscapes: Geographical Essays* (New York: Oxford University Press, 1979), 2.

4 Tomas F Gieryn, "A Space for Place in Sociology", *Annual Review of Sociology* 826 (2000): 464–5.

space with embedded cultural and social meanings, "a projection from an actual landscape and society."[5] Therefore, it is a construct in which a sense of place, human activities, cultural values, and memories coalesce.

Why Euromaidan? Historical Continuity, Aura, and Religion

Since the dissolution of the Soviet Union, Independence Square has become more than the main square of Kyiv. It is a landmark of historical continuity. It was the location of a student hunger strike called the "the Revolution on the Granite" in 1990, a center for "Ukraine without Kuchma" actions from 2000 to 2001, the heart of the Orange Revolution in 2004, the location of a protest against the new tax code in 2010, and finally in 2013 the location of Euromaidan, a demonstration against the breakdown of European integration. This continuity was intensely stressed in the interviews with Euromaidan participants: "This is the third Maidan that I have attended. In 2010, [during] the 'Taxmaidan'—I lived in a tent for a whole week.... Then I felt the spirit of freedom. The same as now" or "I've participated in every revolution in this country, I even have a picture of myself at the age of three with a flag in 1991."[6] Consequently, it is not just a chronology but also an incorporated part of personal experiences and in the case of Euromaidan—personal experiences of protest actions. It involves experiential memory of events.

Maurice Halbwachs' seminal work on collective memory catalyzed sociological and historical debates about the social contextualization of memory.[7] The idea that individual memory can be recalled only within a social framework and that it needs the support of the group, which limits space and time for the totality of past events, was developed fruitfully. As such, references to the personal history of protest on Independence Square could be an important point in collective memory. According to Su-

---

5   Donald W. Meinig, Symbolic Landscapes. Some Idealizations of American Communities in *The Interpretation of Ordinary Landscapes: Geographical Essays* (New York: Oxford University Press, 1979), 165.

6   Interview with 51-year-old man, Kyiv, December 6, 2013 (only information about gender and the age of interviewees will be provided. Interviews were conducted in Ukrainian or Russian—I translated all quotes); Interview with 25-year-old woman, Kyiv, February 9, 2014.

7   See the key work by Maurice Halbwachs, *On Collective Memory*, trans. Lewis A. Coser (Chicago: University of Chicago Press, 1992), and the most prominent review of Halbwachs' ideas by Paul Connerton, *How Societies Remember* (Cambridge: Cambridge University Press, 1989).

san Crane, this "expresses a sense of the continual presence of the past."[8] Therefore, the historical continuity of Independence Square is the way that it constantly recalls the past, justifies the present, and looks to the future with hope. As was mentioned in one of the interviews: "maybe places become important when they touch something personal."[9] Independence Square became a valuable marker for collective memory because it was connected with deeply personal and collective experiences.

The understanding of Independence Square as a crucial location for protest action draws parallels to events in 1991 and during the Orange Revolution. For example, one interviewee noted, "I am part of the generation that in its youth, I was 16, stood on the Maidan and gained Ukrainian independence. So this is a matter of honor."[10] Another mentioned, "it is Independence Square and we fought for our independence here. There is some continuity with 2004."[11] However, there were strong voices expressing the uniqueness of Euromaidan: "On the first [of December] there was such a large number of people, the likes of which I have never seen before in Kyiv on the streets, neither in the 1980s when independence was proclaimed, nor during 2004–2005, when there was the Orange Revolution. It was something incredible."[12] Even when people acknowledged and referenced a historical continuity between previous protests and the Euromaidan, there was a feeling of exceptionalism, of something unique in Ukrainian history.

Other types of justification relied either on practical reasons or simply on the name of the square. For example, one respondent stated that, "it is a center, a heart of Ukraine, and it is close to the main government and ministries, to the Presidential Administration, so it is possible to conduct active actions against the regime."[13] Another mentioned that, "it is very symbolic that protest actions take place in Kyiv at Independence Square. The name itself—the "Maidan of Independence"—should serve to ensure that every person in Ukraine can express their opinion."[14] However, such justifications were not as common as references to historical continuity.

8 Susan A Crane, "Writing the Individual Back into Collective Memory," *The American Historical Review* 102 (1997): 1373.
9 Interview with 44-year-old woman, Kyiv, February 9, 2014.
10 Interview with 56-year-old woman, Lviv, December 5, 2013.
11 Interview with 30-year-old man, Kyiv, February 9, 2014.
12 Interview with 51-year-old man, Kyiv, February 7, 2014.
13 Interview with 20-year-old man, Kyiv, December 8, 2013.
14 Interview with middle-aged woman, Kyiv, December 8, 2013.

Moreover, the physical space of the square was described as unique and somehow supernatural. When talking about the location in which protests took place in Kyiv, interviewees explained its exceptionality with words like energy, spirit, and aura. One interviewee contended, "Probably there is some energy that works [here] which is not felt physically, but it makes people go to these places. This is Khreshchatyk [Street], and Independence Square."[15] Another said, "here, at the Square, I have changed a lot. There is a spirit here, which makes you stronger."[16] While another said there is a "positive aura, if I could say so. You come here and feel completely different."[17] The Square turned into a sacred place in a very personal and mystic way. As such, it was difficult for interviewees to describe or share experiences or feelings of "energy." It was possible only to state its presence or absence. On the other hand, people used traditional religious justifications; however, such explanations were associated mainly with Mykhailivska Square. One young man said, "it is important that they gathered at Mykhailivska Square. Why did they gather there? Because students ran there. Right? Children [ran] to the church. The church protected them."[18] This space was considered "under the wing of God,"[19] so people were safe there. References to the religious significance of places were part of a larger framework that entwined religious and nationalist discourses, and created a strong base for the justification of "maidan" as a space and "maidan" as a protest.

Even when Independence Square might be connected with nationalist discourse, especially linked to Ukrainian Independence and self-determination, there were people who supported protest actions and shared a Soviet-like view of the space in which those actions took place. One elderly woman related, "personally for me protest begins and ends on Kalinin Square, [Maidan of] Independence. (...) For me they are native places. There was a library of the CPSU [Communist Party of Soviet Ukraine] here, (...) there was a Lenin museum."[20] Such expressions were rather rare but showed the intersection of completely different symbolic landscapes. Conflicting and exclusionary discourses, in this case, co-exist.

---

15 Interview with 56-year-old man, Lviv, December 3, 2013.
16 Interview with 40-year-old man, Kyiv, December 6, 2013.
17 Interview with 69-year-old man, Kyiv, February 8, 2014.
18 Interview with 29-year-old man, Kyiv, December 13, 2013.
19 Interview with 47-year-old man, Kyiv, December 12, 2013.
20 Interview with 76-year-old woman, Kyiv, February 9, 2014.

Euromaidan brought together not only people with different political views and social positions, but also with different visions of the same location.

From Euromaidan-Square to a Euromaidan-State-of-Mind

The perception of "maidan" ranges from a specific, geographically defined place to an abstract, intellectually constructed concept—from a neutrally recognized location to a highly personal and emotionally significant space. The events of the winter of 2013–14 and their subsequent discussion in Ukrainian society provided strong evidence that Independence Square became a powerful *lieu de mémoire*, a place of remembrance.

Independence Square was a concrete space with well-defined boundaries. "I have a wish that this territory would grow all the time and that the borders of Maidan would expand," recounted one interviewee.[21] The events of Euromaidan privatized public space.[22] People lived in tents on and in buildings around Independence Square and Khreshchatyk Street for up to three months. They established all necessary facilities: kitchens, hospitals, information and coordination centers, chapels, etc. There was a feeling of closeness and safety that one usually associates with home. Interviewees reported that, "there is one family here," "for me, symbolically speaking, I am at home. I feel at home," and "the Maidan is the safest place in Ukraine even with this terror around" respectively.[23] In addition, this place was connected with very personal perceptions, such as a smell: "There is a small moment when it smells like Lviv [here]."[24] "Now, the smell of bonfires," related one interviewee "has become a symbol of this Maidan, which you can identify even on the furthest metro stations."[25]

As a domestic space, Independence Square was strongly separated from the frenetic, depersonalized, metropolis that surrounded it. As one of the interviewee mentioned: "On [Mykhaylo] Hrushevskyi [Street] there are barricades, on Hrushevskyi [people] might throw fireworks, or they might

21 Interview with 33-year-old man, Kyiv, February 9, 2014.
22 For more about the privatization of the public sphere, see Lyn Lofland, *The Public Realm: Exploring the City's Quintessential Territory* (New York: Transaction Publishers, 1998).
23 Interview with 57-year-old man, Kyiv, February 13, 2014; Interview with 55-year-old man, Kyiv, December 7, 2013; Interview with 35-year-old man, Kyiv, December 7, 2013.
24 Interview with 47-year-old man, Kyiv, December 12, 2013.
25 Interview with 33-year-old man, Kyiv, February 9, 2014.

shoot. You travel a few meters, and there are cafés, people are sitting with computers and writing, girls are walking, cars drive by."[26] Even though it is Kyiv's main square, it was not considered part of Kyiv. It was a *Ding an sich*, a thing-in-itself. However, the Euromaidan, as determined by protest signs, was still referencing Kyiv, either when asking for support ("we need Kyiv") or when creating its own identity ("we are not Kyiv"). Generally speaking, Kyiv served as "the other" for the Euromaidan. The process of "othering" Kyiv was accentuated when carnage and slaughter visited Independence Square. It completely became disassociated from the space of Kyiv. The difference between Independence Square and its nearest streets, especially in the first months after the events of February 18–20, 2014, was striking. Nevertheless, this conclusion is based only on personal experiences and observations since the second wave of interviews finished just before the conflict escalated.

In addition, the Square evoked strong and powerful emotions, especially comparing to other places where protests occurred: "Lviv is Maidan-support, but Kyiv is the real Maidan."[27] Such a feeling, perhaps, stemmed from the projection of live feeds from Kyiv onto screens in public spaces in Lviv. As such, individuals outside the capital could understand the importance and scale of events in Kyiv, while forced to be passive viewers without the possibility to influence the process.

The Maidan of Independence can be considered either a solid entity or a fragmented space, which consists of different parts with different symbolic meanings. For example, one of the landmarks on the square itself was the Monument of Independence, or the Stella. It was one of the key places on the night of November 30, 2013, when students were beaten, which led to large-scale actions. The importance of the monument in this context was reflected by a young woman who stated, "after we fled, we agreed to go back to the Stella because everyone wanted to stay there. We just started to flock there ... we cannot physically leave because it is our Stella. It is native for us; such memories."[28] Interviewees also referred to the blood spilled nearby that brought new meaning to this space. This monument was the "starting point" of Euromaidan.

After the attempt to disperse the protesters on the night of December 11, 2013, barricades, which lined the perimeter of the square, became one

---

26 Interview with 51-year-old man, Kyiv, December 7, 2013.
27 Interview with 25-year-old woman, Kyiv, December 6, 2013.
28 Interview with 22-year-old woman, Kyiv, December 5, 2013.

of the symbols of Maidan. It was the first time since the Second World War that barricades appeared in Kyiv—generally, they became quite a surreal image. Initially constructed for practical reasons, they later gained an artistic value. The Maidan itself was even described as "a huge complex with different steampunk barricades."[29] Barricades became a generalized image associated with the location. A good example of this perspective is a quote from a man who came to Kyiv after the first protesters were killed on Hrushevskyi Street in January 2014: "I did not come to the Maidan, I came to the barricade."[30]

Another illustration of fragmented space is the distinction between the stage and the rest of the square. This may be explained by the growing divergence between the politicians on stage and the people who lived on the Maidan. Also, the stage, as it was a raised platform, was distinct from the surrounding area: "a stage itself, I feel, is something completely separated from Maidan."[31] It was a part of the landscape of the Maidan, but with its own meaning separate from the everyday life of the people who lived there. Moreover, different groups of people had different spaces that they thought significant: the monument for students, the prayer tent for believers and clergy, barricades for those more militant. Artists also created a special, practical place: "We decided that we want to have a permanent picket on the Maidan and built such a space entitled the 'Artistic Barbican'...it is a symbolic name because it is an open gallery, where there is a permanent exhibition and a cultural program with a wide range [of topics]."[32] This space, as well as the "Free University," were highly functional and had their own well-defined audience.

The distinction between the solid and fragmented views of Independence Square can be well illustrated with the drawings made during the second wave of the "Voices of Resistance and Hope: Kyiv-Lviv-Kharkiv" project. There were twenty-eight pictures: twenty-seven from Kyiv and one from Lviv, made by a girl whose narration centered on her volunteering experience in Kyiv. Some of them were mental maps that represented physical environments, others depicted either very specific elements of the space or symbolic images. Generally, the drawings by men were more schematic, while females drew more personal and detailed pictures. Spa-

---

29 Interview with 35-year-old man, Kyiv, February 7, 2014.
30 Interview with 50-year-old man, Kyiv, February 7, 2014.
31 Interview with 33-year-old man, Kyiv, February 9, 2014.
32 Interview with 35-year-old man, Kyiv, February 7, 2014.

tially, the Maidan is shown in Figure One. The interviewee drew a street map and pointed out important places such as the stage, Ukrainian House, City Council, the barricades, etc. This drawing represents a combination of a bird's eye view and a side view that includes the Christmas tree[33] and Independence Monument. Figure Two shows a side view of only two elements—the Christmas tree and one of the houses made by the members of the interviewee's nongovernmental organization on the Maidan. These markers of space were the most significant and exclusive to Independence Square; however, they did not represent the whole view of the place.

Figure One. Drawing by a 28-year-old woman, February 15, 2014
Figure Two. Drawing by a 29-year-old woman, February 11, 2014

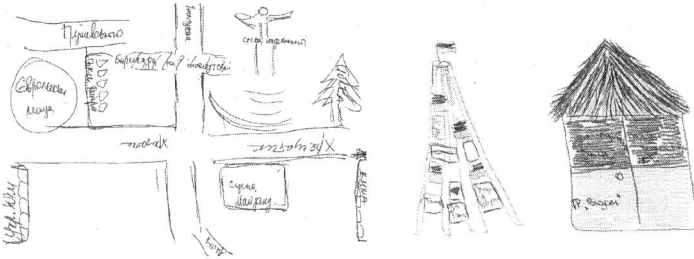

Maidan is perceived not only as a spatial phenomenon but also as a group of people with similar ideas, values, and expectations. "Places themselves are not important at all, only people who came to the protests are important...their inspiration, their positive disposition matters."[34] "Maidan is not *the* barricades, it is *the* people," said one interviewee.[35] Maidan became a synonym for social movement in Ukraine—it lost its grounding in physical space and gained new meaning. People who were involved in protest actions did not have to be physically at the Square: "You know, there are many people in Kyiv who are not physically at the Maidan but are virtually there. I mean informational support, coordination of friends through social networks and so on."[36]

People, as the main actors of the protest, were visible in the drawings. They were either personified, as shown in Figure Three, or drawn as

---

33 The Christmas tree, or *Yolka*, was one of the symbols of the protest. It was constructed and decorated with homemade flags and posters.
34 Interview with 22-year-old woman, Kyiv, December 6, 2013.
35 Interview with 32-year-old man, Kyiv, February 7, 2014.
36 Interview with 51-year-old man, Kyiv, February 7, 2014.

shown in Figure Four. In some form, people appear in seven of the twenty-eight pictures, five drawings of women and two of men. As interviewees were asked to draw their understandings of the space of the Maidan, there is evidence to conclude that people are connected to this locality. As of mid-February, the Euromaidan had a human face.

Figure Three. Drawing by a 19-year-old man, February 16, 2014
Figure Four. Drawing by a 28-year-old woman, February 7, 2014

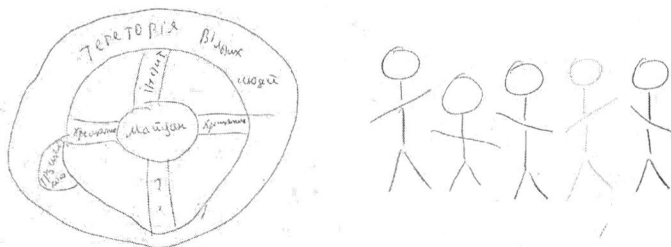

Starting as an external and tangible space, the Maidan transformed into a key component of protesters' internal sense of self. Some of the interviewees described it as an idea: "Maidan starts inside. I mean people inside themselves created the Maidan. Everything here is just an area, which, by the way, can be conquered. This is not a problem at all. The area could be occupied, but the Maidan cannot be destroyed. (...) The tents of the Maidan will go home. But Maidan as a state of mind will continue until the destruction of the current system of power."[37] According to one man, "Maidan starts in every person somewhere deep in their soul, in their heart. When they want to be independent, when they no longer want to be, I would say, a slave."[38] As an idea, Maidan goes far beyond Kyiv. As shown in Figure Five, the Maidan stands with the concepts of "Europe," "Ukraine," and "Victory"; they were drawn together at the local place that is depicted with tents around the square.

Figure Six is fascinating. It was drawn on February 9, 2014, before the Russian annexation of Crimea and the conflict in eastern Ukraine. Note that the Maidan, the red dot in the center, and Kyiv, the red figure around the dot according to the interviewee, together bring light to Ukraine. The star on the Crimea and crosses on the right side of the drawing were explained as "it is like the game Battleship: ships will strike from there. And

---

37 Interview with 40-year-old man, Kyiv, February 7, 2014.
38 Interview with 29-year-old man, Kyiv, February 7, 2014.

here I put a cross. It is a threat from Russia."[39] The picture in Figure Six shows a map of Ukraine. Besides these drawings, two other pictures contained either the word "Ukraine" or a map. For the authors of those pictures, Maidan was not just a main square in the capital, it was the entire country.

Figure Five. Drawing by a 35-year-old man, February 13, 2014
Figure Six. Drawing by a 35-year-old man, February 13, 2014

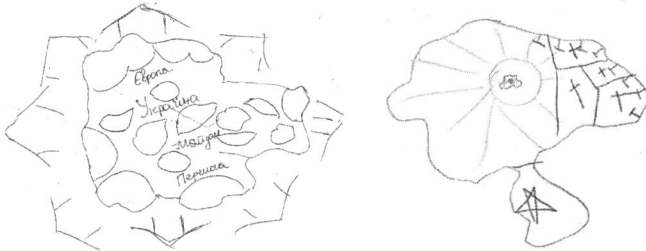

The events of Euromaidan caused a revaluation of public spaces and brought new meaning to buildings and monuments. For example, as was already mentioned, the perception of the Stella changed: "Stella, baba on a sphere—that was the name before everything started—now looks more human because of the people [around]."[40] Some clashes happened near Ukrainian House, which finally came under the control of protesters, and its meaning was similarly changed: "Though Ukrainian House seemed to me to be one of the coldest buildings in Kyiv in general, now it became, well ... I thought it impossible to warm it and do something with it, but now it became warmer."[41] Ultimately, Mykhailivskyi Cathedral was reinterpreted, too: "Time and historical events change concepts suddenly, change places. People thought of the Mykhailivskyi Cathedral as a decoration.... Then the abbot of the monastery, the monk, gave shelter to beaten students.... Later came the funeral of that boy, on January 22, 2014. That was the consecration of the place and it became quite different."[42] This rethinking of space occurred based on a new system of values and according to broader understandings of events. Past events influenced a new and better vision of the future as they were reevaluated positively. However, some

39 Interview with 58-year-old man, Kyiv, February 9, 2014.
40 Interview with 29-year-old woman, Kyiv, February 8, 2014.
41 Interview with 25-year-old woman, Kyiv, February 9, 2014.
42 Interview with 51-year-old man, Kyiv, February 7, 2014.

places after the violence of February 18–20, 2014, gained a strong negative connotation due to the bloodshed and loss of life. But, this is an issue
which cannot be addressed in the scope of the "Voices of Resistance and
Hope: Kyiv-Lviv-Kharkiv" interviews because the second wave of the survey ended just before the further escalation of the conflict between protesters and Ukrainian authorities.

Outside Kyiv: Euromaidan and Taras Shevchenko

The main events of winter 2013–14 undoubtedly occurred in Kyiv. However, without support from across Ukraine, Euromaidan would have been impossible: "Here we have a Maidan of Independence, a piece of freedom. It
is like a center. But, we have places not only in Kyiv, we have places in the
regions. There are squares and Maidans where people defend [freedom]
too."[43] Therefore, it is important to add to the discussion about the symbolic landscape of Euromaidan comments about protest spaces outside of Kyiv, particularly in Kharkiv in the east and Lviv in the west. These two cities,
while historically, socially, culturally, and economically different, both had
local Maidans with several similarities. The main and the most visible similarity was the inspirational figure of Taras Shevchenko who served as a
spatial marker in both centers.

In Kharkiv, people had to move to the square near the Shevchenko
monument, because Freedom Square, a traditional gathering space, was
fenced off. One interviewee noted, "absolutely, Freedom Square was
fenced off by the Kharkiv authorities. It is a cool, symbolic, real space. It is
freedom in a cage and freedom for the people. In a Kharkiv-way, in our
own way, it has tremendous significance." [44] However, even though Freedom Square is larger, the square near the Shevchenko monument had
more symbolic meaning: "Today, the Shevchenko [Monument], thank God,
has not been fenced off and it is unlikely it will be because if they try to do
so, the fences will surely fail. So there is certainly significance, the
Shevchenko Monument is a symbol of a certain struggle of a passionate
attitude toward everything, toward injustice."[45] The references to
Shevchenko created historical continuity between his ideas and contempo-

---

43 Interview with 31-year-old man, Kyiv, February 9, 2014.
44 Interview with 36-year-old man, Kharkiv, December 8, 2013.
45 Ibid.

rary protest actions. They also formed associations between his thoughts and dispositions, and those of the protesters.

Taras Shevchenko (1814–61), Ukrainian poet, writer, and painter, is one of the key figures in the Ukrainian pantheon. He constantly gains top positions in lists of Ukrainian heroes, either in sociological surveys or on television shows.[46] He was considered a uniting and unifying symbol for the Euromaidan as well: "It is very good that from Freedom Square in Kharkiv we went to Taras Shevchenko Square because he is like some coryphaeus of the Ukrainian spirit. I believe that the Shevchenko monument is a symbol as it is in every city of Ukraine, so it will be a symbol of Euromaidan."[47] Similarly, one young woman reported, "well, I think that Shevchenko was a revolutionary-minded person, so it is kind of a symbol of the Ukrainian revolution, the Ukrainian protest."[48] Protest actions near the Shevchenko monument accentuated the link between his poetry and the mood of people on the square. Harmony between his ideas and the aspirations of the protesters created a specific bond with the square near the Shevchenko monument.

Similar explanations were provided in Lviv as interviewees linked the space to the works of Shevchenko: "I think it is very symbolic now that this is happening near the Taras Shevchenko monument. Many times the speakers from the stage have turned to his work, quoted it, said that he is watching us. This may be partly true because there is something in the phrase 'fight and you shall overcome', which sounded a dozen times in my mind between us, between those people who are there."[49] Finally, constant reminders about Shevchenko, both visual, the monument, and verbal, quotes from the stage, inspired people to victory: "When you look in this direction and see Shevchenko, I do not know, it adds some kind of spirit, faith in what we are doing. And Shevchenko once stood for this. And we are continuing this cause, and we should just finish it."[50] This combination

---

46 Sotsiolohichna hrupa "Reitynh," "'Narodnyi Top' spetsialnyi proekt: Vydatni ukraintsi usikh chasiv [The People's Top Special Project: The Most Prominent Ukrainians of All Time]," May 2012, http://ratinggroup.com.ua/upload/files/RG_TOP_Ukrainian_05 2012.pdf (accessed June 25, 2014). In the 2007–08 program "The Greatest Ukrainians," Shevchenko placed fourth.
47 Interview with 25-year-old woman, Kharkiv, December 7, 2013.
48 Interview with 20-year-old woman, Kharkiv, December 4, 2013.
49 Interview with19-year-old man, Lviv, December 3, 2013.
50 Interview with35-year-old woman, Lviv, December 8, 2013.

of real and symbolic, material and immaterial landscapes shaped the "protest spaces" in Kharkiv and Lviv.

Conclusion and Discussion

During February and March 2014, the phrase "we looked for Europe and found Ukraine" was frequently shared on Facebook. Euromaidan became the driving force for Ukrainians to rethink themselves and the spaces around them. Old places gained new meanings, and Independence Square emerged as a place of memory, separated from the rest of Kyiv, that was very private and very solitary at different points in time.

To give figurative weight to the place of protest in Kyiv, interviewees referred both to the historical continuity and to the uniqueness of the actions during the winter of 2013–14 in the context of Ukrainian history. The Maidan of Independence emerged as a symbol of Ukrainian protest because of crucial events past and present that took place there—independence from the Soviet Union, the Orange Revolution, and the Euromaidan. These events were experienced either directly or indirectly, through personal experience or through media, and they became a component of the collective memory of victorious protests. In the case of Euromaidan, the past was extremely important for the present, and it gave hope for the future.

The central part of Kyiv was described by protesters with a mix of patriotic and religious imagery. Various interviewees commented on the exceptional energy of the place that drew people in and revitalized. The perception of protest spaces was either uniform or fragmented, depending on the personal experience of the interviewee and their relationship to the protest. It was described as a network of streets, buildings, and highly specialized places, in addition to a concrete element of space, symbolic and functional. Moreover, notions of the Maidan went far beyond the square; it was perceived as a group of people with the same dreams and aspirations—it was an idea of protest, freedom, independence, and self-determination. Euromaidan as a social movement created an innovative system of values, which was shared by a huge number of people. According to this system of values, spaces and places were reinterpreted.

Outside of Kyiv, the main reference point both in terms of marking space and symbolic justification was Taras Shevchenko. He is the most recognizable and unifying historic figure across Ukraine, as his monuments appear in every Ukrainian administrative center and in most towns. Prophetic quotes from Shevchenko's poetry were constantly recalled in interviews, and his monuments in Kharkiv and Lviv were perceived as equal participants in and inspirations of the protest.

The conclusions for this article were based on materials obtained by mid-February 2014. After the intensification of the conflict, space was again reinterpreted. The main question now to be answered by society and by authorities is: how do we deal with these spaces, especially with Independence Square in Kyiv? Do we preserve it as it was at the end of February, or somehow try to revitalize it? The death of more than 100 people in the center of Kyiv was a very traumatic experience for contemporary Ukrainian society, and it was rooted in the space of the Maidan and its environs. Events during the winter of 2013–14 divided Ukrainian history in two—before and after—and created one of the most prominent places of Ukrainian memory.

"Voices of Resistance and Hope": On the Motivations and Expectations of Euromaidaners

Anna Chebotariova

The Euromaidan protest movement unified Ukrainians of various ideological, political, ethnic, religious, and socio-economic backgrounds. It functioned literally and figuratively as a lively and heterogeneous public sphere in which the visions and strategies of different groups interacted, merged, and sometimes clashed. It was also one of the biggest protest movements, which due to repeated clashes with riot police, also became one of the bloodiest events in the history of post-Soviet Ukraine. This article will explore the motivations, goals, and expectations that drove protesters to risk their well-being and, ultimately, their lives by participating in civil unrest. I argue that after protests were violently dispersed on November 30, 2014, protesters joined the civil unrest due to issues of Ukrainian governance, particularly corruption and the violation of human rights, and not so much due to issues of European integration, particularly Yanukovych's rejection of the Association Agreement. Inspired by the Orange Revolution, and despite repeated police attacks, protesters at first expected to achieve their goals peacefully. However, the lack of political dialogue, the arrest and torture of protesters, and finally the adaptation of "dictatorship laws"[1] resulted in the radicalization of the Euromaidan movement. Participants started to perceive the conflict as a "now or never" struggle, the outcome of which would define the nature of Ukrainian politics and society.

From their very beginning in late November 2013, Euromaidan rallies were closely watched and studied by journalists, documentary filmmakers and photographers, scholars, and analysts from all over the world. The aim of the "Voices of Resistance and Hope" project, December 2013 to February 2014, undertaken by the Center for Urban History (Lviv) in cooperation with the University of Warsaw, was to give a voice to Euromaidan participants by recording their personal stories, emotions, and attitudes towards

---

1   A set of anti-protest laws, passed on January 16, 2014, by pro-Yanukovych MPs, criminalizing most of the peaceful methods and forms of protest (i.e. by introducing fines and prison terms for wearing facemasks and helmets).

163

actual events.[2] The 140 in-depth interviews with activists and participants, recorded at the height of the rallies in Kyiv, Lviv, and Kharkiv, allow us to look at this social movement from below. Since Euromaidan also had considerable response abroad, five interviews were conducted with protesters in Lublin and Warsaw. Although the sample was not statistically representative, our goal was to reflect the specifics of the situation in each city, and to conduct interviews with people of different socio-demographic and cultural backgrounds representative of the protesters. This paper will concentrate on analyzing the fifty-one interviews recorded on or around protest spaces in Kyiv. Respondents were recruited randomly among protesters in different locations (Independence Square, House of Trade Unions, Hrushevskyi Street etc.), though interviewers also used personal networks to conduct interviews with activists of Maidan sub-initiatives and organizations (such as "the Civic Sector" or "People's Hospital"). Twenty-five of those interviews were conducted from December 6- 22, 2013, after the first violent attacks on protesters. The other twenty-six conversations were recorded February 7–16, 2014, after the first violence and bloodshed on Hrushevskyi Street, and before the sniper attacks that killed more than 100 people and resulted in Yanukovych's flight from Ukraine. The timing of the interviews, those in December 2013 and February 2014, allows us to observe and track potential changes to the motivations and thoughts of the protesters. It is also important to note, that in December 2013 people were more eager to talk and share their experiences, while in February 2014 people were more reticent. Obviously, the threat of violent reprisals reduced protesters' willingness to answer questions from and tell their stories to strangers.

"People who have got things to lose"[3]: A Socio-Demographic Sketch of the Maidan

One of the most speculated subjects in media during Euromaidan was to what extent the movement represented Ukrainian society in general. Among several sociological research projects conducted during the protests, a statistical survey (see Table One below) by Ilko Kucheriv's Demo-

---

2   More information on the project can be found at: Lviv Center for Urban History "Voices of Resistance and Hope," http://www.lvivcenter.org/en/researchprojects/Pro testVoices/ (accessed June 30, 2014).
3   Interview with Female, 28, from Kyiv, February 7, 2014, in Russian.

cratic Initiatives Foundation (DIF) in cooperation with the Kyiv International Institute of Sociology (KIIS) is of particular interest.[4] Collected in early December 2013 and February 2014 from protesters on Maidan Square,[5] these data allow us to describe and identify changes to the socio-demographic profile of protesters in comparison to wider Ukrainian society. All-Ukrainian data, provided below, are derived from the representative statistical survey "Region, nation and beyond: interdisciplinary and intercultural reconceptualization of Ukraine," conducted on the eve of Euromaidan (March 2013) by St. Gallen University in cooperation with Lviv Center for Urban History in East-Central Europe.

Table 1. Socio-demographic profile of protesters

	All-Ukrainian data (February-March 2013) N=6000	DIF/KIIS survey (7–8.12.2013) N=1037	DIF/KIIS survey (03.02.2014) N=502
	%	%	%
Gender			
Male	44.7	57.2	88.2
Female	55.3	42.8	11.8
Age			
18–29	22.8	38	33.2
30–54	43.9	49	56
55 and older	33.3	13	10.8
Education			
Incomplete secondary	4.9	0.8	4.3
Secondary/specialized	60.4	22.1	43.1

---

4 For more detailed survey results, see Fond Demokratychni Initsiatyvy "Vid Maidanu-taboru do maidanu-sichi: shcho zminylosia?" [Democratic Initiatives Foundation "From Maidan-camp to Maidan-Sich: what has changed?"], http://www.dif.or g.ua/ua/polls/2014_polls/vid-maidanu-taboru-do-maidan.htm (accessed June 30, 2014).

5 Methodological challenges of conducting representative sociological research of Maidan as a mass-scale social movement, scattered in space and time, were described in the article by one of KIIS' leading sociologists, Volodymyr Paniotto: see Volodymyr Paniotto "Euromaidan: Profile of a Rebellion," *Global Dialogue* 4, no. 2 (2014), http://isa-global-dialogue.net/euromaidan-profile-of-a-rebellion/ (accessed July 30, 2014).

Incomplete higher/student	6.2	14.4	9.5
Higher education	28.5	61.7	43.1
Occupation			
High-skilled specialists with higher education	17	47.5	31.2
Students	4.8	13.2	6.2
Entrepreneurs, business-men	7.2	9.3	17.4
Workers/ service sector employers	21.9	9.1	19.4
Farmers	1.7	0.6	0.6
Pensioners	28.8	9.4	7.4
Unemployed	11	6.2	13.3
Others	7.6	4.1	3.2
Activism[6]			
Political party activist	12.9	3.9	7.7
NGO/informal group activ-ist		4.7	22.6
Non-affiliated	87.1	91.8	69.9
Region[7]			
Western Ukraine	20.1	51.8	54.8
Central and Northern Ukraine	32.9	30.9	23

6   Since the question about civic and political activism was not asked in "Region, na-tion and beyond" survey, the all-Ukrainian data on activism are derived from 2013 sociological monitoring "Ukrainian society—the dynamics of social changes," con-ducted by the Institute of Sociology of Ukrainian Academy of Sciences in Kyiv. See Serhiy Dembitskiy, "Sotsiolohichna diahnostyka stanu hromadianskoi aktyvnosti v Ukraini" [Sociological diagnostics of the current state of civil activity in Ukraine], *Ukrainske suspilstvo 1992–2013. Dynamika sotsialnykh zmin. Sotsiolohichnyi moni-toryng,* (Kyiv, Institute of Sociology, 2013): 113–20, http://i-soc.com.ua/institute/ soc-mon-2013.pdf (accessed July 30, 2014).

7   Western Ukraine included: Volyn, Zakarpatska, Lviv, Ternopil, Ivano-Frankivsk, Rivne, and Chernivtsi regions; Northern and Central Ukraine: Zhytomyr, Kyiv, Cher-kasy, Vinnytsya, Khmelnytskyi, Kirovohrad, Poltava, Chernihiv, and Sumy regions; Eastern and Southern Ukraine: Odesa, Kherson, Mykolaiv, Zaporizhzhya, Dnipropetrovsk, Kharkiv, Donetsk, Luhansk regions and AR Crimea.

Eastern and Southern Ukraine	47.1	17.3	21
Native language			
Ukrainian	50.9%	54.6%	59%
Russian	21.2%	25.9%	15.6%
Both	23.2%	18.6%	24%
Other	4.7%	0.4%	0.8%

Thus, men prevailed among Maidan participants, especially in February, after the radicalization of protests and the escalation of violence. Younger and middle-aged people constituted the backbone of protestors—the average age of Maidan participants in February was 37, compared to a national average of 45. An absolute majority of protesters, especially in December, were well-educated people, while skilled specialists with higher education were also the biggest professional group. The presence of entrepreneurs and workers/service-sector employers had increased significantly by February (from 9.3% to 17.4% and from 9.1% to 19.4% respectively).

Despite the widespread belief that the Euromaidan was a protest movement of people from western and central Ukraine only, we see that the share of protesters from eastern and southern Ukraine was quite significant, around 20%—however, the actual percentage of Ukraine's population in the eastern and southern region is double this figure. Euromaidan was a movement of urbanites: rural protesters constituted roughly 18% of participants, while Ukraine's total rural population stands at just over 31%. According to the December survey, almost half of Maidaners were from Kyiv; by February, protesters from other parts of Ukraine numerically dominated at about 88%. Only a fraction of Maidan participants, up to 8%, represented political parties, while the majority was not politically or socially affiliated. The share of NGO or informal activists increased four-fold from roughly 5% in December to over 22% in February. In our opinion, this tendency also indicates the processes of the institutionalization of groups and organizations on the Maidan, for example, self-organized initiatives such as the "People's Hospital," the "Civic Sector of Euromaidan," and the "Free University," to name but a few.

The share of protesters who listed Ukrainian as their sole native language was slightly higher than in the broader society, roughly 55–59%

compared to about 51%. The percentage of Russophones and bilinguals among Maidaners was around 40%.

Language and ethnic backgrounds of protesters interviewed during both waves of our qualitative research were also quite diverse. Eleven interviews were conducted in Russian and forty in Ukrainian, according to the respondents' preference. When it came to ethnic belonging and identities of interviewees, there were three respondents who identified themselves as Russians, two as Jews, and two as Crimean Tatars—all of them residents of Ukraine. Among our respondents there were also three people from abroad—two Diaspora Ukrainians (from the US and Czech Republic) and one Georgian. When asked about hierarchies and meanings of territorial (local, regional, civic, ethnic, and transborder) identities during the "second wave" of our research in February,[8] a majority of respondents—16 out of 26—described themselves primarily as Ukrainian citizens. This allowed us to speak to issues regarding identity and what "being Ukrainian" meant for those at the Maidan. These issues, however, require considerable attention, beyond the scope of this article.

Forms of participation in the protests varied from simply being present on the square "expressing my own civic position by being present at the Maidan"[9] to supporting the protest materially with money, medicine, or material goods, and to highly specialized and professionalized roles. As one of our respondents, a twenty-six-year old public relations manager from Kyiv, described:

> I came the next day after the "students' revolution,"[10] and I spent a lot of time here. Later, I began, actually, to live here (laughs) and one of the editors of a magazine offered me a freelance reporter job. So for some time I have worked as a journalist. Then the Automaidan[11] was created, and...I

---

8   The question was formulated in the following way: "Please answer the questions "Who am I? Who do I feel myself as?" differently. Among the following options please choose the one that is most important for you and explain why: a resident of your city/village (which one), resident of your region (which one), citizen of Ukraine (or another country), representative of a certain nationality (which one), European, representative of another community (which one)?" This question was added in February and was not asked during the first wave of our research.

9   Interview with 32-year-old man, from Kyiv region, February 13, 2014, in Ukrainian.

10 Here the respondent refers to pro-EU protests in late November 2013 before the first attack of *Berkut* police. It was often called "students' Maidan" by protesters and journalists because of the high presence and activity of university youth there.

11 A movement within the Euromaidan made up mainly of drivers who would protect the protest camps and block streets with their cars. Numerous car processions

joined them...I have offered my help with creative work.... But after the persecution against the Automaidan protesters and we were attacked by Berkut, I realized that we needed to strengthen ourselves further and help each other even more. As a result, I became the press secretary of Automaidan.... Well, the real value of both Euromaidan and Automaidan is the absence of leaders. People are so organized that even if you remove the leadership, there will be others who will continue the operation. This is the main reason why the protests will not be destroyed.[12]

The above quotation, and others, tells us that the development, organization, and diversification of Maidan infrastructure were catalyzed by outbreaks of physical and symbolic violence against protesters. Thus, the first barricades appeared on Independence Square during the large rally of December 1, 2013, the day after the violent dispersal of peaceful pro-EU demonstrators. By February 2014, after numerous clashes with riot police, the application of anti-democratic laws, and the deaths on Hrushevskyi Street, the Maidan became a city-state with its own sophisticated infrastructure. This included demarcated and well-protected frontiers, living spaces, tents and administrative buildings, kitchens, field hospitals, coordination centers, and numerous sub-initiatives. Many protesters used their professional skills to contribute to the movement. Thus among our respondents, around one-third mentioned that their role at Maidan corresponded to their occupations, for example a priest would conduct a liturgy at a "prayer tent" or a librarian would volunteer for the Maidan "library." At the same time, the Maidan was an opportunity for many protesters to grow accustomed to new social roles. For example, a hairdresser, an artist, and a child psychologist were among our respondents from militarized self-defense units. Apart from direct participation in Maidan life, sixteen interviewees highlighted the importance of communication and awareness-raising activities, particularly via social networks: "My Facebook profile has turned into a mini-agitation platform. As much as I can and with the few tools available to me, I write about the Maidan. Continuously, I see some results. People join us, they become interested, and they offer to help."[13]

---

were organized to the president's residence in Mezhyhirya and other officials' luxurious properties to voice protests. Automaidan was a repeated target of violent attacks by government forces and "*Berkut*" riot police.

12 Interview with 26-year-old woman from Kyiv, February 8, 2014, in Russian.
13 Interview with a 33-year-old woman from Kyiv, February 9, 2014, in Russian.

"This blood, blood on the cobblestones—I'll never forget it...."[14] On the Motives of Joining the Civil Unrest

More than half of the respondents decided to join the protests at the end of November in response to Yanukovych's refusal to sign the Association Agreement with the European Union. Protesters hoped that European integration would strengthen the rule of law and would weaken the rule of the *bespredel*.[15] A number of respondents were particularly disappointed with this broken promise—they felt cheated by the government's sudden decision not to sign the Association Agreement. Six respondents emphasized their own positive experience of living in or traveling to EU countries, while ten others saw Europe as an escape from Russian influence or Ukraine's Soviet legacy. A fifty-two year-old artist from Kyiv explained his position as follows:

> *I was very happy about perestroika. Any move from the Soviet model to European democratic civilization always pleased me and any rollback disappointed me. Since then, I have no doubts. I remember that jeans are produced in America and The Beatles sing in a country where being strong means something different.... My parents and relatives all listened to Western radio stations, and since childhood I have understood that Soviet newspapers lied. Otherwise, they would not be looking for alternative sources of information. I knew that all I loved was prohibited. Since then my choice has been clear.*[16]

The violent crackdown on November 30, 2013, had a key impact on the nature of the Euromaidan and on the main motivations of those who later joined the movement. As the majority of injured protestors were youth, fifteen respondents described this event in paternalistic terms by, for example, calling protesters "our children" who had to be protected from state violence. A fifty-nine-year-old army veteran, a member of a self-defense unit, from a village in Ivano-Frankivsk said:

> *I cannot speak. I have tears in my eyes for our beaten children. I am here for their future. I came so that they could live with dignity and provide for me a decent retirement. Those politicians get a salary as well as social bene-*

---

14 Interview with a 33-year-old woman from Kyiv, February 9, 2014, in Russian.

15 A word in Russian denoting those individuals, politicians and officials, who nurture and benefit from a situation of *bespredel* (lawlessness). The adjective is frequently used by respondents to describe the situation in Ukraine under Yanukovych.

16 Interview with a 52-year-old man from Kyiv, February 7, 2014, in Russian.

fits. I am retired and my pension is 1,000 hryvnias.[17] Try to survive a month on that! While they get 30–40 thousand, pension and salary. That is still not enough for them![18]

Violence against protesters, therefore, catalyzed growing resentment not only against the state security apparatus, but with the country's general situation, too. In particular, more than one-third of respondents mentioned social problems, such as inequality, unemployment, high taxes, and corruption, as the main triggers for their decision to join the Maidan. Pensioners and entrepreneurs particularly emphasized these concerns. As a result, this original pro-European Union protest metamorphosed into anti-governmental rallies that united people with often contradictory ideological and political views. For example, a nineteen-year-old activist from a leftist youth NGO in Lviv described her hesitation over the presence of right-wing groups at the Maidan, the protest's shift of priorities, and her subsequent decision to join the mass protest:

It all started with our own leftist "Anarchomaidan." The Maidan is blurred, everybody understands Europe differently. Among left-wingers, we had discussions whether we should even support Euro-Association. What would be the benefits? For which social guarantees should we stand?... On Sunday [December 1, 2014], thousands of people gathered and there were far fewer black and red flags[19]... In this context, after the crackdown, our rhetoric changed, our only desire became to stand there against the police state and the Yanukovych regime.[20]

Only two respondents said they came to the Maidan to support certain opposition politicians; the others were rather critical about the activities of such people. Interestingly, almost a quarter of respondents said that the high number of people at the Maidan was the main motivating factor for them to join the protest. A florist, aged thirty-three years, from a village in Dnipropetrovsk region said: "I was motivated by seeing people gathering here. These are the people who do care about Ukraine's fate, and the fate

---

17 Approximately €70 or $85 at the time of writing.
18 Interview with a 59-year-old man from Ivano-Frankivsk region, December 9, 2013, in Ukrainian.
19 Symbol used by Ukrainian nationalist movement, derived from the battle flag of the Ukrainian Insurgent Army (UPA) during World War II.
20 Interview in Ukrainian with a 19-year-old woman from Lviv, December 8, 2013.

of each of us, and our children. When I saw thousands of such responsible people, I could not sit on my sofa anymore."[21]

Only five respondents still mentioned the Association Agreement as the ultimate goal of the protest movement. A majority, twenty-seven respondents, mentioned that the main goal of the protests was the resignation of the president and his government and the re-election of the parliament. One-third of respondents emphasized the restoration of the rule of law, the release of imprisoned activists, and the punishing of those responsible for beating, torturing, and killing people. Twenty respondents argued that the main goal of protesters was a deep structural change of a deeply rotten system. This was to be accomplished through lustration and anti-corruption policies, as well as constitutional and democratic reforms to the Ukrainian state. Therefore, they perceived Yanukovych's possible resignation as only one-step towards achieving this goal. As a forty-year-old entrepreneur from the south-eastern city of Dniprodzerzhynsk noted: "[If Yanukovych resigns], the tents of Maidan will disappear. But Maidan as a state of mind will stay until the whole system collapses. It is not just a question of changing the leadership."[22]

"I wish they all would resign, then we will come to Khreshchatyk [Street], wearing summer dresses, to plant flowers and paint benches...."[23]— On Changing Expectations and Hopes

Maidaners articulated their strong hopes for a change of government, for the restoration of justice and for profound reforms of a corrupt political system in general. At the same time, respondents were quite cautious and rather pessimistic about their predictions. Even in December, they emphasized the high possibility of the government's use of force and the zero-sum character of tensions between protesters and the regime:

> *If we retreat, there is no way back. Because if Maidan gives up or is marginalized, the result will be mass arrests and the strengthening of dictatorship. All those people, most active people, will be imprisoned. Then it is for*

---

21 Interview in Ukrainian with a 33-year-old woman from Dnipropetrovsk, February 8, 2013.

22 Interview with a 40-year-old man from Dniprodzerzhynsk, February 7, 2014, in Russian.

23 Interview with a 28-year-old woman from Kyiv, February 7, 2014, in Russian.

a long time.... It is not like with Kuchma.... These people won't surrender their power so easily. They will cling to it till the very end.[24]

Mentioning Leonid Kuchma, the interviewee, a fifty-one-year-old entrepreneur from the town of Slavuta in the Khmelnytskyi region, gave an important reference to the events of late 2004. The Orange Revolution became a crucial historical-biographical experience that was a constant reference point for participants of Euromaidan. Approximately 62% of our respondents, even the very young, had taken part in the civil unrest of 2004: "During the Orange Revolution I was a third-year student. I also came to protest. This protest is more mature, less romantic, and more conscious. People do not expect that their life will improve tomorrow.... Honestly, people do not trust politicians. This Maidan is much more decisive."[25]

The experience of the Orange Revolution, that of a non-violent, bloodless protest achieving its primary goal, was described as crucial by Euromaidan participants, despite general disappointment with Viktor Yushchenko's politics. People, however, became much more skeptical about the role of particular politicians, and relied on self-organization rather than on opposition politicians. One-third of interviewees expressed strong hopes for the possibility of a peaceful outcome, even after numerous waves of bloody clashes with police. At the same time, the escalation of the conflict dashed these hopes. A thirty-three-year-old Russian-Jew who had lived in Kyiv for five years stated: "Well, I would certainly like it to be over, to end peacefully, without blood, without horrors, so that justice would triumph ... But the only thing we can predict right now is that the worst is probably ahead... There was a chance to win peacefully, but I think that chance has ended...."[26]

The clashes at the Administration of the President building on Bankovyi Street on December 1, 2013, highlighted one of the first attempts to radicalize the protest from inside by right-wing groups. Interestingly, in our December interviews, a clear majority of the respondents referred to these events as "provocations." In contrast, the use of force by protesters during the Hrushevskyi Street clashes in late January was perceived as a desperate but appropriate response to the regime's policies and actions. Three respondents fully supported radical groups, particularly the Right

---

24 Interview with a 51-year old man from Khmelnytskyi region, December 6, 2013, in Ukrainian.
25 Interview with a 28-year-old woman from Kyiv, December 6, 2013, in Ukrainian.
26 Interview with a 33-year-old man from Kyiv, February 9, 2014, in Russian.

Sector and their "effective methods of fighting."[27] Four respondents disagreed with the use of violence by protesters. The majority, sixteen interviewees, described radicalization as a bitter but unavoidable consequence of the lack of political will to solve the situation. Both Yanukovych and opposition leaders were blamed; the former for "not hearing the protesters for two months" and the latter for lacking unity and decisiveness. [28] A fifty-one-year-old film director from Kyiv reflected:

> Of course, I would prefer this all not to have happened. However, it has happened for a reason... Certainly, it is terrible when people are beaten and shot.... I am an absolutely peaceful person. I do not want to use arms.... I have the experience of serving in the army, but God forbid shooting at anyone. It is so difficult! I must point out that the lion's share of responsibility for these events lies with the government and the president personally. They had to react adequately to the events of November 30. Then it was still possible to settle things, trying to punish those who are guilty. But, obviously there was no political will for that. Now, this flywheel started to unwind, "the escalation of confrontation," as you can call it.[29]

Though men and women both supported and opposed radicalized tactics, the arguments used to justify these positions often had distinctive gendered frameworks. As the entrepreneur from Dniprodzerzhynsk mentioned:

> In fact, Maidan as another viche[30] has lost its meaning. People have been gathering on the square, but they ceased to understand why. Our opposition reported repeatedly that they [the president and the government] do not see us.... I will tell you what; we are normal people so violence is something unacceptable... But, at the same time, we are men, and a man is a warrior. That is why we do not deny force.[31]

Another example of these gendered phenomena comes from an interview with a female volunteer of the People's Hospital who described her

---

27 Interview with a 60-year-old man from Lviv region, February 9, 2014, in Ukrainian.
28 Interview with a 23-year-old man from Mykolaiv region, February 8, 2014, in Ukrainian.
29 Interview with a 51-year-old man from Kyiv, February 7, 2014, in Ukrainian.
30 In old-Slavonic language it literally means popular assembly or mass gathering. This word was used as the name of weekly Sunday gatherings at Maidan during December 2013-February 2014 when opposition leaders and activists spoke from the stage.
31 Interview with a 40-year-old man from Dniprodzerzhynsk, February 7, 2014, in Russian.

emotions after the first killings, and the destruction of the medical center by *Berkut*:

> *It was the moment that morally broke me. It became clear that I needed to transform my feelings into something very, very positive because not everyone can resist the temptation of tunneling such emotions into the neck of thrown bottles.[32] I recommend everyone who feels aggression because of what is happening, and we all feel a huge, incredible anger, to turn it into something positive.... This is a real challenge for women that makes things more difficult, but may also be a source of inspiration. Our attitude to violence is different, we feel things differently. We can direct our empathy not into the channel of Molotov cocktails, but into the channel of saline solution.[33]*

A variety of factors caused the Euromaidan protests to escalate violently. Whether it was the protesters' despair, disappointment, or desire for revenge and justice, the government's neglect of reasonable demands or the growing cruelty of the police, the initial hope for peaceful protest quickly evaporated.

Conclusions

This article has covered only certain aspects of a very complex phenomenon, and has tried to give a prominent voice to the Maidaners themselves. One must remember that the data analyzed above reflect protesters' moods and aspirations before the mass killings of February 19–20, 2014 and the subsequent events.

Highly educated professionals and middle-class people of different ethnic, regional, and language background drove the protest forward. The Maidan represented various segments of Ukrainian society and had a very patchwork structure. The glue that united different groups was not so much the idea of European integration but the struggle for social justice and human dignity. The protesters opposed the monopolization of power, wealth, and security forces in the hands of one person—President Yanukovych— together with his confederates. The majority of Maidaners saw the civil unrest as a chance to trigger urgently needed reforms to the economic and

---

32 The respondent refers here to "Molotov cocktails" or petrol bombs—bottle-based improvised incendiary weapons used in many urban protests, including the Euromaidan.

33 Interview with a 28-year-old woman from Kyiv, February 7, 2014, in Russian.

political systems of Ukraine. While the experience of the Orange Revolution played a significant role, unlike in 2004 people did not rely on opposition politicians as their representatives. The ability of civil society to mobilize and organize against a corrupt political system is one of the crucial achievements of the Euromaidan.

Though staunchly against the use of violence after the events of November 30, 2014, some Maidaners experienced a difficult realization that some degree of force would eventually be required. There was a whole spectrum of attitudes towards the radicalization of protesters—from full support and participation in the attacks to rejection of violent forms of resistance. Exhausted by the regime's cynical disregard of their demands and police brutality, the majority of protesters saw the situation of mid-January as a deadlock. The question whether a non-violent effective alternative was possible will probably never be answered.

Digital Civil Society: Euromaidan, the Ukrainian Diaspora, and Social Media

Svitlana Krasynska

A variety of factors, groups, and individuals played many roles in the 2013–14 events popularly called Euromaidan, events that are discussed in considerable detail elsewhere in this collection. This chapter explores the intersection of two influential Euromaidan forces—the Ukrainian Diaspora and social media—with a particular focus on how information was disseminated and how pressure was placed on foreign governments.

In the last decade, the proliferation of social media platforms has redefined how the world participates in social movements, advocacy, and anti-government demonstrations.[1] Although not without limitations, social media have played a significant role in various uprisings globally. For example, Philip N. Howard and Muzammil M. Hussain concluded in their article on the role of social media in the Middle East and North Africa: "Social media have become the scaffolding upon which civil society can build, and new information technologies give activists things that they did not have before: information networks not easily controlled by the state and coordination tools that are already embedded in trusted networks of family and friends.[2]

Ukraine's Euromaidan was no exception. Without a doubt, social media has played a crucial role in the progression of Euromaidan protests,

---

1   For further discussion, see Philip N. Howard and Muzammil M. Hussain, "The Role of Digital Media," *Journal of Democracy* 22, no. 3 (July 2011): 35–48; Christina Neumayer and Celina Raffl, "Facebook for global protest: The potential and limits of social software for grassroots activism," in *Proceedings of the 5th Prato Community Informatics & Development Informatics Conference 2008: ICTs for Social Inclusion: What is the Reality?* (2008), http://cirn.infotech.monash.edu.au/assets/docs/p rato2008papers/raffl.pdf; Babak Rahimi, "The Agonistic Social Media: Cyberspace in the Formation of Dissent and Consolidation of State Power in Postelection Iran," *The Communication Review* 14, no. 3 (2011): 158–78; Joel Penney and Caroline Dadas, "(Re)Tweeting in the service of protest: Digital composition and circulation in the Occupy Wall Street movement," *New Media and Society* 16, no. 1 (March 2013): 74–90; Summer Harlow, "Social media and social movements: Facebook and an online Guatemalan justice movement that moved offline," *New Media and Society* 14, no. 2 (August 2011): 225–43.

2   Philip N. Howard and Muzammil M. Hussain, "The Role of Digital Media," *Journal of Democracy* 22, no. 3 (July 2011): 48.

allowing for the instantaneous dissemination of information, the deployment and coordination of protesters, and the organization and delivery of critical supplies, to name but a few.[3]

Additionally, social media allowed those who were not physically present in Kyiv to participate in protests in a variety of ways. This group included Ukraine's rather substantial Diaspora. While definitions of the term "Diaspora" vary in the literature and a great "dispersion of the meaning of the term in semantic, conceptual and disciplinary space" exists, this article uses the term rather inclusively.[4] As comprehensive data on Euromaidan supporters outside of Ukraine does not currently exist, the term "Diaspora" here comprises a wide range of individuals who identify themselves as Ukrainian, either by national or ethnic origin, who reside outside of Ukraine—from second and third generation immigrants to those who have arrived recently with or without intention to stay in the host country permanently. This article uses "Diaspora" and "Ukrainians abroad" interchangeably, emphasizing the term's encompassing definition.

According to the Ukrainian World Congress, the Ukrainian Diaspora comprises approximately 20 million people, while the International Organization for Migration purports that "Ukraine has one of the largest diaspora in the world, many of them maintaining cultural and economic linkages with the homeland."[5] Indeed, Ukrainians living abroad keenly support their compatriots, annually contributing roughly $9.3 billion in remittances, a formidable amount that constitutes almost 5 percent of the country's gross

---

3 For further discussion, see Pablo Barberá and Megan Metzger, "Tweeting the Revolution: Social Media Use and the #Euromaidan Protests," *The Blog* (blog), *Huff-Post Politics*, July 23, 2014, http://www.huffingtonpost.com/pablo-barbera/tweeting-the-revolution-s_b_4831104.html (accessed August 20, 2014); Olga Onuch, "Social networks and social media in Ukrainian 'Euromaidan' protests," *The Washington Post*, January 2, 2014, http://www.washingtonpost.com/blogs/monkey-cage/wp/20 14/01/02/social-networks-and-social-media-in-ukrainian-euromaidan-protests-2/ (accessed August 20, 2014); Tanya Talaga, "How social media is fuelling Ukraine's protests," *thestar.com*, February 5, 2014, http://www.thestar.com/news/world/201 4/02/05/ukraines_revolutionary_movement_euromaidan_stays_organized_with_soc ial_media.html (accessed August 20, 2014).
4 Rogers Brubaker, "The 'diaspora' diaspora," *Ethnic and Racial Studies* 28, no. 1 (January 2005): 1–19.
5 "About the UWC," *Ukrainian World Congress*, http://www.ukrainianworldcongr ess.org/index.php/id/259 (accessed August 11, 2014); "Migration in Ukraine: Facts & Figures," *International Organization for Migration Mission in Ukraine*, September 2011, 5, http://www.iom.int/jahia/webdav/shared/shared/mainsite/activities/countries /docs/Ukraine/Migration-in-Ukraine-Facts-and-Figures.pdf (accessed June 6, 2014).

domestic product.[6] At times of crisis, as it turns out, Ukrainians abroad also mobilize in substantial numbers. During Euromaidan protests, Ukrainians on every populated continent participated in rallies, raised and transferred funds, signed petitions, contacted their host countries' politicians, and engaged in many other activities, some of which are described in more depth in this chapter.[7] While it is likely that a fraction of Ukrainians living abroad did not uphold the views or aspirations of the Euromaidan movement, this chapter focuses on the events and initiatives undertaken exclusively in support of the Euromaidan as no significant mobilization of the regime's supporters, or the "Antimaidan", was observed outside of Ukraine.

A comprehensive article by William Lahneman demonstrates that Diaspora communities have the "ability to exert sufficiently focused, organized, and powerful influence to make them significant actors in international affairs."[8] While the actual effect of the Ukrainian Diaspora on the outcomes of Euromaidan and international affairs has yet to be determined, this chapter begins to explore the contributions made by Ukrainians abroad to the movement through social media networks. The chapter asks the following questions: How were Ukrainians abroad involved in the Euromaidan movement through social media? What role did they play in disseminating information about the protests and how did they attempt to pressure foreign governments? And, what are potential implications of these activities for Ukraine's future? I endeavor to answer these questions by conveying three distinct, yet rather typical stories of Ukrainian Diaspora mobilization for Euromaidan on social media.

These stories were constructed from data generated from detailed interviews with leadership representatives of three Diaspora-driven projects. Interview data were supplemented by follow-up correspondence with study participants and by input from other Ukrainian Diaspora groups, along with

---

6   Dilip Ratha, Christian Eigen-Zucchi, Sonia Plaza, Hanspeter Wyss, and Soonhwa Yi, "Migration and Remittance Flows: Recent Trends and Outlook, 2013–2016," *The World Bank*, October 2, 2013, http://siteresources.worldbank.org/INTPROSPE CTS/Resources/3349341288990760745/MigrationandDevelopmentBrief21.pdf (accessed August 21, 2014).

7   *EuroMaidans in the World* [map], January 24, 2014, https://mapsengine.google.co m/map/edit?mid=z1XzcKlIfqxY.kG0iaoWygXkc (accessed August 21, 2014).

8   William J. Lahneman, "Impact of Diaspora Communities on National and Global Politics," *Center for International and Security Studies at Maryland*, July 5, 2005, 8, http://www.cissm.umd.edu/papers/files/lahneman_diaspora_report.pdf (accessed August 21, 2014).

an extensive review of social and mainstream media information about these groups and their activities in the larger context of Euromaidan. Finally, it should be noted that all interviewees provided feedback on drafts of the case studies that focused on them and the organization with which they affiliate in order to eliminate any potential misinterpretation or misrepresentation.[9]

The results of these efforts are the three case studies presented in the following pages. The goal is to provide context and understanding of how the Diaspora participated in Euromaidan on social media by examining how these groups formed, functioned, changed, and how they perceive their future role in Ukraine's development.

I had rather simple criteria through which I selected my case studies. Initiatives had to be predominantly Diaspora-driven and operate exclusively or primarily through social media. In the process of preliminary interviews and correspondence with various online groups, other criteria were added to help portray a typical account of a Euromaidan-related Diaspora initiative on social media. First, while many Diaspora groups existed before Euromaidan, this study focuses on groups that emerged after November 2013. Furthermore, to depict a characteristic grassroots organization, the cases selected were all volunteer, transnational networks of individuals who were located in different countries and on different continents, and who were connected primarily or exclusively through social media.

At the same time, the three Diaspora groups examined in this article varied regarding their missions, directions, structures, and target audiences. Specifically, the first case study presented in this chapter is a WordPress translation blog; the second case focuses on a chiefly Twitter-based group; while the third is a newly registered non-profit organization initially launched as a Facebook group. Notably, however, all three have a significant Facebook presence, which was another selection criterion, as Facebook was the number one social media outlet used by Euromaidan protestors.[10] Furthermore, whereas the first two groups described above were exclusively social media based, for variation, the non-profit was included to provide a slightly different perspective. Though, the majority of its activities took place on social media, the group also had a significant "offline" presence.

---

9   Such a feedback process is sometimes referred to as "member checking."
10 Daniella Peled, "Report News: Ukraine's Social Media Revolution," *Institute for War and Peace Reporting*, March 26, 2014, http://iwpr.net/report-news/ukraines-social-media-revolution (accessed August 21, 2014).

Finally, it should be that stated that I was not simply a detached observer in this project. Being part of the Ukrainian Diaspora, I spent many hours on social media between November 2013 and February 2014. I read, wrote, translated, shared, liked, tweeted, and otherwise viewed or disseminated thousands of Euromaidan related posts on social media, observing and participating, unwittingly at times, in the initiatives studied here. These experiences provided further triangulation opportunities. On the other hand, being a participant, as well as an observer, can introduce bias into a study. I did, however, attempt to isolate my prior knowledge and I used a number of strategies—including extensive document review and member checking mentioned above—to minimize bias in constructing the three cases that follow.

Voices of Ukraine: A Translations Blog

Our Manifesto: Voices of Ukraine was formed in response to an urgent need to accurate information about events in Ukraine to go global in several languages. We are in Ukraine and other countries, and network closely with those involved in current events to verify sources and translate reliable information. We are a volunteer translation and editing project working to give a realistic picture of the ground reality of the Ukrainian political and cultural spaces.[11]

A Canadian-based university professor and second-generation Ukrainian, alias Isis Wisdom, is the English team Editor-in-Chief and an active contributor to "Voices of Ukraine." Initially, she followed the events of Euromaidan, intrigued by what she characterized as the early "manifestation of a functioning civil society and a cultural revolution." The first violent police crackdown, however, spurred her to action, doing more than simply observing events. She said during an interview: "When the first students were beaten, I think that mobilized the entire Diaspora. There was no question about it—I had to do something to help."[12] Like many Ukrainians, she frequently posted to her Facebook profile about Ukraine. However, she wanted to contribute to the movement in other, more tangible ways. "Because we cannot all go flying in and out of Ukraine," she said, "what resources we do have, when they are not solely financial, are ones we can share

---

11 "Voices of Ukraine: Our manifesto," http://maidantranslations.com/our-manifesto/ (last modified December 21, 2013).

12 Interview with Isis Wisdom via Skype, April 15, 2014.

through the Internet."[13] Thus, Isis Wisdom decided to utilize her professional writing and editing skills to advance the causes of Euromaidan online.[14]

Recalling December 2013, she noted the paucity of quality English-language sources about what was happening in Ukraine. Thus, Wisdom took it upon herself to join one of the ongoing initiatives that had live access to events and that needed a professional English-speaking editor and translator. Online, she found a Ukraine-based initiative that met her criteria. Soon after joining the group, she assumed a major leadership role. Subsequently, she helped recruit a team of English speakers from Ukraine and the Diaspora to translate and edit for the project. Not knowing each other personally, having "met" exclusively on social media, the core team seemingly bonded through a common vision. Wisdom stated: "I think everyone in the core group was attracted to and personally shared this same vision—we don't know each other at all, we are all really strangers to each other—but we share the vision: to be an accurate voice, and a … conduit of the lived experiences of Ukrainians in Ukraine."[15]

Behind the Scenes

Responding to the need for reliable and quality information for Western audiences and to the specific request from the Kyiv-based activist group EuromaidanSOS to provide English translation for the Organization for Security and Cooperation in Europe (OSCE), Voices of Ukraine was first launched as the Facebook page "Euro-Maidan As It Is" in December 2013.[16] The main objective of the group was to spread accurate information and eyewitness accounts through social network channels, focusing primarily on the kind of information not typically covered by mainstream media. As part of the project, public statements, personal accounts, blog posts, and social media updates were translated from Ukrainian and Russian, primarily into English and German; however, there were also periodic translations into French, Spanish, Italian, Portuguese, Polish, and Japanese.

---

13 Ibid.
14 Ibid.
15 Ibid.
16 "Euro-Maidan As It Is," *Facebook*, https://www.facebook.com/EuroMaydanTranslat ions (accessed April 29, 2014).

Another Facebook page, "Maidan Needs Translators," was created simultaneously to serve as a platform for recruiting and coordinating volunteer translators.[17] It contains technical instructions on the translation process and texts for volunteers to translate. By the end of 2013, the content of the two Facebook pages, "Euro-Maidan As It Is" and "Maidan Needs Translators," was transferred to a WordPress blog, eventually named "Voices of Ukraine."[18] Both Facebook pages still exist for outreach purposes and serve to supplement the WordPress blog; an additional Facebook page, "Voices of Ukraine-Official," was also created with the same purpose. The blog, however, is the main output for "Voices of Ukraine."

As it was during the Euromaidan, the project remains open to those who can translate from Ukrainian and or Russian; editing and distribution is conducted by native English speakers in the Diaspora. The group is comprised entirely of volunteers and it claims to work as a network rather than a hierarchy. According to Wisdom, coordinators vetted every article through confirmation from several sources, and all translations carry links to their original sources. In addition to the 15–20 permanent volunteer coordinators and editors, and roughly 30 intermittent translators, the team engages seven Ukraine-based experts.

Global Reach

Having posted almost 3,000 articles since December 2013, "Voices of Ukraine" has a truly global reach; according to "Voices of Ukraine's" internal blog analytics, readers from 192 countries have accessed the blog as of August 2014.[19] One of the blog's top viewed articles recorded almost 350,000 views.[20] The article was ranked number one on both Reddit's World News page (prevailing over articles from the BBC, *The Independent*, *Moscow Times*, Reuters and other major news outlets), and on its

17 Maidan Needs Translators' Facebook Page, https://www.facebook.com/pages/Maidan-Needs-Translators/635416686497814 (accessed April 29, 2014).
18 "Voices of Ukraine," http://maidantranslations.com/ (accessed August 13, 2014).
19 Interview with "Isis Wisdom" via Facebook chat, August 13, 2014.
20 Anna Mausi Shvets, "TURKEY: under Ottoman Empire treaty with Catherine the Great if Crimea declares independence it returns to Turkey," Voices of Ukraine, March 17, 2014, http://maidantranslations.com/2014/03/17/turkey-under-ottoman-empire-treaty-with-catherine-the-great-if-crimea-declares-independence-it-returns-to-turkey/ (accessed August 21, 2014).

FrontPage.[21] Furthermore, "Voices of Ukraine" has become a recognized resource for media and international agencies. To illustrate, *Foreign Policy, The Guardian, Forbes Magazine, The Daily Beast* and *USA Today*, among other major news outlets, have linked to the blog as a source.[22] Two senior correspondents at BBC have requested specific contacts in Ukraine. Additionally, *Kyiv Post* carries a regular daily feature on "Voices of Ukraine's" translations and IsraelForeignAffairs.com regularly re-blogs translated articles in several languages.[23]

Although "Voices of Ukraine's" primary focus is on the blog, the group also has a Twitter account, @MaidanOnline, which it uses, among other things, to disseminate its blog posts. The Twitter account has over 2,300 followers and over 4,600 tweets. Followers include several high-ranking European, Canadian, and American politicians, in addition to over 100 well-respected journalists from such media outlets as Reuters, BBC, *Time, Der Spiegel, The Wall Street Journal*, Fox News, Buzzfeed, Observer Herald, Sky News, The Economist Intelligence Unit Europe Team, *Foreign*

21 Reddit, http://www.reddit.com/, is a social networking and news website where registered users can vote submissions "up" or "down" to increase or decrease their popularity and visibility.

22 Alexander J. Motyl, "A House United: Why analysts touting Ukraine's East-West division are just plain wrong," *Foreign Policy*, February 22, 2014, http://www.foreig npolicy.com/articles/2014/02/22/a_house_united (accessed August 20, 2014); Peter Walker, Nabeelah Shabbir, Tom McCarthy and Alan Yuhas, "Ukraine crisis: Obama says Crimea referendum would 'violate international law'—live," *The Guardian— World News*, March 6, 2014, http://www.theguardian.com/world/2014/mar/06/ukrain e-crisis-russia-crimea-eu-un-live#block-53185face4b0c8d9ae9a558e. (accessed August 20, 2014); Andrea Chalupa, "Putin's Fabricated Claim Of A Fascist Threat In Ukraine," *Forbes—Opinion*, April 4, 2014, http://www.forbes.com/sites/realsp in/2014/04/04/putins-fabricated-claim-of-a-fascist-threat-in-ukraine/ (accessed August 22, 2014); Oleg Shynkarenko, "Who Killed One of the Most Notorious Right Sector Leaders in Ukraine?" *The Daily Beast—World News*, March 27, 2014, http://www.thedailybeast.com/articles/2014/03/27/who-killed-one-of-the-most-notorious-right-sector-leaders-in-ukraine.html (accessed August 22, 2014); Olga Rudenko, "Russia says some troops off Ukraine border," *USA Today—Breaking News*, March 31, 2014, http://www.usatoday.com/story/news/world/2014/03/31/ukra ine-border-russia-troops-withdraw-john-kerry-sergey-lavrov/7111893/ (accessed August 22, 2014).

23 Dmitry Tymchuk. "Dmitry Tymchuk's military blog," *KyivPost.com—Opinion*, http:// www.kyivpost.com/content/author/dmitry-tymchuk/ (accessed August 13, 2014); Dmitry Tymchuk. "Dmitry Tymchuk's military blog," *IsraelForeignAffairs.com*, http://israelforeignaffairs.com/?s=tymchuk (accessed August 13, 2014).

Policy, Kyiv Post, Agence France-Presse, *Berliner Tageszeitung,* Greek Public TV, and *Gazeta Wyborcza.*

Personal Focus

Despite having a global reach, "Voices of Ukraine" also prides itself on the personal connections and understanding that it creates between those in Ukraine and those abroad. Wisdom emphasizes: "This is very much a kind of citizen journalism, citizen networking, civil society-type approach.... And it is very much a connecting from person to person, heart to heart."[24] A particular story demonstrates this well. Having translated a personal account of a typical late January 2014 incident that involved a Euromaidan activist whose fiancé was abducted, brutally beaten, and apprehended, and who subsequently faced three to five years in jail on fabricated charges, Wisdom was deeply affected and felt compelled to intervene. She assisted by supplying the activist with information and contacts to pertinent individuals and organizations. She stated during an interview:

> You can empower people just by giving them information.... I know this because when I was a child, my mother got political dissidents out from behind the iron curtain.... And one thing that we have learned out here in the West is we know how to make contacts, we know who they should talk to, we know how it should work, what the legal system works like, when it works, what the processes are, we are used to that.[25]

Wisdom approached the activist through social media and provided her with instructions on how to contact "HromadskeTV," "EuromaidanSOS," and other organizations in Ukraine, as well as directed her to a personal contact at the OSCE. Shortly thereafter, she appeared on social and mainstream media, received legal representation, and eventually secured her fiancé's release. Such a positive outcome not only profoundly affected the two Euromaidan activists in this story, but also Wisdom herself. Conveying that the above story was one of many, she maintained:

> To sit here, in Canada, and be able to so positively affect someone's life so far away, is a demonstration that it is possible to affect positive change in the world as an individual, no matter where you are. I know that everybody

---

24 Interview with "Wisdom," April 15, 2014.
25 Ibid.

who is helping us, who is translating, who is editing... they are all doing this because their hearts, in the Diaspora, are sick for Ukraine.[26]

The Diaspora

Euromaidan embodied an image of Ukraine that many in the Diaspora, especially those of its second and third generation, hold dear. This, in large part, compelled them to take part in the events. As Wisdom emotionally conveyed, "I think that for everybody in the diaspora, Maidan is ... absolutely the Ukraine that we always wanted, and we have always known, in our hearts could be....This is our last chance."[27] Indeed, when the first public call for translators was made by "Voices of Ukraine" on Facebook, the post collected over 500 "likes" within two days, enabling the project's launch with an ample volunteer base. As this case study may also suggest, the Ukrainian Diaspora has played a potentially important role in creating and disseminating information about Ukraine to Western observers, including the mainstream media, politicians, and the general public.

The events, in turn, also affected the Diaspora. Three short months of protests connected Ukrainians abroad on unprecedented levels, creating a new and vibrant digital society of individuals with a shared cause. This intensified networking and communication among the Diaspora, as well as between the Diaspora and Ukrainians living in Ukraine, has fostered a heightened sense of belonging and pride. Determined to continue and further develop the efforts of "Voices of Ukraine," Wisdom concluded:

We are networking with each other, across borders, more than we have before.... So, [we] are not so isolated. And before, in the diaspora, we really were more isolated.... What happened in Ukraine on Maidan...for the first time made the diaspora proud to be Ukrainian. And that, I think, is an experience that has brought with it greater conviction and determination for a lot of the diaspora.[28]

---

26 Ibid.
27 Ibid.
28 Ibid

DigitalMaidan: Twitter Activists

Mission Statement: DigitalMaidan turns up the volume of Euromaidan for the world to hear the truth of what's happening in Ukraine.[29]

Ethnically Ukrainian New York-based journalist and writer, Andrea Chalupa, who became the driving force behind DigitalMaidan, contended: "I believe to be innovative in social media movements, you should look into what they are doing in the animal rights space."[30] Chalupa credits CNN Films' documentary "Blackfish" for inspiring her to participate in her first social media campaign, which intended to protect dolphins off the coast of Taiji, Japan. After participating in an exceedingly effective way to draw attention to a cause, she thought: "If this could work so well to get celebrity and media attention for dolphins, then why don't we use it for Ukraine?" This thought gave life to DigitalMaidan during a period of escalating violence, yet relatively low attention to or apparent understanding of the Euromaidan events in Western media and Western society, generally. Replicating the social media strategy of the Facebook group, "Blackfish Brigade," DigitalMaidan used Twitter as a platform for its activism, with a specific emphasis on twitterstorms, aimed at generating public awareness and putting pressure on foreign governments to respond to the events of Euromaidan.[31]

---

29 Personal correspondence with Andrea Chalupa, May 20, 2014.
30 Interview with Andrea Chalupa via Skype, May 16, 2014.
31 "Blackfish Brigade," *Facebook*, https://www.facebook.com/pages/Blackfish-Brigade/171709709706454 (accessed May 19, 2014). A twitterstorm is defined as "a sudden spike in activity surrounding a certain topic on the Twitter social media site.... Using a certain hashtag, the tweet quickly spreads as people are notified of the message and then reuse the hashtag with subsequent retweets and tweets.... When a specific tweet and hashtag are tweeted and retweeted quickly enough, the hashtag is included on Twitter's 'trending' list and displayed to all Twitter users, even those who are not a member of the hashtag user's list of followers. This often leads to the original message or hashtag crossing to other social media sites or the mainstream media, resulting in much deeper penetration into the collective conscience." Cory Jansen, "Twitterstorm," in *Techopedia*, Janalta Interactive Inc., http://www.techopedia.com/definition/29624/twitterstorm (accessed June 9, 2014).

The Storm

To promote and coordinate the inaugural DigitalMaidan twitterstorm scheduled for January 27, 2014, a Facebook event called "EuroMaidan: #DigitalMaidan Twitter Storm" was created with ninety-nine initial invitees.[32] As part of the initiative, group members were instructed to "tweet" at an appointed time on the day of the event by using the hashtag #digitalmaidan. To produce a more targeted outreach, users had the option of selecting from ninety pre-made tweets available on the DigitalMaidan website.[33] By January 27, on the day of the first twitterstorm and only three days after the launch of the Facebook event, 30,000 individuals were invited to participate.

The first Twitterstorm was primarily directed at notable politicians—US President Barack Obama, Canadian Prime Minister Stephen Harper, then French Prime Minister Jean-Marc Ayrault, and German Chancellor Angela Merkel, among others—urging them to impose sanctions on Ukraine's government. Activists also targeted celebrities and media outlets in North America, Europe, and Israel. The following tweet was used in eight languages besides English: "Ukrainians are being killed fighting for democracy." It included a link to a YouTube video, titled "The Price of Democracy/Tsina Demokratii" that portrayed the initially peaceful protests and the ensuing crackdown by the riot police.[34]

Trending and Response

Exceeding all expectations, #digitalmaidan became the number one trending topic worldwide within minutes of the first Twitterstorm's launch, and remained high on the trending list for most of the day. The initiative was repeated twice within a week of its launch, each time producing similar trending effects. During this time, DigitalMaidan reached a sizable audience: Keyhole, an online hashtag analytic tool, indicated that within one week, between January 26 and February 2, 2014, the hashtag #digitalmaidan was used by 3,667 Twitter accounts in 16,638 posts, reaching almost

---

32 "EuroMaidan: #DigitalMaidan Twitter Storm (2/19)," https://www.facebook.com/eve nts/341170319354082/ (accessed June 1, 2014).

33 "Digital Maidan," http://www.digitalmaidan.com (accessed May 15, 2014).

34 "Price of democracy [Tsina demokratii]," YouTube video, 3 minutes and 12 seconds, posted by Nataliya Bartosik, January 25, 2014, https://www.youtube.com/wa tch?v=TJ8RKhD2WYo (accessed June 4, 2014).

3.7 million Twitter users who collectively saw the hashtag over 11.6 million times.[35]

As a result of the campaign, prominent individuals began using the #digitalmaidan hashtag in their tweets. Among them were Ayrault, Ukrainian journalist and public figure Mustafa Nayem, Russian chess grandmaster and politician Garry Kasparov, Nicaraguan-born human rights and climate change advocate Bianca Jagger, and English comedian and actor Russell Brand. Notably, Oscar-nominated Ukrainian-American actress Vera Farmiga joined Twitter on the day of one of DigitalMaidan's twitterstorms, making @DigitalMaidan one of her first followed accounts. Furthermore, business tycoon and founder of the Virgin Group Richard Branson and former US President Bill Clinton tweeted messages of support for Ukraine shortly after receiving tweets from DigitalMaidan.

> **Richard Branson** @richardbranson · Jan 24
> Leaders in #Ukraine must turn truce into peace, stopping violence & restoring democracy virg.in/ukp
>
> ↩   ⟲ 133   ★ 88   •••

> **Bill Clinton** @billclinton · Feb 3
> # Kudos to brave Ukrainians demanding real democracy. Urge dialogue & peaceful resolution to achieve a strong, united Ukraine. They can do it!
>
> ↩   ⟲ 1.7K   ★ 1.3K   •••

In addition to organizing Twitterstorms, which involved the extensive involvement of DigitalMaidan activists, the core group of volunteers used the initiative's trending success to give interviews and participate in various speaking engagements. Chalupa maintained: "All of us were doing these media appearances, and speaking to schools, and that was really critical. ... DigitalMaidan deputized a core group of passionate volunteers to go out in the world and spread the facts."[36] The initiative was mentioned in such

---

35 "Real-time tracker: digitalmaidan," http://keyhole.co/realtime/hNqqJq/digitalmaidan (accessed May 22, 2014).
36 Interview with Chalupa, May 16, 2014.

online media outlets as *Foreign Policy*, Global Voices, Twitchy, Le Huffington Post, Huffington Post Québec, The Malay Mail Online, *The Japan
Times*, the *London Evening Standard*, The Daily Beast, World Policy Blog,
as well as Russian-language Delo.ua and AIN.ua.[37] Additionally, outreach
to college campuses was fruitful: DigitalMaidan was featured in the online
business journal of The Wharton School of the University of Pennsylvania
and an online audio podcast at Syracuse University.[38]

---

37 Hanna Kozlowska, "From Brooklyn to Kiev, How #DigitalMaidanWent Viral," *For-
    eign Policy, Passport*, January 31, 2014 http://blog.foreignpolicy.com/posts/2014/0
    1/31/from_brooklyn_to_kiev_how_digitalmaidan_went_viral (accessed August 21,
    2014); Tetyana Lokot, "Ukrainian #DigitalMaidan Activism Takes Twitter's Trending
    Topics by Storm," *Global Voices*, January 27, 2014, http://globalvoicesonline.or
    g/2014/01/27/ukrainian-digitalmaidan-protests-twitter-trending-topics-storm/   (ac-
    cessed August 22, 2014); twitchy.com, "#digitalmaidan: Ukrainians ramp up pro-
    tests against government on social media," January 27, 2014, http://twitchy.com
    /2014/01/27/digitalmaidan-ukrainians-ramp-up-protests-against-government-on-
    social-media/ (accessed August 23, 2014); Lauran Provost, "#DigitalMaidan: En
    Ukraine, les Euromaidan prennent Twitter d'assaut [In Ukraine, Euromaidan takes
    twitter by storm]," *Huff Post Le Bon Bien*, January 27, 2014, http://www.huffingto
    npost.fr/2014/01/27/digitalmaidan-ukraine-twitter-euromaidan_n_4674347.html?ut
    m_hp_ref=fb&src=sp&comm_ref=false (accessed August 22, 2014); Malaymail
    Online "Streaming the uprising: Ukraine protests go viral," January 29, 2014,
    http://www.themalaymailonline.com/features/article/streaming-the-uprising-ukraine-
    protests-go-viral (accessed August 22, 2014); Dario Thuburn, "Streaming the upris-
    ing: Ukraine protests go viral," *The Japan Times*, February 3, 2014,
    http://www.japantimes.co.jp/news/2014/02/03/world/politics-diplomacy-world/stream
    ing-the-uprising-ukraine-protests-go-viral/#.U3acLChmPNI. (accessed August 22,
    2014); Andrea Chalupa, "A chance to join Ukraine's protest," *Evening Standard*,
    January 27, 2014, https://twitter.com/JoshNeicho/status/427816188429606912 (ac-
    cessed August 22, 2014); Andrea Chalupa, "When Social Media is Your Only
    Hope," *The Daily Beast—Women in the World*, February, 10, 2014, http://www.t
    hedailybeast.com/witw/articles/2014/02/10/when-social-media-is-your-only-
    hope.html (accessed August 22, 2014); Lydia Tomkiw, "A Digital Movement: Pro-
    tests in Ukraine Go Global," *World Policy—Blog*, February 7, 2014, http://www.wor
    ldpolicy.org/blog/2014/02/07/digital-movement-protests-ukraine-go-global   (ac-
    cessed August 22, 2014)' Delo.ua, "Heshteg #digitalmaidan stal mirovym lid-
    erom/Hashtag #digitalmaidan became the world leader," January 28, 2014,
    http://delo.ua/tech/liderom-sredi-heshtegov-v-mire-stal-digitalmaidan-225683/   (ac-
    cessed August 22, 2014); Maya Yarovaya, "#digitalmaidan vyshel na pervoye mes-
    to v mirovyh trendah Twitter [digitalmaidan reached first place in world trending on
    Twitter]," *Ain.com—Sotzmedia*, January 27, 2014, http://ain.ua/2014/01/27/510447
    (accessed August 23, 2014).
38 "Ukraine's 'Revolution of Dignity' for People and Business," *Knowledge
    @Wharton—Public Policy*, January 31, 2014, http://knowledge.wharton.upenn.edu

Twitter Populace

Interestingly, before the events of Euromaidan, DigitalMaidan organizers could not have called themselves Twitter experts; in fact, they hardly ever used the tool. By contrast, during Euromaidan, Chalupa reported that she was "glued" to Twitter, tweeting roughly twenty times daily. She commented: "Twitter basically became my nervous system. I would go to bed—the last thing I would look at was my Twitter on the phone. The first thing I did when I woke up was look at Twitter on my phone."[39] Hence, during the events of Euromaidan, the DigitalMaidan team became proficient and prolific with Twitter, helping others to join the effort.

Thus, as part of Twitterstorm campaigns, DigitalMaidan expended a substantial amount of time and resources on helping new users sign on and use Twitter: "We have ... gotten hundreds and hundreds of people on Twitter for the first time... [including] moms, middle-aged and elderly people," Chalupa reported.[40] DigitalMaidan's Facebook page provided instructions written on how to use the site, as well as an ongoing forum for people who had questions; questions were answered both by page administrators and other users.[41] Chalupa further noted: "We were really like a customer service—how to use Twitter for Ukrainians."[42]

Beyond Euromaidan

Aside from engaging in extensive outreach and receiving impressive responses, DigitalMaidan also served as a vehicle for Ukrainians abroad and in Ukraine to connect with each other. Chalupa suggests that these activities may have solidified the Ukrainian Diaspora globally, presenting boundless opportunities for future involvement:

/article/ukraines-revolution-dignity-people-business/ (accessed August 23, 2014); Michael Ardaiolo, "Ukraine's Cold War in the Social Media Age," *The Public Diplomat—Digital Diplomacy*, February 4, 2014, http://thepublicdiplomat.com/2014/02/0 4/listen-ukraines-cold-war-in-the-social-media-age/ (accessed August 24, 2014).

39 Interview with Chalupa, May 16, 2014.
40 Ibid.
41 Digitalmaidan Website, *Instructions/Tips*, accessed on August 11, 2014, http://dig italmaidan.com/pre-made-tweets/instructions-tips/; Laura Littlefield's post on "EuroMaidan: #DigitalMaidan Twitter Storm (2/19)" Facebook page (January 26, 2014), https://www.facebook.com/photo.php?fbid=10201518664031876&set=gm.3419271 02611737&type=1&theater (accessed on August 11, 2014).
42 Interview with Chalupa, May 16, 2014.

Another thing [Euromaidan] did, it connected the diaspora around the world.... We know where the Ukrainians are in Tokyo, in Argentina, in Israel, in Norway, in Denmark. We all know each other now. And that's huge. [Euromaidan] has really ... united the diaspora unlike ever before. You can participate no matter where you are. And you can be connected no matter where you are. And that presents so much opportunity for us to work together for a stronger Ukraine.[43]

Much like the previous case study, DigitalMaidan demonstrates a renewed interest in contributing to Ukraine's condition by some elements of the Diaspora. When asked whether DigitalMaidan had intentions to disband at the conclusion of the protests, Chalupa expressed a keen interest in continuing the work, albeit with a slightly different focus. Subsequently, DigitalMaidan would serve as a platform for connecting and supporting all Ukrainians, in Ukraine and elsewhere in the world, by educating them on how to use and leverage social media for their personal, professional, and civic development. Chalupa expressed: "A successful Ukrainian anywhere is a good thing, because each one makes our community stronger."[44]

Razom, Inc.:
From Facebook Group to Transnational Organization

Mission Statement: To foster Ukrainian democracy and civil society through a global network of experts and organizations supporting democracy activists and human rights advocates throughout Ukraine.[45]

A Ukrainian-born and raised software engineer based in New York City, Lyuba Shipovich, conveyed during an interview: "I was skiing on November 30 [2013]. At lunchtime... I opened the phone to look at something on Facebook, and there was the whole thread about students being beaten-up, video, photo.... My sister lives in Kyiv, and I knew she was there that day."[46] Her account sounds familiar to many Ukrainians living abroad. Fortunately, this account had a happy ending: the sister avoided physical harm. The events of the day, however, compelled Shipovich to get actively involved in the protests.

---

43 Ibid.
44 Ibid.
45 "Razom: Our Mission," http://razomforukraine.org/ (accessed June 1, 2014). "Razom" means "together" in Ukrainian.
46 Interview with Lyuba Shipovich via Skype, April 23, 2014.

Trying to determine how to contribute, Shipovich recalled the cold days of the Orange Revolution in which she took an active part. Electricity, she stated, was a big issue, from the need to charge electronics to heating protesters' tents.[47] Thus, her first project entailed pooling resources with her friend, and purchasing and delivering a generator for protesters. Over the next two months, her undertakings grew from purchasing a generator to leading a vibrant, transnational human rights organization.

Rapid Expansion

Much like the events of Euromaidan, Razom developed swiftly. Launched as a Facebook group, "Zakordonni ukraintzi Yevromaidanu/Ukrainians abroad for EuroMaydan," by an Irish-Ukrainian activist in early December, it initially comprised a handful of Ukrainians living on different continents, connected through mutual friends and acquaintances on social media.[48] During one of the first online discussions, the group's members expressed eagerness to contribute but had no idea what to do. Thus, inspired by the success of her first project, Shipovich suggested purchasing another generator. Within three hours of her making the suggestion, the required money was raised and, soon thereafter, the generator was delivered to the Maidan. The venture's success stimulated the group, which ultimately collected over $150,000 worth of humanitarian aid that was distributed in Kyiv and other Ukrainian cities. The Facebook group eventually expanded to roughly 2,500 members by the end of February 2014.

At the same time, located in great numbers on the US East Coast, including New York City, Philadelphia, and Washington, DC, group members gathered in organized rallies in support of Euromaidan, often teleconferencing or driving between the three cities. It was during the organizing of one of these rallies that the core group of volunteers, now Razom's Board of Directors, first met in a bar. Members of the group had never met before; they became acquainted via Facebook.

Expanding exponentially and pursuing multiple initiatives, the grassroots group soon faced several logistical challenges; the need for a formal organization became evident to the group by January 2014. Among the challenges were issues associated with bank transfers, as well as permit

---

47 Ibid.
48 Ukrainians abroad for EuroMaydan's Facebook page, https://www.facebook.com/groups/ukrainians.abroad/ (accessed June 9, 2014).

requests demanded by local authorities to hold rallies. Additionally, Shipovich reports an ostensible lack of communication and cooperation between
Ukrainians representing different waves of Diaspora during that time: "The
existing organizations were based on second and third wave Diaspora, but
the [newer] so-called fourth, or even fifth wave, was kind of separated from
the mainstream Diaspora. So, that gap between the two Diasporas was
unfilled."[49] In order to be regarded "seriously" by the more established diaspora, Shipovich asserted, the group needed a formalized structure.
Thus, in January 2014, Razom, Inc. was incorporated as a non-profit organization in New Jersey. A new Facebook page was launched in late
January 2014, titled "Razom for Ukraine," which as of August 2014 boast-
ed over 14,700 followers worldwide.[50]

Razom Initiatives

Razom functions as a transnational voluntary organization, with three layers of constituents. First, there is a core leadership group primarily located
on the US East Coast. In addition to meeting regularly and organizing
events in their locales, board members are in constant communication with
each other via online chats. The second constituency, comprising over
3,000 individuals, mobilized by Razom for coordinated activities supporting
Euromaidan, is also connected on Facebook, but has a more global presence, encompassing other parts of the US as well as Canada, the EU, Japan, Australia, and New Zealand. Finally, there is an active group of approximately twenty Razom representatives located in seven cities of
Ukraine, Lviv, Ivano-Frankivsk, Kyiv, Cherkasy, Kharkiv, Luhansk, and
Dnipropetrovsk. Together, these different groups of volunteers are engaged in the activities described below.[51]

49 Interview with Shipovich, April 23, 2014. The fourth and fifth waves, according to
   Shipovich, represent immigrants who arrived to the US in the 1990s and 2000s, respectively.
50 Razom for Ukraine's Facebook page, https://www.facebook.com/RazomForUkraine
   (accessed June 9, 2014).
51 Lyuba Shipovich, "Razom," Prezi Presentation, March 16, 2014, http://prezi.com/pn
   -brsfclwl9/razom/ (accessed June 4, 2014).

InfoCenter

The InfoCenter was created by volunteers residing in different time zones—Japan, Eastern, Central, and Western Europe, as well as different parts of the US—to coordinate the work of volunteers distributing humanitarian aid in Ukraine. During the events of Euromaidan, InfoCenter coordinators called several locations in Kyiv city center four times daily to determine the most critical needs of protesters, and to coordinate the Kyiv volunteers' efforts in purchasing and distributing aid that responds to the identified critical needs. Coordination efforts were conducted through online chats and on Facebook.

Event Department

As mentioned previously, multiple rallies were organized in support of Euromaidan in New York, Philadelphia, and Washington. Earlier in the history of the organization, volunteers vowed to hold weekly rallies for as long as Euromaidan endured. The group organized over forty rallies between November 23, 2013 and March 16, 2014. These events attracted considerable media attention and, as result, established regular communication between members of the event department and journalists at *The Wall Street Journal*, *The New York Times*, and the *Washington Post*, among other publications. The group used these contacts and others in its media list for direct and instantaneous access, especially when important and urgent issues need to be covered by the press.

Additionally, the event department also held virtual events, such as a Facebook event called "Letter Storm—USA Help Build Democracy in Ukraine."[52] As part of the initiative, template letters addressed to both the US president and members of Congress were posted on the event's page. The letters asked politicians to take action with regard to political and human rights conditions in Ukraine. To produce a targeted effect, event participants were asked to send letters during certain periods associated with specific events. With almost 5,000 invitees, the Facebook event page listed almost 1,000 individuals confirming their participation at the time of writing.

---

52 Letter Storm "USA, HELP Ukraine!" Facebook event, https://www.facebook.com/events/1410744982513791/ (accessed June 1, 2014).

Legal Aid Group

Responding to a critical need for legal aid for activists in Ukraine, specifically for those detained and facing criminal charges, Razom recruited US-based attorneys to provide legal advice over the phone and Internet. Additionally, after significant security concerns arose, especially for members of the Automaidan movement in Ukraine, *pro bono* attorneys represented individuals seeking asylum in the US. Among other accomplishments, the group released a report titled "The Crisis in Ukraine: Its Legal Dimensions," produced by an international legal team in collaboration with the New York University School of Law, which received notable media attention. [53]

Investigation Groups

As part of its core programming, Razom has three teams conducting research to uncover corruption involving key Ukrainian officials. As part of this initiative, the organization created an extensive volunteer network of Ukrainians working in various professional spheres in the US and the EU. Shipovich reports: "At one point, someone connected me with…the AAC [the Anticorruption Action Center] in Ukraine, and we started helping them with investigations…. It turned out that Ukrainians worked everywhere!" [54] Among the goals of these investigations were increased pressure on foreign governments to sanction Ukraine and to freeze corrupt officials' bank accounts. Shipovich continues: "We also picketed Deutsche Bank, gave documents [implicating officials in corruption] personally to its COO [Henry Ritchotte, Chief Operating Officer of Deutsche Bank], and then later Deutsche Bank froze accounts." [55] Shipovich credits the efficiency of these investigations to the extensive networks of Ukrainians worldwide that were willing and ready to contribute. She recounts:

> AAC calls and says: "We need a copy of the incorporation documents for [X] company in [X] city." I post on Facebook: "Who's near [X]?" And, immediately, someone writes: "I have a friend there." We find that friend. He goes

53 Ivanna Bilych, Alexander Gudko, Kateryna Kuntsevich, Matheus Sena, Malvika Seth, and Olena Sharvan, *The Crisis in Ukraine: Its Legal Dimensions*, April 14, 2014, https://s3.amazonaws.com/razominc/The_Crisis_In_Ukraine_-_Its_Legal_Di mensions.pdf (accessed June 7, 2014).
54 Interview with Shipovich, April 23, 2014.
55 Ibid.

the same day and gets the papers. And we send the documents to AAC—the same day!"[56]

Professionals' Forum

In December 2013, the group took on an initiative to categorize Ukrainians abroad into expertise-specific virtual groups. Shipovich noted:

> *It turns out there are very many highly qualified professional Ukrainians abroad. Some people received education here and stayed, others received education back home and couldn't find a job, so they went abroad to work. These people ... do not want to go back because they got rooted where they are ..., but on a temporary or permanent basis, they are ready to help. ... People of the same professional background can do much more together.*[57]

Almost 200 individuals with varied expertise and levels of education signed up for the forum, forming several professional groups as of April 2014. Their collective impact has yet to be determined, however, the active formation of these groups demonstrates notable good will among Ukrainians abroad to participate in developments.

Outcomes and Impact

This chapter's brief description of Razom's initiatives and accomplishments demonstrates the group's noteworthy contribution to the events of Euromaidan. Furthermore, the group was positively determined to continue and to expand its work in the future. The Euromaidan protests generated a shift in dynamics within the Ukrainian Diaspora.

Along with the findings in the previous two case studies, Razom's activities suggest a trend toward the creation of a more united constituency of Ukrainian activists worldwide. An additional discovery made in this case, however, is that the events of Euromaidan also appear to have united various groups within the Ukrainian Diaspora in the US. Since the events of Euromaidan, according to Shipovich, members of different waves of the diaspora began working more closely together. She stated in an interview: "Euromaidan united everyone, even the old diaspora.... We organized

---

56 Ibid.
57 Ibid.

many things together."[58] Similar to the previous two cases, Razom's expansive international constituency was intent on continuing the work as Ukrainians abroad for Ukraine.

Conclusion

This chapter has endeavored to tell stories of Ukrainians abroad and their extensive involvement in Euromaidan through the vehicles of social media. These cases echoed a great number of other initiatives taking place worldwide. Considered collectively, they make a number of points. First, utilizing various social media tools, the Ukrainian Diaspora was very actively involved in processes taking place in Ukraine between November 2013 and February 2014. The Diaspora had become a visible actor in Euromaidan's developments through various means, including engaging in advocacy and serving as conduits of information. Whether these initiatives will have long-term effects on Ukraine and international affairs remains to be seen; however, the short-term effects are evident. Second, not only did these Diaspora activities resonate both inside and outside of Ukraine, they also served as a pretext to unite Diaspora across borders (and across generations) on unprecedented levels. This development, of course, would not have been possible to such a degree without the emergence of social media platforms and the extensive networks they helped create and maintain. Third, this new digital society of Ukrainians abroad appears willing to continue to invest time, resources, and expertise for Ukraine's development beyond the events of Euromaidan. The availability of various online tools opens many opportunities for Ukraine to engage an active, virtual, *pro bono* workforce of highly educated and skilled professionals to assist with the country's further development.

Will this new digital civil society utilize the momentum and continue active involvement, or will the efforts dissipate, as they did after the 2004–05 Orange Revolution? How will these organizations and grassroots digital groups change over time? What will they collectively accomplish for Ukraine and will they change the country's geopolitical course? Time and future inquiry will show; however, at the very least the three case studies presented here allow for a modicum of optimism.

---

58 Ibid.

Canada's Response to Euromaidan

Aya Fujiwara

The Ukrainian people's protest, which started on the Maidan Square in Kyiv on November 25, 2013 in opposition to President Viktor Yanukovych's decision to discontinue Ukraine's negotiation for the Association Agreement with the European Union had a great impact on the relationship between the Canadian government and the Ukrainian-Canadian community. As soon as the protest became international news, Canada announced its full support for "the Ukrainian people" and denounced Yanukovych's regime for signing the trading and loan agreement with Russia that seemingly offered a better deal than the one advanced by the EU.

As the protests entered a second stage, involving violence and casualties, Canada increased its attention to the issue, spending much time discussing it in the House of Commons and sending medical and financial aid to Ukraine. When Russia's involvement in Crimea and East Ukraine became aggressive in late-February 2014, the Conservative government tried to demonstrate its commitment in the effort to secure democracy, human rights, and sovereignty in Ukraine, imposing financial and travel sanctions on several Russian and Ukrainian individuals and companies, and boycotting the G8 Summit in Sochi. Canada's enthusiastic support for Euromaidan was a response to the large Ukrainian-Canadian population, part of which belonged to a politically active organization. Euromaidan indeed gave the Conservatives a great opportunity to strengthen ties with one of Canada's major minority groups, and to show other growing immigrant communities that Canada would act on their behalf if their homelands should be in political crisis.

Based mainly on records from the Government of Canada and Ukrainian-Canadian communities since late-November 2013, this essay analyzes how Canada and its Ukrainian-Canadians responded to this crisis. It points to the gap between the Canadian government leaders' grand gesture and eloquent statements that they would fight alongside the Ukrainian people, and the actions that they actually took. First, despite the mounting pressure from Ukrainian Canadians and opposition parties, concrete policies were slow to come. Second, the Conservative government tended to be exclusive, only relying on the Ukrainian Canadian Congress (UCC) for advice when it contemplated its plans to deal with Ukrainian crisis. Granted that the UCC played a leading role to urge the government to take action, the government's decision to treat the UCC as the most authoritative and only source of information prevented other Ukrainian people and specialists from being involved in the policy-making process. Third, the government's tendency to accept the UCC's political and historical views without close examination impeded Canadian policy makers from analyzing propaganda and broadening their perspectives.

Even before the start of Euromaidan, which turned world attention to Ukraine, Canada had been working for the promotion of democracy and economic prosperity in Ukraine for many years since its independence in 1991. After Stephen Harper's Conservative government took power in 2006, it gradually began building ties with minority groups in Canada and paying attention to foreign affairs. In May 2008, Canada demonstrated its friendship and support for Ukraine in a grand gesture, hosting an official visit of Viktor Yushchenko, President of Ukraine after the Orange Revolution, and passing a motion to recognize the Ukrainian Famine-Holodomor of 1932–33 as "an act of genocide."[1] The government also dispatched a team of observers to Ukraine for the 2010 presidential and 2012 parliamentary elections. After 2010 in particular, concerned that both the political and economic situation were deteriorating in Ukraine, Canada invested a great deal in investigating the problems in that country. The Standing Committee on Foreign Affairs and International Development sent a delegation led by Bob Dechert, Parliamentary Secretary to the Minister of Foreign Affairs, to hold public hearings in Kyiv, Kharkiv, and Lviv in May 2012.[2] Domestically, the government was sympathetic to the Ukrainian-

---

1   C-459. An Act to establish a Ukrainian Famine and Genocide ("Holodomor") Memorial Day and to recognize the Ukrainian Famine of 1932–33 as an act of genocide, 2nd Session, 39th Parliament, 2008. http://laws-lois.justice.gc.ca/eng/acts/U-0.4/page-1.html; see also, Campbell Clark, "Yushchenko comes to Ottawa: Harper government moves to recognize 1932–1933 Ukrainian famine as genocide," *The Globe and Mail*, May 27, 2008, A4. Among historians, there is some consensus that the Ukrainian famine was largely a human disaster, yet whether or not it targeted Ukrainians particularly and how many people died from it remain controversial. See David R. Marples, *Holodomor: Causes of the 1932–33 Famine in Ukraine* (Saskatoon: Heritage Press, 2011).

2   Canada, Parliament, House of Commons, Standing Committee on Foreign Affairs and International Development, Report on the Rule of Law, Democracy, and Prosperity in Ukraine: A Canadian Parliamentary Perspective, 1st sess., 41st Parliament, 2012, Committee Report 4, June 2012, http://www.parl.gc.ca/HousePublicati

Canadian demand that the newly-established Canadian Museum of Human Rights should include the internment of Ukrainian Canadians during the Great War and pay more attention to the Holodomor.[3] The closer relationship between the government and Ukrainians in Canada was illustrated well by the Shevchenko Medal Award given to Prime Minister Harper by the Ukrainian Canadian Congress in 2011 for his work on a number of Ukrainian issues, including the promotion of Holodomor Memorial Day, human rights in Ukraine, and youth exchange between Canada and Ukraine.[4]

Canada therefore responded quickly to the Ukrainian crisis. The three major parties—the Conservatives, the Liberals, and the New Democratic Party (NDP)—all agreed that the Ukrainian situation was one of the most urgent matters for Canada because of its strong belief in democracy and human rights and because of Ukrainians' longstanding contribution to the country. Specifically, Canada's Foreign Minister, John Baird, took action to show his nation's position, meeting with Ukraine's opposition leaders and Maidan demonstrators in Independence Square when he attended the Organization for Security and Co-operation in Europe's (OSCE) meeting on December 5–6, 2013. The UCC reported that his visit was highly valued at Independence Square, where people "chanted 'Thank you Canada'."[5] On December 9, Minister Baird made his country's position clear: "We stand on the side of the Ukrainian people in their fight for democracy."[6] The House of Commons then immediately passed a motion to create a Committee of the Whole solely to discuss the Ukrainian situation on December 10, 2013 and to hold an emergency debate on January 27, 2014. When Russia took over Crimea on February 27, the House of Commons again had a lengthy debate to denounce Russia.

ons/Publication.aspx?Language=E&Mode=1&Parl=41&Ses=1&DocId=5690981&File=0 (accessed October 15, 2014).

3   Marco Levytsky, "CMHR should maintain balance, PM says," *Ukrainian News*, November 21- December 4, 2013, 1.

4   "Canadian PM Stephen Harper to receive Shevchenko Medal," *Ukrainian Weekly*, 20 March 2011, 1.

5   "Canada's Foreign Minister the Honourable John Baird visits the Maidan in Kyiv, Ukraine," *Community News*, December 5, 2013, http://www.ucc.ca/2013/12/05/news-canadas-foreign-minister-the-honourable-john-baird-visits-the-maidan-in-kyiv-ukraine/ (accessed December 10, 2013).

6   Canada, House of Commons Debates, December 9, 2013 (Hon. John Baird, CPC). http://www.parl.gc.ca/HousePublications/Publication.aspx?Language=E&Mode=1&Parl=41&Ses=2&DocId=6379548 (accessed October 15, 2014).

The Government of Canada justified its apparently one-sided position, stressing the "global" nature of the Ukrainian problem. President Yanukovych's use of violent methods to crack down on the people's peaceful demonstrations, Canadian leaders argued, was a threat to widely shared principles of democracy and human rights. The common spirit of the Canadian parliament was well illustrated by Paul Dewar of the NDP, when he said, "Let us be clear: all Canadian political parties are united in their desire for a free, democratic, and prosperous Ukraine."[7] From the earliest stages, some suggested that it was an international conflict, hinting at Russian intentions to halt the installation of an effective democracy in Ukraine. Leon Benoit, Tory MP from Vegreville-Wainwright, Alberta, for example, regarded the crisis as "the start of a movement to an expansion on the part of Russia to a new Soviet-style regime."[8] Ted Opitz, the chair of the Canada-Ukraine Parliamentary Friendship Group, went further, criticizing the Russian leader directly, "It is Mr. Putin who is unfairly leveraging Ukraine with the hold he has on Ukraine right now with Gazprom and the other trade levers he is pulling. There is no reason Ukraine cannot trade with the European Union and trade with Russia."[9] Even J. L. Granatstein, historian and a fellow of the Canadian Defence and Foreign Affairs Institute, who opposes ethnic minorities' tendencies to insert their homeland politics into Canadian multiculturalism, encouraged Canada's involvement in Ukraine, writing, "....there is the national interest concern for the protection and advancement of freedom and democracy, a national interest shared by all NATO members, including Canada." Thus, "the Russian threat to Ukraine surely is a challenge to this Canadian national interest."[10]

In reality, the extent to which Canada should or could prioritize the Ukrainian situation over other foreign affairs or domestic issues remains controversial. Another historian, Michael Bliss, pointed out the lack of de-

---

7   Canada, House of Commons Debate, December 9, 2013 (Mr. Paul Dewar, NDP). http://www.parl.gc.ca/HousePublications/Publication.aspx?Language=E&Mode=1& Parl=41&Ses=2&Docld=6379548 (accessed October 15, 2014).

8   Canada, House of Commons Debate, December, 10 2013 (Mr. Leon Benoit, CPC). http://www.parl.gc.ca/HousePublications/Publication.aspx?Language=E&Mode=1& Parl=41&Ses=2&Docld=6384300 (accessed October 15, 2014).

9   Canada, House of Commons Debate, December 10, 2013 (Mr. Ted Opitz, CPC). http://www.parl.gc.ca/HousePublications/Publication.aspx?Language=E&Mode=1& Parl=41&Ses=2&Docld=6384300 (accessed October 15, 2014).

10 Jack L. Granatstein, "Freedom in Ukraine is a Canadian national interest," *The Globe and Mail*, May 6, 2014, A15.

bate over Canada's military involvement in the Ukrainian situation, when Canada announced its decision to station its fighter aircraft in Poland. He asked, ".... should not Canadians disregard our voluble Ukrainian lobby long enough to ask some hard questions about investing our resources in what much of the world sees as another of the West's dubious crusades?"[11] How far ethnic groups' demand to assist their homelands should be incorporated into Canada's ethnic pluralism and foreign policy has been debated publicly and academically for many decades in Canada.[12] Euromaidan once again resumed this discussion, yet indicated that the distinction between "their" or "our" politics was difficult to make when Ukraine was searching for democracy.

Political leaders, in general, proclaimed the Ukrainian crisis a "Canadian" issue, following the ethnic pluralist rhetoric that Canada would listen to problems that concerns its ethnic groups. *The Globe and Mail* reported in early-February 2014 that Canada's interest was not so much vote-seeking than a strong historic tie between Canada and Ukraine on the grounds that the Ukrainian vote alone could not affect the result of domestic elections.[13] There is some truth in this argument. But the message sent to all ethnic communities by the government, that it could advocate for its domestic ethnic constituents internationally, had a great impact, given the increasing number of immigrants in Canada. The ethnic vote was undoubtedly in the mind of several members of Parliament, who competitively

---

11 Michael Bliss, "Why is Canada sending fighter jets to Poland?" *The Globe and Mail*, April 23, 2014, http://www.theglobeandmail.com/globe-debate/why-canadian-fighter-jets-in-poland-will-embolden-putin/article18122221/ (accessed May 1, 2014).

12 For a comprehensive scholarly look at the multiculturalism debate, see, for example, David Carment and David J. Bercuson, *The World in Canada: Diaspora, Demography, and Domestic Politics* (Montreal: McGill-Queen's University, 2008); Phil Ryan, *Multicultiphobia* (Toronto: University of Toronto Press), 2010; and Vic Satzewich, "Multiculturalism, Transnationalism, and Hijacking Canadian Foreign Policy: Pseudo-Problem?" *International Journal*, Vol. 63, No. 1 (Winter 2007–2008): 43–62. For public argument, see, for example, Jeffrey Simpson, "Multiculturalism: Don't let diaspora politics twist Canada's foreign policy," *The Globe and Mail,* April 24, 2010, p. A19; Natalie Brender, "Diasporas in Foreign Policymaking: Just Another Ploy of Neoliberal Multiculturalism?" Center For International Policy Studies (blog), University of Ottawa, February 5, 2013. http://cips.uottawa.ca/diasporas-in-foreign-policymaking-just-another-ploy-of-neoliberal-multiculturalism/ (accessed October 15, 2014); and Sarah McGregor, "Granatstein's Immigration Views Cause Some Unease," *Embassy*, November 2, 2005, 1.

13 Kathryn Blaze Carlson, "Ukrainian-Canadians have a strong voice in Ottawa," *The Globe and Mail*, February 1, 2014, A15.

stressed the presence of the large Ukrainian population in their own ridings. Bernard Trottier, an Ontario MP, for example, stated, "This weekend I met and shared my concerns with Ukrainian Canadians in Etobicoke-Lakeshore, who were exercising their freedoms, demonstrating outside the Ukrainian consulate in solidarity with those in Ukraine."[14] Robert Sopuck, who represents a district with a long history of Ukrainian settlement, Dauphin-Swan River-Marquette, Manitoba, also emphasized the significance of Ukrainians in this district, stating, "My constituency has the largest population of Ukrainians in Canada. They make up roughly 35% of my constituency. When I look at what the Ukrainians in my constituency have done, it is truly remarkable. They are successful farmers, successful small business people."[15]

Yet many argued that the Ukrainian contribution to Canada was not limited to a particular ridings or districts. Some MPs Canadianized the Ukrainian crisis, referring to the long history of contributions made by Ukrainians to Canada's nation building. "Pioneer myths," as Frances Swyripa has shown, have been traditionally used by Ukrainian Canadians to propagate their political rights in Canada.[16] Interestingly, mainstream politicians, not necessarily Ukrainian in origin, now embraced them widely, mainly to justify their involvement in this issue and to strengthen their popularity. Bob Dechert, Parliamentary Secretary to the Minister of Justice, for example, argued, "The first wave of Ukrainian immigrants to Canada came in, rode on a railway to the end of the line, were given a bag of seed and a shovel, and were told to walk another 100 miles, where they would find some land. Then they were to make it work. They opened up western Canada."[17] Lawrence Toet, MP for Elmwood-Transcona (Winnipeg), expanded on the story and went beyond the pioneer era: "As members know, the historic ties between our two nations extend back through generations

---

14 Canada, House of Commons Debate, December 2, 2013 (Mr. Bernard Trottier, CPC).   http://www.parl.gc.ca/HousePublications/Publication.aspx?Language=E& Mode=1&Parl=41&Ses=2&DocId=6357774 (accessed October 15, 2014).

15 Canada, House of Commons Debate, December 10, 2013 (Mr. Robert Sopuck, CPC),   http://www.parl.gc.ca/HousePublications/Publication.aspx?Language=E&M ode=1&Parl=41&Ses=2&DocId=6384300 (accessed October 15, 2014).

16 Frances Swyripa, *Wedded to the Cause: Ukrainian-Canadian Women and Ethnic Identity, 1891–1991* (Toronto: University of Toronto Press, 1993), 5, 216.

17 Canada, House of Commons Debate, January 27, 2014 (Mr. Bob Dechert, CPC), http://www.parl.gc.ca/HousePublications/Publication.aspx?Language=E&Mode=1& Parl=41&Ses=2&DocId=6391978 (accessed October 15, 2014).

of Ukrainian migration to Canada. For more than 120 years, Ukrainian-born Canadians have contributed to the social, economic and political fabric of Canada. Today, Ukrainians make up almost four per cent of the total Canadian population."[18]

Thus both global and national causes united the House of Commons in terms of its support for the Euromaidan protestors, but party lines surfaced at times. The Conservative government, despite its support for the Ukrainian people, took a cautious approach to the adoption of specific policies initially, emphasizing the "global" dimensions of the issue adroitly. As all Western nations share the values of human rights, democracy, and sovereignty, they argued, Canada should work together with others, particularly the United States and EU nations. Liberals, however, expected Canadian leadership in intervention as a middle power, which they regarded as Canada's traditional role on the world stage. They pushed for concrete sanctions at the earliest stage and often expressed frustration. For example, Chrystia Freeland, MP for Toronto Centre, who is of Ukrainian descent, eloquently urged the government to take more concrete policies on January 27, 2014, claiming that the government had not put all suggestions into practice:

> Ukraine listens to us and the world listens to what we do and what we say about Ukraine. This is an opportunity, as my hon. colleague suggested, for us to do what Lester B. Pearson taught us, which is to punch above our weight in international affairs, by taking the lead on Ukraine. It is really clear what we can do. It is wonderful for me as a Ukrainian Canadian to hear so much anguish, worry and sympathy for the people of Ukraine, but now is the time to act. There are three very clear things for us to do. The first is targeted sanctions against President Yanukovych and his allies in government. That will have an impact. Indeed, one of the jokes that people tell in the former Soviet Union now is that their dictators want to rule like Stalin but live like Abramovich. That is what globalization allows nowadays, that one can be a dictator at home but have a villa on Cap Ferrat. We cannot allow that to happen and must say that they cannot have it both ways.
> The second thing that we have to do is to provide expedited visas for the people who have put their lives at risk on the Euromaidan. Again, this would be a very important symbolic statement that we are with them.

---

18 Canada, House of Commons Debate, January 27, 2014 (Mr. Lawrence Toet, CPC), http://www.parl.gc.ca/HousePublications/Publication.aspx?Language=E&Mode=1& Parl=41&Ses=2&DocId=6391978 (accessed October 15, 2014).

Third, we have to send high-level observers. Sunlight is the best disinfectant, and if we are watching, I can assure everyone there will be less brutality.[19]

While the NDP was skeptical of taking such a one-sided position initially, its past support of socialism prompted its MPs to dispel the public image that they might side with Russia and pressured the government to take more aggressive policies in support of the protestors. Philip Toone, a member of the NDP and a Quebec MP, stated, "The United States announced that it was revoking the visas of individuals linked to violence in Ukraine against people in favour of a European democratic movement. Why has the Canadian government not done the same as the Americans by banning visas to Ukrainians linked to the violence going on now?"[20] To this comment, the Conservative party member retaliated, "Mr. Speaker, obviously the member's points were bogus. The point is that his party and the other party over there, over the decades, enabled Communist and left wing regimes to thrive and prosper."[21] Obviously, all rival parties agreed on the same cause, but how to approach the crisis met with challenges.

The Conservatives were also criticized for excluding other interested groups from the policy-making process, except for a small executive group of the Ukrainian Canadian Congress. All the policies that Canada implemented—to recognize the Ukrainian parliament's decision to deprive Yanukovych of all powers, to send an official delegation "to meet with transitional government in Ukraine," to support Ukraine financially and keep pressuring Russia politically and economically all came from the UCC's letter sent to Prime Minister in late February.[22] As Taras Kuzio points out,

19 Canada, House of Commons Debate, January 27, 2014 (Ms. Chrystia Freeland, Lib), http://www.parl.gc.ca/HousePublications/Publication.aspx?Language=E&Mode=1&Parl=41&Ses=2&DocId=6391978 (October 17, 2014); see also ibid., (Mr. Marc Garneau, Lib); ibid., December 10, 2013 (Hon. Ralph Goodale, Lib), http://www.parl.gc.ca/HousePublications/Publication.aspx?Language=E&Mode=1&Parl=41&Ses=2&DocId=6384300 (accessed October 17, 2014).
20 Canada, House of Commons Debate, January 27, 2014 (Mr. Philip Toone, NDP), http://www.parl.gc.ca/HousePublications/Publication.aspx?Language=E&Mode=1&Parl=41&Ses=2&DocId=6391978 (accessed October 17, 2014).
21 Canada, House of Commons Debate, January 27, 2014 (Mr. Robert Sopuck, CPC), http://www.parl.gc.ca/HousePublications/Publication.aspx?Language=E&Mode=1&Parl=41&Ses=2&DocId=6391978 (accessed October 17, 2014).
22 Ukrainian Canadian Congress, "Ukrainian Canadian Congress: Positive Steps towards Resolution of Crisis in Ukraine," *Community News*, February 22, 2014,

specialists of Ukrainian politics and history were rarely consulted when the government dealt with the Ukrainian problem.[23] It does not mean that these specialists were silent. They organized a number of talks, conferences, and roundtables. Inclusion of all interested parties was essential as it would have provided the government with much broader knowledge, creating an opportunity for open debate. Indeed, only two academics— Timothy Snyder and Bohdan Harasymiw—have been very briefly cited in the House of Commons since late November 2013. At the same time, neither Liberal nor New Democratic Party MPs, regardless of their knowledge of Ukraine, were among official delegates sent to Ukraine in late February 2014.

The Liberals, in general, expressed frustration when the Conservative government did not summon their members to join an official delegation to Kyiv. One Liberal MP, Marc Garneau, avowed that the government's exclusiveness to its own party in diplomacy was not limited to the Ukrainian case, mentioning the example where a Liberal MP from Mount Royal, Quebec "was barred from a reception in Israel during the Prime Minister's trip." A similar gesture, he continues, was shown again, when "the Canadian delegation (to Ukraine) does not include MPs from other parties, even though all parties share the same concerns about Ukraine."[24] Linda Duncan, the NDP member for Edmonton Strathcona, also criticized the government for failing to incorporate other parties' members in the delegation. She argued that Canada should have shown the Ukrainian parliament an example of party unity, stating, "the sitting government of Ukraine is now a combination of all of those opposition parties, which shows how they can come together, even though they have a diversity of views, to reform the way that they operate under the government and move forward together."[25] Elizabeth May, leader of the Green Party, also joined this debate, stating

http://www.ucc.ca/2014/02/22/ukrainian-canadian-congress-positive-steps-toward-resolution-of-crisis-in-ukraine/ (accessed October 17, 2014).

23 Taras Kuzio, "Ukrainian Canadian Congress, Shymko, Grod ignore experts on Ukraine," YouTube video, March 27, 2014, posted by Taras Kuzio, http://www.youtube.com/watch?v=wgLqr-q3ZRY (accessed October 18, 2014).

24 Canada, House of Commons Debate, February 26 2014 (Mr. Marc Garneau, Lib), http://www.parl.gc.ca/HousePublications/Publication.aspx?Language=E&Mode=1&Parl=41&Ses=2&DocId=6445246 (accessed October 18, 2014).

25 Canada, House of Commons Debate, February 26 2014 (Ms. Linda Duncan, NDP), http://www.parl.gc.ca/HousePublications/Publication.aspx?Language=E&Mode=1&Parl=41&Ses=2&DocId=6445246 (accessed October 18, 2014).

that the delegation should have "represented Canada and not just the ruling party."[26]

Yet for the UCC leaders who were an integral part of this mission, it
was a great opportunity to demonstrate and confirm their officially granted
leadership among Ukrainian Canadians. The UCC's involvement in Canada's official policy-making process in support of Euromaidan was not surprising. It is the largest such organization, which consists of a number of
provincial councils, branches, and other membership organizations such
as the Ukrainian Self-Reliance League and the Ukrainian Canadian Professional and Business Federation, but it rarely represents all Ukrainians'
voice in Canada. Organized as an umbrella organization by Ukrainian nationalists for the collective war effort for Canada in 1941, the UCC has
been acting as the most politically influential lobby group for Ukrainians in
Canada. Concerned with the spread of Communism, the Canadian government and its agents played an integral role in the organization's birth,
mediating among several rival factions of Ukrainian nationalists in a quest
for strong unity and the struggle against Communism.[27] The UCC, as the
only non-governmental organization that represented the Ukrainian community and homeland in Canada until 1991, built strong ties with the Canadian government. After the independence of Ukraine, the UCC lost its
raison d'être—attaining the independence of Ukraine—but quickly adopted
the promotion of human rights and democracy in Ukraine as its major goal
and replaced the Soviet Union with Russia as a common threat and enemy. Yet the UCC's status as the primary body to negotiate with Canada
might have declined slightly when newly independent Ukraine established
formal diplomatic relations with Canada and opened its Embassy in 1992.

In this light, Euromaidan was a fortuitous occasion for the UCC to advance its status as the Ukrainian people's representative.[28] As appointed

26 Canada, House of Commons Debate, February 26 2014 (Ms. Elizabeth May, GP),
http://www.parl.gc.ca/HousePublications/Publication.aspx?Language=E&Mode=1&
Parl=41&Ses=2&Docld=6445246 (accessed October 18, 2014).
27 For Canada's involvement in the establishment of the Ukrainian Canadian Committee during World War II, see, for example, N. Fred Dreisziger, "Tracy Philipps and
the Achievement of Ukrainian-Canadian Unity," in *Canada's Ukrainians: Negotiating
an Identity*, ed., Lubomyr Luciuk and Stella Hryniuk (Toronto: University of Toronto
Press), 326–41; and Bohdan S. Kordan, *Canada and the Ukrainian Question,
1939–1945* (Montreal and Kingston: McGill-Queen's University Press), 95–136.
28 The mechanism by which the Ukrainian elite gained political power in Canada historically is explored best by Orest Martynowych, *Ukrainians in Canada: The Forma-
tive Years, 1891–1924* (Edmonton: Canadian Institute of Ukrainian Studies, 1991).

government officials replaced the UCC leaders in many political spheres, the latter has been working to promote its position as the non-official body of the worldwide Ukrainian Diaspora as opposed to the government. For example, when its president, Paul Grod met President Viktor Yanukovych in 2010 through the Ukrainian World Congress, a New York-based international non-profit organization of the Ukrainian Diaspora, he celebrated the occasion, calling it "a critical meeting for both the government of Ukraine and the Ukrainian people," for the promotion of Ukraine's "democratic institutions, economic stability, civil society, and national identity."[29] Although such efforts for cooperation were thwarted by the president, the incident exalted the UCC above the government on the international political stage. The UCC thus emphasized the fact that the protest was the people's movement against an undemocratic, corrupt, and violent government, and thus had to lead the way. In its petition to the Canadian government issued on December 22, 2013, the UCC urged Canadians to "stand with the Ukrainian people during the difficult time and forcefully oppose all efforts to repress their rights and freedoms."[30] In late February, Grod criticized President Yanukovych for declaring "war against his own people."[31] In this way, the UCC, as a people's body, consolidated its power. In late June, Grod successfully confirmed his status as the people's representative, meeting Ukraine's new president, Petro Poroshenko for the rebuilding of the cooperative relationship between "the global Ukrainian Diaspora" and "the state of Ukraine."[32]

The UCC's elite's self-portrayal as the leaders who were endeavoring to save the Ukrainian people first from the threat of the dictator and second

29 Ukrainian Canadian Congress, "Ukrainian Canadian Congress Meets with President Viktor Yanukovych," *Community News*, June 23. 2010, http://www.ucc.ca/20 10/06/23/ukrainian-world-congress-meets-with-president-viktor-yanukovych/ (accessed October 18, 2014).
30 Ukrainian Canadian Congress, "Canada must impose personal sanctions against corrupt officials and those responsible for human rights abuses in Ukraine," petition submitted to the House of Commons, December 22, 2013, http://www.ucc.ca/wp-content/uploads/2014/01/Petition.pdf (accessed October 19, 2014).
31 Ukrainian Canadian Congress, "UCC deeply outraged by Yanukovych regime's use of terror against people," UCC *Communiques & News*, http://www.ucc.ca/ 2014/02/20/ucc-deeply-outraged-by-yanukovych-regimes-use-of-terror-against-ukrainian-people/ (accessed October 19, 2014).
32 Ukrainian World Congress, "Ukrainian World Congress President Eugene Czollj meets with President Petro Poroshenko," *News*, June 11, 2014, http://www.ukrainia nworldcongress.org/news.php/news/1070 (accessed October 19, 2014).

from Russia was quite effective. The UCC's political monopoly testifies that intentionally or not it advanced its political power and was unofficially designated as a significant participant in Canadian diplomacy. Paul Grod was invited to participate at every stage of Canada's action. James Bezan, Parliamentary Secretary to the Minister of National Defence, emphasized how the UCC played a significant part of Canadian delegation in early December 2013:

> Just last week, the OSCE had a meeting. Its 20th ministerial council was held in Kiev and our Minister of Foreign Affairs, who has had such a strong, principled stand on how we engage with Ukraine, was there. I was very proud when I saw him and Paul Grod, who is the president of the Ukrainian Canadian Congress, walking through Independence Square with the Canadian maple leaf strapped to their backs, showing the people of Ukraine that Canada stands in solidarity with them, that we will stay engaged and we will make sure that their aspirations will be realized.[33]

Paul Grod was again invited to join the Canadian delegation to Ukraine led by Foreign Minister John Baird in late-February.[34] The Liberals, while not invited to join this delegation, regarded the UCC as a valuable organization, which bridged the government and the Ukrainian people. Liberal MP, Kevin Lamoureux, in particular, who kept close ties with the UCC executives, applauded the work of the UCC repeatedly in the House of Commons. On one occasion he commented that "the foreign affairs critic has had communications with organizations such as the Ukrainian Canadian Congress." He acknowledged UCC executives such as Taras Zalusky and Paul Grod for the "excellent and wonderful job they have done in ensuring that whether a member is the leader of the Liberal Party, members like myself, members of the Conservative Party or the New Democratic Party, we are kept abreast of their point of view on what is actually taking place."[35] The NDP also urged the government to follow recommenda-

33 Canada, House of Commons Debate, December 10, 2013 (Mr. James Bezan, CPC), http://www.parl.gc.ca/HousePublications/Publication.aspx?Language=E&Mode=1&Parl=41&Ses=2&DocId=6384300 (accessed October 19, 2014).
34 http://www.pm.gc.ca/eng/news/2014/02/25/pm-send-canadian-delegation-ukraine
35 Canada, House of Commons Debate, December 10, 2014 (Mr. Kevin Lamoureux, Lib), http://www.parl.gc.ca/HousePublications/Publication.aspx?Language=E&Mode=1&Parl=41&Ses=2&DocId=6384300 (accessed October 19, 2014); see also his address at the House of Commons, February 26, 2014, http://www.parl.gc.ca/HousePublications/Publication.aspx?Language=E&Mode=1&Parl=41&Ses=2&DocId=6445246 (accessed October 19, 2014).

tions—for example, "cracking down on money laundering in Ukraine"—put forward by the UCC.[36] The question whether or not UCC executive members, who were neither official diplomats nor political leaders elected by Canadians, should be participants in higher state diplomacy was never debated.

The Canadian Parliament thus adopted the UCC's version of Ukrainian politics and history unquestionably as the most authoritative, notwithstanding its inclination towards far right political views, which hindered a balanced interpretation of the Ukrainian past. All parties regarded the UCC's recommendations as guidelines, which the government should follow. Quite naturally, the UCC, as a nationalist organization, emphasized the history of a lengthy struggle for Ukrainian independence, depicting the Soviet Union and Russia (after 1991) as its enemies. Such victimhood has sometimes led to controversial gestures, which, accurately or not, reinforced its image as an extremist entity. One such example is its enshrinement of a historical figure like Stepan Bandera, leader of the Organization of Ukrainian Nationalists (OUN), who collaborated with Nazi Germany at the beginning of World War II, thereby building close links with a group of "Banderites" who promote ultra-nationalism. When former president Viktor Yushchenko designated Bandera as a "hero of Ukraine" in early January 2010 in order to regain some popular support, the UCC praised the decision, referring to it as "long overdue recognition."[37] Its leaders, as John-Paul Himka argues, never recognized the fact that "the OUN was an anti-Semitic organization that orchestrated pogroms and recruited for the Ukrainian police in German service (a primary instrument of the Holocaust in Ukraine)."[38]

36 Canada, House of Commons Debate, December 10, 2013 (Ms. Peggy Nash, NDP), http://www.parl.gc.ca/HousePublications/Publication.aspx?Language=E&Mode=1& Parl=41&Ses=2&DocId=6384300 (accessed October 19, 2014).
37 UCC, "Ukraine's President Recognizes Ukraine's Freedom Fighters," UCC Comuniques & News, February 1, 2010, http://www.ucc.ca/2010/02/01/ukraines-president-recognizes-ukraines-freedom-fighters/ (accessed October 19, 2014); for the study of the Bandera dispute, see, for example, Eleonora Narvselius, "'The Bandera Debate: the Contentious Legacy of World War II and Liberalization of Collective Memory in Western Ukraine," *Canadian Slavonic Papers* 53, no. 3–4 (September-December 2012): 469–90.
38 John Paul Himka, "Ukrainian Memoirs of the Holocaust: Destruction of Jews as Reflected in Memoirs Collected in 1947," *Canadian Slavonic Papers* 54, no. 3–4 (September-December 2012): 430.

While Russia's advance into Crimea in March 2014 astounded the world, both the UCC and Canada became active participants in the "propaganda war." As both Ukrainians and Russians exaggerated the other's political stance, Ukraine's crisis was understood internationally as a political struggle between Russian expansionists led by Vladimir Putin and ultranationalistic Ukrainians. Russia's portrayal of the Maidan supporters as "fascists," which spread quickly throughout the West, was intended to justify its military invasion of Crimea, thereby attempting to focus media attention on a small group of radical right-wing elements among Ukrainian protestors.[39] The UCC retaliated against this Russian-made image of the Ukrainian people. Grod's co-authored article with Shimon Fogel argued that such comments were part of Putin's "propaganda campaign geared to discredit Ukraine's Maidan and the principles of democracy, freedom, ethnic and human rights for which millions stood, and for which more than a hundred died."[40] "The Russian Federation," according to Grod, was "engaged in dangerous brinkmanship, which together with the disinformation campaign it is waging in Eastern and Southern Ukraine, has reignited a new cold war."[41] Such links between the Soviet past and the current political crisis became a common thread in Canada.

Canadian politicians quickly adopted the storyline that the crisis was Ukraine's struggle against intended Russian expansionism, which had often deprived Ukrainians of freedom and human rights in the past. Even before the Russian military intervention in Crimea, some MPs nuanced the Russian conspiracy, repeatedly referring to the Cold War era. Leon Benoit, of Ukrainian descent and Conservative MP for Vegreville-Wainwright, called "what is happening in Ukraine" as "a re-Sovietization of the area" and "a new Soviet-style regime."[42] Although Jason Kenny, Minister of Em-

39 Olexiy Haran, "Don't believe the Russian Propaganda about Ukraine's 'Fascist' protestors," The Guardian, March 13, 2014, http://www.theguardian.com/commentisfree/20 14/mar/13/russian-propaganda-ukraine-fascist-protesters-euromaidan (accessed October 19, 2014).

40 Paul Grod and Shimon Fogel, "Ukraine faces many challenges—anti-Semitism is not one of them," The Globe and Mail, March 30, 2014, http://www.theglo beandmail.com/globe-debate/ukraine-faces-many-challenges-anti-semitism-is-not-one-of-them/article17720817/ (accessed October 19, 2014).

41 http://www.ucc.ca/2014/03/01/russian-military-intervention-in-ukraine-condemned/ (accessed October 20, 2014).

42 Canada, House of Commons Debate, December 10 2013 (Mr. Leon Benoit, CPC), http://www.parl.gc.ca/HousePublications/Publication.aspx?Language=E&Mode=1& Parl=41&Ses=2&DocId=6384300http://www.parl.gc.ca/HousePublications/Publicati

ployment and Social Development and Minister for Multiculturalism, noted that "today's Ukraine" differed from "the period of Soviet darkness," he recalled how North American leaders during the Cold War such as Pierre Trudeau and Ronald Reagan had responded to the crisis.[43] Intriguingly, Canadian politicians now begun to embrace the version of Ukrainian history painted by stories of struggle and a sense of injustice due to wars and Soviet occupation, which formed the core of Ukrainian nationalist identity. They repeatedly talked about past tragedies such as the Holodomor and the linguistic and cultural oppression that Ukrainians suffered. In Laurie Hawn's terms, "their struggle is our struggle."[44] Quoting CNN journalist Antonia Mortensen and political commentator David Frum, an NDP MP, for example, reinforced Ukrainian victimhood, "No nation suffered more from the Soviet regime than the Ukrainians."[45] Another NDP member, noting the Ukrainian past, including the wartime internment in Canada and the history of the Holodomor, cited a ninety-year old Ukrainian man's concern: ". . . this is not just about trade, but about building another Russian empire today, as under Stalin."[46] Prime Minister Harper also joined in this propaganda war, calling Putin "evil,"[47] an "extreme nationalist," and "an imperialist,"[48] who had retained a "Cold War mentality."[49] He went further, comparing Putin's annexation of Crimea to Hitler's annexation of Austria in 1938.[50]

on.aspx?Language=E&Mode=1&Parl=41&Ses=2&DocId=6384300 (accessed October 19, 2014).

43 Canada, House of Commons Debate, December 10, 2013 (Hon. Jason Kenny, CPC), http://www.parl.gc.ca/HousePublications/Publication.aspx?Language=E&Mode=1&Parl=41&Ses=2&DocId=6384300 (accessed October 19, 2014).

44 Canada, House of Commons Debate, January 27, 2014 (Hon. Laurie Hawn, CPC), http://www.parl.gc.ca/HousePublications/Publication.aspx?Language=E&Mode=1&Parl=41&Ses=2&DocId=6391978 (accessed October 19, 2014).

45 Canada, House of Commons Debate, January 27, 2014 (Mrs. Carol Hughes, NDP), http://www.parl.gc.ca/HousePublications/Publication.aspx?Language=E&Mode=1&Parl=41&Ses=2&DocId=6391978 (accessed October 19, 2014).

46 Canada, House of Commons Debate, January 27, 2014 (Ms. Christine Moore), http://www.parl.gc.ca/HousePublications/Publication.aspx?Language=E&Mode=1&Parl=41&Ses=2&DocId=6391978 (accessed October 19, 2014).

47 Darren Calabrese, "Stephen Harper attacks Vladimir Putin and 'evil' Communism," *CBC News*, May 31, 2014, http://www.cbc.ca/news/world/stephen-harper-attacks-vladimir-putin-and-evil-communism-1.2660700 (accessed on June 1, 2014).

48 Adrian Wyld, "Harper calls Putin 'extreme nationalist, imperialist'," *Toronto Star*, June 8, 2014, http://www.thestar.com/news/canada/2014/06/08/harper_calls_putin_extreme_nationalist_imperialist.html (accessed on June 9, 2014).

Although the government of Canada demonstrated that it would side with the UCC completely, embracing the latter's political and historical vision and incorporating UCC suggestions into its policies, its performance was somewhat superficial. Criticism for Canada's lack of action came from both Canada and Ukraine, though it did not represent the majority voice. Roland Paris, Director of the Centre for International Policy Studies best described the problem, arguing that Canada did not stand out globally:

> *Ottawa's language has been unusually strong, including Mr. Harper's comparison of Russia to Nazi Germany. Canada's actions—including targeted sanctions against a limited number of the Kremlin's supporters, political and economic support for the Kiev government, modest deployment of military assets as part of NATO's 'reassurance package' in Eastern Europe, and the contribution of observers for Ukraine's election—have been comparable to actions by many other allies.*[51]

UCC leaders were well aware that it would need intensive lobbying in order for Canada to take concrete measures against both President Yanukovych and Russia. Local UCC leaders, not the government, spearheaded all the movements in Canada, including organizing political rallies in major cities, collecting petitions, and urging people to pressure the prime minister, foreign minister, and their local MPs to act against the violation of human rights and freedom. They also published an on-line "daily briefing" on Ukraine. In January, Borys Wrzesnewskyj, a former Liberal MP, wrote, ". . . we expect concrete actions, as well. We call upon the Prime Minister to be a leader among Western democracies. . . ."[52] Yet Canada's slowness was obvious and after spring 2014, the voices of frustration increased. For example, Vadym Prystaiko, then-Ukraine's Ambassador to Canada, com-

---

49 Lee-Anne Goodman, "PM Harper cautions Putin is trapped in 'Cold War mentality'," *CTV News*, March 26, 2014, http://www.ctvnews.ca/politics/pm-harper-cautions-putin-is-trapped-in-cold-war-mentality-1.1746400 (accessed on April 1, 2014).

50 Steven Chase, "Harper Compares Russia's Crimea moves to Third Reich aggression," *The Globe and Mail*, March 4, 2014, http://www.theglobeandmail.com/news/politics/canada-suspends-military-activities-with-russia/article17289679/ (accessed on May 1, 2014).

51 Roland Paris, "Harper's heroic message does not reflect reality," Center for International Policy Studies (blog), University of Ottawa, June 3, 2014, http://cips.uottawa.ca/harpers-heroic-ukraine-message-does-not-reflect-reality/ (accessed October 20, 2014).

52 Borys Wrzesnewskyj, "The next chapter in Ukraine's fight for freedom," *Ukrainian News*, January 1–13 2014, 6.

mented that Canada's promised financial aid had not reached Ukraine in late July.[53] Even the UCC's Paul Grod, who decided to keep Canada's high-ranking politicians as his friends and very rarely expressed frustration with the Canadian government, informed a *Globe and Mail* reporter, "We're very surprised that Canada, which considers itself one of Ukraine's best friends on the international stage, has still not delivered what Ukraine really needs today."[54] As Russia supported the advance of separatist troops in southeastern Ukraine in late August, Ambassador Prystaiko once again urged Canada to send "'real' military support" to Ukraine.[55]

When Euromaidan began in November 2013, Canada responded with a firm stance to support the people of Ukraine due to its strong belief in democracy and freedom, and its historic ties with Ukraine. Collaborating with Canada's largest Ukrainian organization, the Ukrainian Canadian Congress, the Government of Canada stood up for the protection of freedom and democracy in Ukraine. Its commitment was praised by many Ukrainians and Canadians and helped promote Prime Minister Harper's image domestically and internationally. Yet in many ways, Canada's collective effort to support Ukraine did not always match official rhetoric. It rarely took the initiative in taking concrete measures, waiting for other countries to impose financial and travel sanctions. The UCC leaders, for their part, strengthened the UCC's status in Canada as the "people's" representative, declaring their political interests in Canada's foreign policies and befriending Canada's highest-ranking politicians. Yet the real issue—how to cope with Ukraine's political, financial, and military problems—remained unresolved. The intermediate and balanced role that Canada had played in the past, integrating all experts' ideas and opening up opportunities for debate, was sorely lacking.

53 Steven Chase, "Ukraine asks Ottawa: Where's our money?" *The Globe and Mail,* 24 July 2014, A1.

54 Ibid.

55 Ukrainian ambassador begs for troops to counter Russian invasion," *Ottawa Citizen,* August 29, 2014, http://ottawacitizen.com/news/national/canada-assails-russia-for-invasion-of-ukraine (accessed on August 29, 2014).

Belarus and Euromaidan: Lukashenka's Response

Uladzimir Padhol and David R. Marples

Introduction

Euromaidan had a significant impact on Ukraine's neighbors. Within the EU, perhaps the most sympathetic responses came from Poland and the Baltic States. Russia's response is dealt with separately in this volume. Perhaps the most difficult situation to assess, however, is the reaction from its northern neighbor, Belarus, a country that has proved a difficult neighbor for Russia, particularly in terms of its integration within structures such as the Eurasian Economic Community, although the ties in many areas are very close. The president, Aliaksandr Lukashenka, had been in office over nineteen years when Euromaidan took place. During that time he not only cracked down on opposition and defied the EU's requests to introduce a more democratic political system, but also warned repeatedly of revolutions from within and sheltered a refugee president on the run, Kurmanbek Bakiyev of Kyrgyzstan in April 2010. Still, traditionally Ukraine and Belarus have been good neighbors and the border between them is open. Lukashenka has been always careful not to antagonize his Kyiv counterpart and has maintained harmonious relations with most Ukrainian presidents to date, including the pro-Western Viktor Yushchenko and, until spring 2011, the more Russia-oriented Viktor Yanukovych.

This paper examines the responses of the Belarusian authorities and the main opposition leaders to Euromaidan and the events that followed in Crimea in March. It places special focus on the president, given his relative control of all aspects of decision-making. In many respects, official Belarus signifies Lukashenka—there is no supporting cast. We seek to answer the following questions: How did Belarus react to the crisis in Ukraine? How did the attitude of President Lukashenka toward Ukraine change and was it consistent? What is his opinion about a federalist system in Ukraine or about the latter country joining NATO? Does he have better opportunities for resolving energy issues with Russia because of Euromaidan and its aftermath? Are Belarusian military bases being deployed for a possible attack on Ukraine? What impact has the war in Ukraine had on the Belarusian economy? Could Belarus maintain neutrality in the event of a full-scale war between Russia and Ukraine? If Ukraine should lose its eastern regions to Russia, could Belarus survive as an independent state?

The Initial Response

On February 23, 2014, after President Viktor Yanukovych fled from Kyiv following the violent altercations in the streets of the Ukrainian capital, Lukashenka issued a public statement that there would be no Euromaidan in Minsk.[1] A month later, in a speech to the Belarusian Parliament he elaborated his position and summarized his perspectives on the situation in Ukraine. He noted that there were two reasons for the crisis in Ukraine: first, the weakness of the economy, which essentially collapsed, and "total corruption." The two factors in his view were completely interlinked. He analyzed the potential situation for Belarus that would be posed by the entry there of the Russian army: "God forbid," he stated that there should ever be an attack on Belarus from the West or from the East, but in either event, Belarusians would defend their soil. Even the Russian president, Vladimir Putin, would be detained in such an instance. Lukashenka also had doubts whether Russian troops would be loyal to their leaders if they advanced on Belarus—the implication was that the leader of Belarus is extremely popular in Russia and the troops would be reluctant to turn against him. Hence, he concluded, he was not afraid.[2]

His stance was reiterated, according to the Belarusian Telecommunications Agency [BELTA], when he stated, half in jest, that he had recently been asked the question what he, as a man with roots buried between Chernihiv and Kyiv would do to overcome the crisis in Ukraine. He replied that "There is no need to exert yourself, you just need to work, trust us with the country, and by the end of the year we will ensure that there is both stability and unity of the people, along with integrity of the state."[3] His officials were somewhat more circumspect. According to the news agency "REGNUM," on March 3, Foreign Minister of Belarus Uladzimir Makei stat-

---

1   http://naviny.by/rubrics/politic/2014/03/01/ic_articles_184746/ (accessed August 26, 2014).
2   Belarusian Television, April 22, 2014.
3   Vladimir Matveev, "Lukashenko pro Ukrainu: Esli vy ne znaete, chto delat, doverte nam etu stranu, i k kontsu goda my obespechim tam stabilnost [Lukashenko on Ukraine: If you do not know what to do, entrust us with this country, and by year's end we will ensure stability there]," *Tut.by*, March 12, 2014 http://news.tut.by/politics/390423.html (accessed August 26, 2014).

ed: "We are interested in Ukraine as our stable partner and close friend. Between us is a huge border in the south of the country, ratified last year" (2013). The two sides were now working out the demarcation "on the ground" and "we would like to, once again, see Ukraine as our good friend and trading and economic partner." Concerning the civil uprising in Kyiv and other cities, Belarus was observing the situation, but it appeared the situation was far from clear with the victory of "the so-called Maidan." It would be necessary to assess the legitimacy of the new government, but already official Minsk was in contact with Kyiv and intended to maintain "normal communications."[4]

Lukashenka's seemingly harsh attitude to a potential Russian incursion into Belarus may also have been linked to the period of frosty relations with Russia during the 2010 presidential elections. At that time Russia mounted a psychological war against Lukashenka aimed at reducing the latter's popularity, and he did not discount the possibility that Russia could launch a real war against him, as it subsequently did against Ukraine in Crimea. The hostility ended with a compromise on December 9, only ten days prior to the election. Nevertheless, in late March 2014, when the UN General Assembly issued a resolution on its refusal to recognize the results of the Crimean referendum, Belarus was among the countries that voted against it, along with ten other states: Armenia, Bolivia, Cuba, Nicaragua, North Korea, Russia, Sudan, Syria, Venezuela, and Zimbabwe.[5]

Response of the Belarusian Opposition

For the Belarusian opposition leaders, the situation was more clear-cut: this was a revolution against an authoritarian regime similar to their own and therefore should be supported. On March 25, the "Day of Freedom," when Belarusians commemorate annually the independent state of 1918, an opposition rally chanted the slogans "Glory to Ukraine!" and "Long live Belarus!"[6] The protest's organizers condemned Russia's actions in Crimea.

---

4   Vladimir Makei, "Belorussiya zainterosovana v 'yednoy i stabilnoy Ukraine' [Belarus is interested in a united and stable Ukraine]," *REGNUM*, March 3, 2014, http://www.regnum.ru/news/polit/1773776.html (accessed August 26, 2014).

5   See, for example, "Ministry of Foreign Affairs Daily Briefing," *Ministry of Foreign Affairs of Ukraine*, March 28, 2014, http://mfa.gov.ua/en/press-center/briefing/1211-brifing-v-mzs (accessed August 26, 2014).

6   See, for example, the coverage provided at "Dzen Voli: Heroyam Slava—Zhvye Belarus [Day of Freedom: Glory to the Heroes—Long Live Belarus]," *Nasha Niva*, March 25, 2014, http://nn.by/?c=ar&i=125397 (accessed August 26, 2014).

Dzmitry Dashkevich, the leader of the Young Front, and a former political prisoner, declared that the two republics historically had in common that they had general interests in the West and general problems with Russia. "We all want to see a free Ukraine, which would have great significance for many countries, "and without doubt for Belarus."[7]

Opinion Polls

A useful means of assessing public reaction to events is through opinion polls. The Independent Institute of Social-Economic and Political Studies [IISEPS] has been conducting such surveys for more than twenty years and is one of the most reliable sources of popular opinion in Belarus. Its surveys held in March and June 2014 included questions on the Ukrainian Revolution (March) and "If war comes tomorrow" (June). The authors of the March survey make it clear that opinion had turned against former Ukrainian president Viktor Yanukovych because of the bloody events of late February when snipers fired on demonstrators, as well as his hasty exit from Kyiv. Thus the responses may have been different had he remained in office. The March survey affirms that 89% of respondents followed the events in Ukraine to a lesser or greater degree, with 16.1% taking the side of Yanukovych and 21% that of the opposition (Euromaidan); 56.2% maintained that they were neutral.[8]

On the question of responsibility for the protests, the responses were 32.4% for the Ukrainian opposition, 22.9% the Ukrainian government, 13.1% the European Union (EU), 11.9% the Ukrainian people, and 9.1% Russia. As after the Orange Revolution of November-December 2004, respondents were equally divided on the question of what the protests comprised: a subjective process based on Western political technology and weakness of the authorities or else an objective process deriving from the dissatisfaction of the people with the political powers. Yet over 54% considered Euromaidan to be a seizure of power (state revolution), with about half that number of the view that the removal of Yanukovych was a just punishment for the "spilling of blood." The questions here were rather limited since presumably some might have considered his removal a response to the corruption of his regime and abuses of power. A further 78%

---

7   http://charter97.org/ru/news/2014/3/25/91884/ (accessed January 4, 2015).
8   "Ukrainskaya Revolyutsiya v zerkale obshchestvennogo mneniya Belarusi [The Ukrainian Revolution in the mirror of Belorussian public opinion]," *NISEPI*, April 19, 2014, http://www.iiseps.org/analitica/571 (accessed August 26, 2014).

did not think that it was necessary to spill blood in order to attain a better life, i.e. the costs of Euromaidan were too high.

In general, Belarusian responses to Euromaidan were negative. Almost 80% thought that regime change should take place only through elections or elections accompanied by peaceful protests, and 70% did not want something similar to occur in Belarus. If protests did happen, then 65.5% declared they would not take part on either side, while 15% stated they would support a Belarusian Maidan and 10.7% the authorities. Of the Belarusian Maidan supporters, 43.1% thought that regime change could take place only by peaceful means and 39.7% were prepared to countenance change by any means. One could perhaps therefore posit that a small section of the population (under 10% and probably more like 6–7%), could be described as militant radicals. The survey also demonstrated that age affected responses, with those aged 18–29 more likely to favor the opposition in the Ukrainian conflict and those over 60 inclined to favor the authorities and former president Yanukovych. Regarding the future of Ukraine in the overall survey, 35.2% believed a new government would be established through elections and the situation would stabilize, 33.8% foresaw the collapse of Ukraine, 16.7% thought civil war would begin, and 9.8% were undecided or declined to respond. A tiny minority anticipated the return to power of Yanukovych.[9]

In the survey conducted in June 2014, the focus was war and the potential for a Russian takeover as well as reaction to continuing events in Ukraine. A minority of 26.3% felt that it was entirely possible that Russia might annex Belarus or parts of it, whereas 30% did not think it was credible, and a further 36.4% thought it possible but unlikely. An overwhelming majority of over 93% rejected the notion that rights of Russian-language speakers were threatened in Belarus, while 78.9% did not see any threat to Belarusian speakers. In the event of a Russian annexation of all or part of Belarus, almost half of respondents (47.7%) were prepared to adapt to the new situation, 16.5% would support it, and only 14.2% were willing to take up arms to stop it. Most of these, as shown from Table Five of the survey, were supporters of the opposition. The annexation of Crimea—an "historical part of Russia"—in general was quite well received, even among supporters of the opposition, but especially so among supporters of the president, who also (77%) consider that the events in eastern Ukraine (the

---

9   Ibid.

establishment of people's republics in Donetsk and Luhansk) represented a popular protest against "illegitimate authorities."[10]

Ukraine and the Popularity of Lukashenka

The war in Ukraine also benefited Lukashenka personally, raising his popularity to new heights. In the first quarter of 2014, for example, his rating rose to 39.8%, compared to 34.8% the previous December. In terms of those who trust the head of state, the rise was from 37.7 to 45.5%. On paper at least, there were no obvious reasons for the surge in confidence and appeal. GDP was not growing, inflation was at 4.9% by the end of March, public transport prices were "soaring" and the public was expecting the sharp collapse of the national currency. In a similar situation the previous year, Lukashenka's rating had fallen almost 8%. Experts linked the spring 2014 surge directly to the events in Ukraine. Belarusians were first frightened of the "bloody Maidan," then the political plot of Crimea, and now they were horrified to watch events unfolding in Eastern Ukraine. The most popular expression in the country was "at last there is no war here." Political analyst Andrei Fiadarau commented that because of the upheaval in Ukraine, Belarusians had a better appreciation of the kind of stability brought about by the twenty-year leadership of Lukashenka. Valery Karbalevich, a well-known sociologist, noted that "the fear of chaos and destabilization had intensified the desire of Belarusians for a strong and ruthless power."[11]

Still, official Belarus was not unprepared for potential changes to the status quo. Lukashenka had been inspecting the combat readiness of the Belarusian Air Force in Baranovichi in order "not to repeat the sad experience of the Ukrainians." He was also critical of the interim government in Ukraine: "Yatsenyuk thinks that the revolution can write everything off" but the price of gas had risen by 50–70% and the population cannot afford such prices. The EU in turn has simply "thrown away" Ukraine. What help have they provided, he asked? The United States, which had adopted the chief role [in the change of regime in Ukraine], provided dry rations for the Ukrainian army and the IMF had promised $1 billion—"you know under

---

10 "Esli zavtra voyna [If war comes tomorrow]," *NISEPI*, May 7, 2014, http://www.iis eps.org/analitica/592 (accessed August 25, 2014).

11 "Lukashenko vyrastil reyting blagodariya Ukraine [Lukashenko's approval rating rises thanks to Ukraine]," *Rosbalt*, April 21, 2014, http://m.rosbalt.ru//exussr/2014/ 14/21/1259611.html (accessed August 25, 2014).

what conditions." Ukraine had taken a course of action and now had no idea what to do. Belarus had also "sorted out" the fundamental problem of corruption, according to a 56-year old accountant (her full name was not given). A freelance programmer informed Rosbalt that "Ukrainians and Belarusians are not Europeans, it must be admitted. The difference between us is that we like order, and the Ukrainians anarchy." The report concluded by noting that there are likely to be few surprises in the 2015 presidential elections in Belarus because Ukrainian events have already predetermined the outcome.[12]

Federalism and NATO

The president was scathing about the concept of federalism, the expressed preference for system of government in Eastern Ukraine by Russian president Putin. During an interview on the Kyiv program "Shuster Live," he stated strongly "I am categorically opposed to all federations!" He referred to federalism as "idiocy." The result today is the destabilization of the largest country in Europe, he continued in a twist of logic, since Ukraine has not actually introduced a federalist form of government. Such a state attracts the militants, bandits, and others who want to make easy money. Rather Ukraine should remain a united and integral state. In any case, he pointed out, amid the present turmoil and confusion, it was impossible to hold referendums on the creation of a federal state. The results would be biased and lead to talk that they are illegitimate. And who would recognize them? First it is necessary to bring peace to Ukraine, to stabilize the situation, and only then think about resolving through a referendum the question of whether the future state should be a federation, a confederation, or a unitary state. But again, Lukashenka reiterated "I am totally against it!"[13] There is a certain irony about the Belarusian president's condemnation of referendums given his own fondness of them and manipulation of their results. He used them, for example, in 1995, 1998, and 2004 to enhance his powers and lengthen his presidency—but perhaps above all he had in mind a potentially similar situation taking place in Belarus.

---

12 Ibid.

13 "Intervyu Lukashenko Ukrainskoy Programme 'Shuster LIVE' [Lukashenko Interview on the Ukrainian Program 'Shuster LIVE']," *Novosti Belarusi*, March 28, 2014, http://www.belta.by/ru/all_news/president/Intervju-Lukashenko-ukrainskoj-programmeShuster-LIVE_i_664335.html (accessed August 26, 2014).

Another question on the agenda after the uprising in Ukraine was the potential for joining NATO, an idea that has always been strongly opposed in Belarus.[14] The president's response to the question of Ukraine entering the alliance was firm but quite reasoned, if not always logical. He would not conceal that the key issue was ensuring the NATO alliance did not approach our borders. This was important for Russia and Belarus. The Slavic peoples are closely linked and Belarus would like to trade and live with its Slavic neighbors, who share similar culture and languages. "We want to continue to live in this way." The choice, however, is for the Ukrainian people to make. "They must organize their lives as they see fit, but not create problems for their neighbors," he added.[15] The comments ignored the fact that NATO already has been on the border of Belarus since Poland joined in 1999. Admittedly, however, Belarus is much closer to Ukraine than it is to Poland, a country that was not part of the Soviet Union. NATO is also perceived in Minsk as a direct threat, partly because of the events during the dismantling of the former Yugoslavia and the removal of Slobodan Milosevic from power. The Belarusian leader ended his statement more emphatically: "Ukraine will not be in the West. No one is waiting for it there."[16]

Lukashenka's Attitude to Yanukovych and Turchynov

Lukashenka's attitude to Ukraine prior to the crisis brought on by Euromaidan was of a dual nature. First, it was determined by pragmatic goals. In terms of trade turnover with Belarus, Ukraine ranks third, after Russia and the EU (the question is discussed below). Second, Lukashenka had suffered a public humiliation at the hands of the former president of Ukraine. When Ukraine commemorated the 25th anniversary of the Chernobyl disaster (April 26, 2011), Lukashenka was invited to attend the Chernobyl summit and international conference in Kyiv. The EU suggested that Prime Minister Mikhail Myasnikovich might attend rather than the president, but Lukashenka insisted that he intended to fly to Kyiv. The invitation

---

14 Both of the IISEPS surveys cited above indicate that opposition to joining NATO in Belarus has remained very high.
15 "Lukashenko: Pust Ukrainskiy narod ustraivayet svoyu zhizn, kak schitayet nuzhnym, no chtoby ne sozdaval problem svoim sosedyam [Lukashenko: Let the Ukrainian people be satisfied with their lives as they see fit, but avoid creating problems for your neighbors]," *Tut.by*, May 12, 2014, http://news.tut.by/politics/39850 2.html (accessed August 26, 2014).
16 Ibid.

was rescinded, however, when President of the European Commission, Jose Manuel Barroso, threatened to pull out if Lukashenka attended.[17] Visa bans had been imposed on the Belarusian leader and the Europeans had no wish to be seen in public with him. Lukashenka was furious and publicly insulted Yanukovych, declaring that he was not about to serve as a "yes man" to the European president. He referred to Barroso and other EU leaders as "scoundrels" and "goats" among other insults.[18] No doubt the rebuff rankled.

After Yanukovych's flight from Kyiv, Lukashenka could not resist sarcastic and scathing comments, centered on the duties of a president. Referring to the last part of a speech made in exile by Yanukovych, Lukashenka retorted: "Immediately the question arises: "and where is your army?" A president, he continued, should remain with his people, no matter how hard it may be, even if "tomorrow" he might be shot and killed. "This is your destiny." A president should be prepared to sacrifice himself. Instead, Yanukovych had sat in his residence reveling in his power, and then had run away when the situation became difficult. Thus when the *Rada* claimed that he had fled and given up his office, what could be said to contradict it? He did not wish to be perceived as a "changeling" with regard to his former amity with Yanukovych. Rather "I condemn him as a friend."[19] There is a certain irony about Lukashenka's remarks given that, as noted earlier, he opted to shelter another fleeing president, Bakiyev of Kyrgyzstan. During Euromaidan in the early spring of 2014, there were a number of rumors that the Ukrainian president might flee to Belarus, his ancestral homeland on his father's side of the family, where there are still a few families living in the village of Ianuki, in Viciebsk region.[20] Likely his poor relations with Lukashenka precluded that escape route.

---

17 See, for example, "Row breaks out around Lukashenko over Chernobyl summit," *Kyiv Post*, March 20, 2011, https://www.kyivpost.com/content/politics/row-breaks-out-around-lukashenko-over-chernobyl-su-100345.html (accessed August 26, 2014).

18 "Lukashenko finds scapegoats in Ukraine, EU," *Russia Today*, April 27, 2011, http://rt.com/politics/lukashenko-belarus-ukraine-barroso/ (accessed August 26, 2014).

19 "Lukashenko dal intervyu 'Shuster Live': Yanukovicha ya osuzhdayu kak druga [Lukashenko gave an interview on 'Shuster Live': As a friend I condemn Yanukovich]," *Naviny.by*, March 26, 2014, http://naviny.by/rubrics/politic/2014/03/26/ic_new s_112_434042/ (accessed August 26, 2014).

20 For an account of Yanukovych's family background in Belarus, see, for example, "Viktor Yanukovich, An Ethnic Belarusian, Elected As President Of Ukraine," *Bela-*

In contrast to Lukashenka's withering contempt for Yanukovych was his sympathetic attitude toward Oleksandr Turchynov, the Speaker of the Parliament, who took on the role of Acting President after the flight of the former leader. Lukashenka declared that he had only positive emotions toward Turchynov, a man he had known for some time and who had visited Minsk during the Yushchenko era (2005–10). The Belarusian leader depicted him as a very honest and decent man, religious, and the author of dozens of books. He had defended his doctoral dissertation, but not in order to make money out of it. Admittedly, Turchynov was extremely nationalistic and is "absolutely pro-Ukrainian." At times his views cause him to speak sharply but he should not be considered an "absolute evil for Russia or us."[21] At a recent meeting in the West Belarusian city of Homiel, Turchynov was not concerned that Belarus had joined Russia and Armenia in voting against the UN resolution (cited above). He was concerned only that Lukashenka and his army might invade northern Ukraine. Lukashenka had reassured him that if he came to Ukraine, it would be on a tractor with a plow to assist Ukrainians with agriculture, which was currently a problem for them.[22]

Perhaps because of his sympathy for Turchynov, Lukashenka disagreed with the Russian stance that the post-Yanukovych interim government of Ukraine (i.e. the Euromaidan government) was illegitimate. In the first place, he noted, the current leaders of the Ukrainian state were elected by the legitimate Parliament, and had legally amended the Constitution. Further, the Moscow leaders once sat quietly around a table with the leaders that had come to power as a result of the "coup." During an interview with the Russian station NTV, Lukashenka reiterated that as far as he was concerned, Turchynov was the legitimate president of Ukraine. According to the Ukrainian Constitution, in the absence of a president, the duties fall

rus Digest, February 14, 2010, http://belarusdigest.com/story/viktor-yanukovich-ethnic-belarusian-elected-president-ukraine-1868 (accessed August 26, 2014).

21 "Lukashenko podderzhal yedinstvo Ukrainy i pokhvalil Turchinova [Lykashenko supported Ukrainian unity and praised Turchinov]," Liga.Novosti, April 22, 2014, http://news.liga.net/news/politics/1458717-lukashenko_podderzhal_edinstvo_ukrainy_i_pokhvalil_turchinova_.htm (accessed August 26, 2014).

22 Tatyana Melnychuk, "Lukashenko v poslanii k natsii vystupil za yedinuyu Ukrainu [In his message to the nation Lukashenko called for a united Ukraine]," BBC-Russkaya Sluzhba, April 23, 2014, http://www.bbc.co.uk/russian/international/2014/04/140422_belarus_lukashenko_ukraine_view.shtml (accessed August 26, 2014).

upon the head of the Parliament. "So for me, it is absolutely legitimate and the *Verkhovna Rada* is absolutely legitimate." Turchynov had correctly interpreted the situation formed by the unusual events in Kyiv.[23] "We will work with our Ukraine, no matter how difficult it is," Lukashenko stated. "We are very worried about what is happening in Ukraine." His attitude toward the southern neighbor was based as much on personal sentiment as his duties as president.[24] Thus by spring 2014, it seemed that Belarus' position was ambivalent. On the one hand, it stood alongside Russia in the UN General Assembly. On the other, it refused to join any coalition against Ukraine; on the contrary the president's public rhetoric was very positive in support of the newly formed regime in Kyiv. Emotions and personal feelings aside, one reason for such apparent fence sitting may have been the perilous state of the Belarusian economy and the need to keep borders open for trade. Let us now turn to the economy and the impact of Euromaidan on Belarus.

Economic Issues

Lukashenka has long stressed the importance of Belarus to Ukrainian agriculture, providing tractors, sowing, and harvesting assistance. Belarusians, he declared, have an excellent relationship with Ukrainian farmers, especially in the western regions. They have "planted their grain" and used harvesters to gather it, not only in Ukraine, but also in Russian regions such as Bryansk, Pskov, and Smolensk. "There is a good neighborhood belt around Belarus." Fifteen years ago, he gave the command: "no matter how difficult it may be, we will help our neighbors," and such aid was offered to Kyiv Oblast.[25] At the same time, good neighborliness did not detract from Belarus' role as a geostrategic partner of Russia. He spoke of problems at the Orsha Aircraft Repair Plant, in which one of the stakeholders is the Ukrainian company Motor Sich. "This is not a problem," stated

---

23 "Lukashenko schitat legitimnym naznachenie Turchinova i.o. prezidenta Ukrainy [Lukashenko considers the appointment of Turchinov as the acting President of Ukraine legitimate], "*ITAR-TASS*, April 13, 2014, http://www.itar-tass.com/mezh dunarodnaya-panorama/1117507 (accessed August 26, 2014).

24 "Lukashenko protiv federalizatsiy Ukrainy [Lukashenko is against the federalization of Ukraine]," *BBC-Ukraina*, April 23, 2014, http://www.bbc.co.uk/ukrainian/ukrain e_in_russian/2014/04/140423_ru_s_lukashenko_appeal.shtml" (accessed August 26, 2014).

25 "Intervyu Lukashenko [Lukashenko Interview]," *Novosti Belarusi*, March 28, 2014.

Lukashenka. But Belarus needs to produce its own planes, which should be marketed primarily to Russia.[26] In other words, Lukashenka wished to emphasize that Russia was the chief military partner of Belarus.

Both Ukraine and Russia are key trading partners. In 2013, according to information from the State Statistical Service of Ukraine, Belarus was its second largest trading partner after the Russian Federation among CIS countries, and occupied sixth place overall. In 2013, however, general trade turnover between the two states fell by almost 23% from the level in 2012. Exports dropped by 11.2% and imports by 28.1%. Figures from October 2013 indicate that Ukrainian investment in the Belarusian economy was $4 million, or 33.1% less than in January-October 2012. In turn, Belarusian investment in the Ukrainian economy had risen by over 22% from 2012. Although Ukraine by 2013 was the third largest market of Belarusian exports after Russia and the United Kingdom, trade continued to decline, "because of the current situation" and not because of the fall of the Ukrainian currency, which had dropped against the dollar from 8 to 11.6 (in 2014 it declined further to over 15). Enterprises of Homiel Region traditionally sold a lot of goods to Ukraine, but business had slowed down, though here the problem was evidently that Homiel factories were demanding 100% prepayment for deliveries. Belarusian meat and dairy products have long been popular in Ukraine, but even before the beginning of Euromaidan, Homiel meat was no longer being sold to its southern neighbor. Ukraine had closed its border to the import of pork products in fall 2013 because of foot-and-mouth disease and the ban has not been lifted. Dairy products, however, were delivered in the same amounts as earlier, according to the management of Homiel Meat and Dairy Company.[27]

The largest industrial enterprise in the country, *Homselmash* [Homiel Agricultural Machinery], had also reduced considerably its exports to Ukraine. All contracts remained in force, but few orders had arrived. The Embassy of Belarus in Ukraine noted the decline, but maintained that relations between the two states remained the same. Belarus was still interested in the Ukrainian market according to Ihar Milidovich, the Consul

26 "Lukashenko poruchil aviazavodu delat samolety i vertolety [Lukashenko instructed the aviation factory to build planes and helicopters]," *Index-press.by*, April 2, 2014, http://www.intex-press.by/ru/news/society/15817/ (accessed August 27, 2014).

27 Olga Yerokhina, Pavel Mitskevich, "Prodazhi belorusskogo moloka v Ukrainy sokratilis [The sale of Belorussian milk in Ukraine declines]," *Komsomolskaya Pravda*, April 8, 2014, http://www.kp.by/daily/26216/3100343 (accessed August 27, 2014).

General in Kyiv. The issue was that different businesses were responding in various ways to the existing "objective risks," which, Milidovich noted, there was no point in denying. Each company had to decide with which currency to enter contracts and conditions under which to conduct the supply of products given the current situation on the Ukrainian market. There was no single "recipe for today" and some temporary setbacks had occurred. But once again it was emphasized that relations between the two states had not changed.[28] The situation was likely to become more complicated early in 2014 as Euromaidan turned into a violent confrontation between demonstrators and the Yanukovych presidency.

By late April 2014, trade between the two states had suffered a further decline. In January-February it had fallen 17.1% compared to the same period in 2013. Exports of Belarusian goods to Ukraine dropped by 9%, and imports from Ukraine fell dramatically by almost one-third from the previous year. About 70% of Belarusian exports to Ukraine are oil products. Moreover, economic indicators were continuing to decline. The volume of industrial production in Ukraine declined by 4.2% in January-February 2014. After the removal of Yanukovych, the new Ukrainian government set itself a target of reducing the budget by 40%, which had a negative impact on economic growth.[29] By May 2014, the prices for some Ukrainian imports (including beer and confectionery) were so low that Belarus imposed an embargo on their import unless the prices of the goods were at least as high as local ones. The result was that some Ukrainian companies went out of business. By August, however, the embargo was lifted and all duties on goods traded between the two countries were removed.[30] Nevertheless, both countries had been adversely affected by the continuing conflict in Eastern Ukraine and the instability in the country overall in the summer of 2014.

---

28 Ibid.
29 Dmitriy Zayats, "Tovarooborot Belarus s Ukrainoy sushchestvenno snizilsya [The commodity trade between Belarus and Ukraine has significantly decreased]," *Tut.by*, April 23, 2014, http://www.news.tut.by/economics/396343.html (accessed August 27, 2014).
30 Aleksandr Yaroshevich, "Belarus i Ukraina zaklyuchili torgovoe peremiriye [Belarus and Ukraine sign a trade truce]," *NAVINY.BY*, August 19, 2014, http://naviny.by/ru brics/economic/2014/08/19/ic_articles_113_186345/ (accessed August 27, 2014).

Russian Military Bases in Belarus

One of the key questions to be addressed here is whether the Russian military bases in Belarus might be used for an attack on Ukraine. The answer appears to be: at the time of writing there was no indication that this would be the case. Belarus until recently had two Russian bases on its territory: a radar station near Hantsavichi (Baranovichi) and a naval communications center near Vileyka that communicated with Russian nuclear submarines. In April 2014, Russian Minister of Defense Sergey Shoygu announced that a Russian Air Force regiment would be based in Belarus at a new base to be constructed by 2015. An air force headquarters would be established later in 2015 in order to test fighter jets. Further, also in this same year, Russia would deliver four battalions of S-300 surface-to-air missiles. In this way, Shoygu noted, Russia would be increasing its contribution to Belarusian defense capabilities.[31] Similar arrangements had evidently been made with Russia's other partner in the newly formed Customs Union, Kazakhstan.

Lukashenka from the outset had declared emphatically that there were no plans now or in the future to use Belarusian troops in Ukraine. Yet there were some obvious concerns. Despite his statement, Lukashenka provided military airfields for use by Russian planes for the deployment of their troops. These planes could strike at the territory of Ukraine—or for that matter the EU countries—at a range of several thousand kilometers. Once Russian aircraft arrived in Belarus, Ukraine was effectively surrounded. Lukashenka's explanation for his action—though one must consider the possibility that he was given no choice by his Russian counterpart Putin—was that permits were provided for the Russian aircraft to counter the location of NATO troops in Poland and the Baltic States.[32] He also maintained that he intended to increase the independent strength of the Belarusian Army, yet the portion of military spending in the budget was below 1%, which placed Belarus below countries such as Albania and Papua New Guinea in terms of military spending per capita. As Siarhei Bohdan notes,

---

31 "Russia to deploy fighter jets, anti-aircraft missiles at new Belarus base—Defense Minister," *Russia Today*, April 23, 2013, http://rt.com/politics/dm-base-belarus-new-256/ (accessed August 27, 2014).

32 "Lukashenko: If forced to choose, Belarus will always choose Russia," *Belarusian Telegraph Agency*, March 23, 2014, http://eng.belta.by/all_news/president/Luk ashenko-If-forced-to-choose-Belarus-will-always-choose-Russia_i_67412.html (accessed September 19, 2014).

"Since gaining independence, Belarus has had a history of spending the bare minimum on its armed forces." He also notes that most of the funds expended are also on the defense of the country in the event of an attack and that offensive capability is very limited.[33]

In March, responding to a question about the potential deployment of an additional twenty-four Russian aircraft in Belarus, Lukashenka declared that there were no urgent questions facing his country, but if Russia wished to give them extra planes, he would only be happy. He claimed that Belarus was in the process of modernizing weapons and military equipment for its Armed Forces and that his main concern was not to receive airplanes and helicopters, but rather special operations forces that could cause irreparable damaged to the enemy. Also of importance was the defense of the country against planes, helicopters, and cruise missiles, i.e. the air defense system. That was why Belarus was willing to buy the C-300 and other weapons. He was also committed to upgrading Belarusian aircraft and the inclusion in its ranks of the SU-27 and MiG-29 by the end of 2014. Thus, he said, it was Belarus that had demanded the additional planes. They would remain on Belarusian territory "as long we want them." He also noted that the two countries continued to hold regular military exercises.[34] By March 13, six Russian SU-25 fighter jets and three military transport aircraft had been relocated to the Babruisk airfield in Belarus.[35]

Responses to Events in Crimea and Odesa

Two events that escalated the conflict in Ukraine were the March 1 invasion of Crimea by Russian forces followed by a referendum to join Russia, and the May 2 deaths of dozens of separatist supporters in a burning building in Odesa. The position of the Belarusian leader on both events, which

33 See, for example, Siarhei Bohdan, "Belarusian Army: Capacity and Its Role in the Region," *Belarusian Digest*, August 18, 2014, http://belarusdigest.com/story/belarus ian-army-capacity-and-its-role-region-18931 (accessed August 27, 2014).

34 "Lukashenko ne protiv razmeshcheniya v Belarusi dopolnitelno 24 rossiyskikh samoletov, no ostroy neobkhodimosti v etom net [Lukashenko is not against the deployment of 24 Russian planes in Belarus, but there is no pressing need for this]," *Novosti Belarusi*, March 23, 2014, http://www.belta.by/ru/all_news/president/L ukashenko-ne-protiv-razmeschenija-v-Belarusi-dopolnitelno-24-rossijskix-samoleto v-no-ostroj-neobxodimosti-v-etom-net_i_663696.html (accessed August 27, 2014).

35 "Belarus razmestila v Bobruyske shest rossiyskikh istrebiteley [Belarus deploys six Russia fighters in Babruysk]," *24smi. Novosti*, March 13, 2014, http://www.24smi .org/news/14364-belarus-razmestila-v-bobrujske-shest-rossijskikh-is.html (accessed August 27, 2014).

elicited widespread condemnation internationally, provides an interesting perspective on how Belarus has tried to avoid any commitment to either side as well as a lack of consistency. Lukashenka also noted that some people maintained that there had never been a state called Ukraine and that it still did not exist. He declared this attitude to be cynical. He pointed out that many states had emerged only from the wreckage of the Soviet empire, and they included Belarus as well as Ukraine. In a typical rhetorical flourish he declared that he "had never been [treated like] toilet paper" no matter with whom he had dealt, but referring specifically to the Russian leadership. Though people had accused him of being silent, "I could not sit like a mouse under a broom and keep quiet."[36]

On Crimea, Lukashenka responded that the peninsula was *de facto* part of Russia, but not *de jure* since there had been no international agreements or recognition. It was not an independent state like South Ossetia and Abkhazia, but belonged to the Russian Federation. He blamed the Ukrainian authorities for the loss of Crimea. They had made "a lot of errors." Some claimed that Russia had simply grabbed the peninsula, but Russia had seen what was happening there and was concerned about the fate of 2.5 million ethnic Russians. Therefore it intervened. Everything that was happening in Ukraine was "absolutely disgusting and I don't like it," he added, contradicting completely everything he was to say about the interim government three weeks later. He was scathing in turn about the weak response of the West and its imposition of relatively mild sanctions on Russia. Twenty Russian officials had been banned from traveling to EU countries, but some had never been to Europe and others had no need to go. And the annexation of Crimea by Russia would be widely recognized as a fact, whether or not it ever became legally accepted. Belarus was not about to create problems for its neighbor. Notably his position on Crimea was much more forthright and pro-Russian than his stand on events in Ukraine generally.[37] It also appeared to negate his March 11 statement

---

36 Melnychuk, "Lukashenko v poslaniy k natsii [Lukashenko in his message to the nation]," *BBC-Russkaya Sluzhba*, April 23, 2014.

37 Tatyana Melnychuk, "Lukashenko priznal Krym de-fakto chastyu Rossii [Lukashenko admits Crimea is a de-facto part of Russia]," *BBC-Russkaya Sluzhba,* March 23, 2014, http://www.bbc.co.uk/russian/russia/2014/03/140323_lukashenko _crimea_russia_speech.shtml (accessed August 26, 2014). He was not as forthright, however, as former Soviet leader Mikhail Gorbachev, who stated that the Crimean referendum had corrected a "historical mistake" and should be "celebrated, not sanctioned." The "mistake" to which he referred was the agreement by the

that the principal position of Minsk was to ensure the territorial integrity of Ukraine.[38]

Concerning the tragedy in Odesa, Lukashenka, during a meeting with the presidents of Russia, Armenia, Kyrgyzstan, and Tajikistan (the countries that in part formed the Collective Security Treaty Organization), implicitly at least equated the perpetrators with the events at Khatyn, a Belarusian village that was burned by the 118th Security Police Battalion operating with the Germans on March 22, 1943.[39] Lukashenka stated "We remember Khatyn, when several hundred villages in Belarus were burned by the Fascists on this principle (as in Odessa). Therefore such actions are unacceptable in all states, and even more so if we look calmly at what happened."[40] The world, he remarked, was so cramped and dynamic that this plague was quickly spreading, even to the territories of those attending the meeting, and it was time that the CSTO changed the way it responded to such challenges. These were "our people" who were crying out for help and there was a need to respond to such phenomena.[41] Just three years earlier, the Belarusian president had been calling for similar responses to protests in Minsk that followed the 2010 presidential elections of December 2010. Though he could accept the Turchynov presidency, therefore, he was concerned about what he considered more extremist actions that accompanied Euromaidan.

Soviet leadership in 1954 to transfer Crimea from Russia to Ukraine, to commemorate the 300th anniversary of the Treaty of Pereyaslav. Cited at "Gorbachev Says Outcome of Crimea Referendum Corrected Historical 'Mistake'," *The Moscow Times*, March 19, 2014, http://www.themoscowtimes.com/news/article/gorbachev-says-outcome-of-crimea-referendum-corrected-historical-mistake/496386.html (accessed August 27, 2014).

38 "Lukashenko priznayet novuyu vlast v Kieve nazlo Kremlyu [Lukashenko recognizes the new government in Kiev in order to spite the Kremlin]," *BBC-Russkaya Sluzhba*, March 12, 2014, http://www.bbc.co.uk/russian/international/2014/03/140312_ukraine_minsk_react.shtml (accessed August 27, 2014).

39 See, for example, Per Anders Rudling, "The Khatyn Massacres in Belarus: a Historical Controversy Revisited," *Holocaust and Genocide Studies* 26, no. 1 (Spring 2012): 29–58.

40 "Lukashenko sravnil sobytiya 2 Maya v Odesse s tragediey v Khatyni [Lukashenko compares the events of 2 May in Odessa to the tragedy of Khatyn]," *Tut.by*, May 8, 2014, http://news.tut.by/politics/398203.html (accessed August 27, 2014).

41 "Lukashenko ob Odesskoy tragedii: 'Po takomu zhe printsipu fashisty sozhgli sotni belorusskikh dereven' [Lukashenko on the Odessa tragedy: 'By the same token, the Nazis burned hundreds of Belorussian villages]," *Regnum*, May 8, 2014, http://www.regnum.ru/news/polit/1799875.html (accessed August 27, 2014).

Euromaidan and the Independence of Belarus

Euromaidan immediately raised questions about the freedom of actions of states included in various agreements with Russia, such as the CSTO and Customs Union. Would it pose a threat to Belarusian independence? Would Belarus be drawn inevitably into the conflict? Two caveats should be noted to the first question posed. First, Belarus is not an independent state in the political sense. It has been obliged to enter different forms of alliances with Russia and use a common customs duty on goods. For example, since its entry into the Customs Union, Belarus has been forced to raise taxes on passenger cars to Russian levels, which has affected almost every Belarusian family, and limited their ability to exchange their cars. And second, it is not an independent state in the economic sense either since it survives only through the financial support of Russia and through the latter country allowing access to its markets for Belarusian products.

Lukashenka has acknowledged his limited freedom of maneuver: "Remember, no matter what I do now, talking with Ukraine, the West, the East, etc., I do not take a single step without the agreement of the Russian Federation if the question touches Russia." Thus—another startling volte-face—if it were necessary to operate in Ukraine to ensure the survival of the Russian state, "We will do this."[42] In another example of the lack of political independence of Belarus in foreign affairs, at a meeting with the Secretary of the Security Council of the Russian Federation, Nikolay Patrushev on May 12, 2014, Lukashenka stated: "The situation around us is not simple, we do not hide this and we discussed it with the Russian President and Prime Minister. Probably it is a good thing that I have an opportunity to discuss with you, [who] are conducting consultations at the level of State Secretaries of the Security Council. Because it is necessary to see what tomorrow brings and coordinate our positions and our actions, if this will be necessary it is very important for us."[43] In short, Belarus lacked the freedom to act independently in the conflict.

---

42 "Aleksandr Lukashenko vstretilsya s gubernatorom Kaluzhskoy oblasti Anatoliyem Artamonovym [Aleksandr Lukashenko met with the governor of Kaluga Region Anatoliy Artamonov]," *Ofitsialnyi internet-portal Prezidenta Respubliki Belarus*, April 4, 2014, http://president.gov.by/ru/news_ru/view/aleksandr-lukashenko-vstretitsja-s-gu bernatorom-kaluzhskoj-oblasti-8428/ (accessed August 27, 2014).

43 "Lukashenko: Pust Ukrainskiy narod... [Lukashenko: Allow the Ukrainian people...]," *Tut.by*, May 12, 2014.

An example of the Kremlin's influence over Belarus, can be gleaned from the 2014 World Hockey Championships in Minsk, which took place during the crisis in Ukraine (May 9–25). Member of the European Parliament for Poland Marek Migalski was refused permission to enter Belarus at the request of the Russian authorities. Migalski had been among those who opposed the holding of the event in Minsk on the grounds that many Belarusians hardly welcomed the occasion with many of their relatives in prison because they lacked democracy and freedom. Nonetheless, Migalski stated, he and two friends had decided to attend because for two weeks, it would be possible to meet with community leaders, relatives of political leaders, and ordinary Belarusians. In order to enter the country they had purchased tickets for the Belarus-Switzerland match. At passport control, however, they were detained and their passports confiscated. The border guards informed Migalski that his two friends could enter, but he would not be allowed into Belarus. The three friends disagreed with this decision, and were held for three hours in the transit zone. Ultimately, they were informed that the judgment had come from the Russian authorities and the decision was "irrevocable." They were put on a return train to Warsaw.[44] Visitors to Minsk receive a customs form informing that they have entered the "Russia-Belarus Union." It would seem that it is becoming a real entity.

Can Belarus act independently in any situation that involves the interests of Russia? The answer, according to some political experts, is that it is becoming increasingly difficult, particularly in view of the forthcoming Belarusian presidential election of 2015. Analyst Andrey Suzdaltsev perceived a direct link between Lukashenka's apparent malleability and his need for Moscow to fund his election campaign. Across the former Soviet countries, socio-economic and political situations continue to deteriorate and it would be rash for Lukashenka to resort to his usual appeal to the population by offering wage increases. In the past he could count on financial and material backing from Russia, but today in order to obtain such support he must agree to deeper and real integration. Already the Belarusian leader had agreed to all the conditions demanded by Putin for the establishment of the Eurasian Economic Union, which resulted in a loan of $2

---

44 Marek Mihalski, "Miane ne pustsili u Belarus pa ukazanni raseiskikh uladau [I was not allowed to enter Belarus as directed by Russian authorities]," *Khartyia'97*, May 12, 2014, http://www.charter97.org/be/news/2014/5/12/98275 (accessed August 27, 2014).

billion for Belarus.[45] But evidently much more funding would be required in the months ahead.

Conclusion

It is evident from the examples provided that although the Belarusian leader's rhetoric sometimes suggested that he intended to follow an independent course, he was drawn more and more into the conflict on the side of Russia. There is a certain logic to this in that his support for Turchynov withstanding—and the latter was essentially an interim figure—he was appalled by Euromaidan and some of its more extreme manifestations. Moreover, it became very difficult to remain neutral given the intransigence of and constant pressure from the Kremlin, which had several economic weapons at its disposal to "persuade" Belarus to make its choice clear. The fact that the Belarusian opposition came out strongly in support of the Ukrainian civil uprising may also have been a contributory factor. The war demonstrated in this respect the relative weakness of Lukashenka. Though in his view, Ukraine stands beside Russia as part of his Slavic world, if Kyiv seeks to sever these links, then Belarus must ultimately, however reluctantly, take the side of Russia.

On the other hand, Euromaidan provided some unexpected benefits for Lukashenka. Immediately, Belarus could pose as a bastion of stability alongside Ukraine. As residents watched with horror on their TV screens the bloodshed in Kyiv and later in the Donbas, no doubt many reflected that whatever economic problems they were facing, such as price rises and a relative decline in living standards over the past few years, at least they were not living in Ukraine. The economic crisis and political corruption in Ukraine were far more intense than in Belarus. In addition, whatever the practical consequences of supporting Russia militarily, Lukashenka was able to pose as a mediator between the warring sides by the late summer of 2014. In August 2014, he hosted a summit in Minsk that brought together the leaders of Russia, Ukraine, the EU, and the Eurasian Customs Un-

---

45 Andrey Suzdaltsev, "Sgovorchivost Lukashenko v Moskve svyazana s vkhodom v predvybornuyu kampaniyu [In Moscow Lukashenko accommodates the Russians due to the start of the election campaign]," *Ekho Moskvy*, May 12, 2014, http://www.echo.msk.ru/blog/politoboz/1318382-echo/ (accessed August 27, 2014).

ion, a meeting described by EU foreign policy chief Catherine Ashton as "cordial, but positive."[46]

The crisis appeared to herald the creation of a new image for a man known as the "last dictator of Europe," i.e. a European statesperson capable of resolving a major international crisis. Thus for Belarus, Euromaidan, at the time of writing, appears to have been a mixed blessing, raising the prestige of official Minsk but at the same time restricting its independent actions. In economic terms, its impact can be considered serious, rather than catastrophic. Trade with Ukraine has suffered, but has not been cut off completely. Further, Russia may offer financial inducements, such as lower gas prices, to ensure Belarus keeps its present course. Ultimately though, the Belarusian authorities need Russian support, rather than the reverse, particularly with an election forthcoming in 2015. It is unlikely that Lukashenka will be remotely threatened by an alternative candidate in that election. On the other hand, Belarus' failure over the past two decades to undertake serious economic reforms leaves it in the position of seeking handouts from all parties, headed by Russia. Belarus' position is stable only compared to that of its southern and eastern neighbors. That statement is not to deny that the president has used the situation to his own advantage and partially succeeded in ameliorating his formerly very negative image in the EU.

---

46 "EU's Ashton says Ukraine talks were 'cordial, positive'," *Reuters*, August 26, 2014, positive"http://www.reuters.com/article/2014/08/26/ukraine-crisis-ashton-cordial-idUSL5N0QW4V020140826 (accessed August 27, 2014).

Understanding the Euromaidan:
The View from the Kremlin

Frederick V. Mills

Introduction

"We do not claim to be any sort of superpower with pretense to global or regional hegemony. We do not encroach on anyone's interests or impose our patronage on anyone..."[1]

Vladimir Putin, December 12, 2013

At no time in recent memory have Russia's actions more confounded and troubled the West than during the events of the Euromaidan. Contradicting Putin's claim during the 2013 State of the Nation Address to have no interest in "imposing patronage" and "encroaching on interests," in late February 2014, following an outbreak of violence in Kyiv and the flight and subsequent impeachment of then President Viktor Yanukovych, the Russian military established *de facto* control over strategic locations and key infrastructure throughout the Crimean peninsula. Subsequently, the Supreme Council of Crimea, the parliament for the Crimean Autonomous Republic, voted to hold a referendum on March 16, 2014. The people of Crimea were tasked with determining their fate—were they to unite with the Russian Federation or restore the 1992 constitution and remain *de jure* Ukrainians?

In what Timothy Snyder termed an "electoral farce...held under military occupation" the people of Crimea voted by a ratio of 24 to 1 to join with Russia.[2] Western politicians and pundits were incredulous about the legality of such a move, the veracity of its results, and Russia's behavior writ large. Catherine Ashton, then High Representative for Foreign Affairs and Security of the European Union, decried Moscow's "unwarranted escalation of tension" while German Chancellor Angela Merkel, in a telephone conversation with American President Barack Obama, questioned whether "[Putin] actually still has contact with reality" as it seems "he lives

---

1 "Presidential Address to the Federal Assembly," *President of Russia*, December 12, 2013, http://eng.kremlin.ru/news/6402 (accessed August 15, 2014).

2 Timothy Snyder, "Far Right Forces are Influencing Russia's Actions in Crimea," *The New Republic*, March 17, 2014, http://www.newrepublic.com/article/117048/crimean-referendum-was-electoral-farce (accessed August 18, 2014).

in a different world."[3] Canadian Foreign Minister John Baird opined that Russia's actions echoed the "ethnic nationalist justification" behind the German annexation of the Czechoslovakian Sudetenland in 1938.[4] Yet, amid all the sound and the fury emanating from Western capitals, a question receiving relatively little attention was "why?" Why has Putin steered the Russian state against the current of international opinion and toward the shoals of confrontation? Answers range from the nuanced, attributing the actions to Putin's apparent desire to subvert Kyiv's domestic and foreign politics and render Ukraine pliable to the Kremlin;[5] to the opportunistic, accusing Obama of being a weak and indecisive leader who invites global challenges;[6] to the pragmatic, offering the possibility that slower economic growth and a restive middle class might invite domestic tension if Russian society is not sufficiently distracted.[7]

This paper approaches Russian actions and the Euromaidan along two axes. First, in an attempt to understand the Kremlin's behaviors, this paper will outline Russia's key interests in Ukraine. What was at stake for Moscow if Kyiv gravitated towards Western institutions such as the EU, and how did Russia benefit when Ukraine decided to abjure the Association Agreement that was scheduled for November 28–29, 2013 in Vilnius?

---

3   "Statement by EU High Representative Catherine Ashton on the developments in Ukraine's Crimea," *European Union External Action*, March 1, 2014, http://eeas.eur opa.eu/statements/docs/2014/140301_01_en.pdf (accessed August 18, 2014); "Ukraine-Krisentelefont mit Obama, Merkel schimpft: Putin lebt in einer anderen Welt [Ukraine-Crisis Call with Obama, Merkel grumbles: Putin lives in Another World]," *Bild*, March 3, 2014, http://www.bild.de/politik/ausland/krim/merkel-schimpf t-im-obama-telefonat-ueber-putin-34911584.bild.html (accessed August 15, 2014).
4   Steven Chase, "Harper compares Russia's Crimea Moves to Third Reich Aggression," *The Globe and Mail*, March 4, 2014, http://www.theglobeandmail.com/ne ws/politics/canada-suspends-military-activities-with-russia/article17289679/ (accessed August 15, 2014).
5   David Blair, "What does Vladimir Putin want in Ukraine," *The Telegraph*, April 15, 2014, http://www.telegraph.co.uk/news/worldnews/vladimir-putin/10765533/What-d oes-Vladimir-Putin-want-in-Ukraine.html (accessed August 20, 2014).
6   Jeanne Zaino, "Did Vladimir Putin Really Invade Crimea Because He Perceives Barack Obama As 'Weak' On Foreign Policy?," *The International Business Times*, March 9, 2014, http://www.ibtimes.com/did-vladimir-putin-really-invade-crimea-bec ause-he-perceives-barack-obama-weak-foreign-policy (accessed August 15, 2014).
7   Anne Applebaum, "Putin Invaded Crimea because he Needs another War," *The National Post*, March 21, 2014, http://fullcomment.nationalpost.com/2014/03/21/a nne-applebaum-putin-invaded-crimea-because-putin-needs-a-war/ (accessed August 20, 2014).

Most western observers have argued that in turning away from Brussels, Yanukovych caved in to Russian economic blackmail. Though Kyiv's decision served Moscow's interests, in reality Ukrainian politicians had few available options to avoid further economic calamity. Second, this paper will document and examine official Russian statements and reactions to the events of the Euromaidan from November 21, 2013, the night of the first protests on Independence Square, to February 22, 2014, the day Yanukovych was deposed by the Ukrainian parliament. By focusing on the period before blatant Russian aggression, this paper will question teleological understandings of Putin's actions. Put another away, when did Putin decide to interfere in Ukrainian domestic politics? Was the Kremlin's meddling post-February 2014 simply the culmination of a "master plan" of power and control, as claimed by *The Economist* and other Western outlets and observers?[8]

Russian interests are inextricably linked to how Russia perceives the international environment. This essay argues that Putin's Kremlin has varied its foreign policy in degree, not in kind. Russia's reaction to the events of the Euromaidan, though simultaneously abhorrent and absurd, demonstrated an inherent logic and consistency directly related to its own understanding of regional and global affairs vis-à-vis its national interests. Though much has been written about the highs and lows of Russia's relations with the West in the twenty-first century, Russia's international behaviors and geo-political and geo-economic interests have been largely consistent. The apparently changing tenor of the relationship, rather, has been determined by an unwarranted polarity in Western thinking, torn between heady optimism—Russia's response to the attacks of 9/11—and indignant disappointment—Moscow's invasion of Georgia in 2008. Ultimately, Russia's actions can be understood through the lens of *Realpolitik*; they were logical, self-interested, and consistent with its worldview and regional objectives.

Russian Interests

Russia's national interests and the role of post-Soviet states are frequently associated in Russian foreign policy documents. The 2013 Concept of the Foreign Policy of the Russian Federation opined:

---

8   "Putin's Inferno," *The Economist*, pg. 4, February 22-28, 2014.

With a tendency for global decentralization, regional governance has emerged as a basis for the polycentric model of the world. New centers of economic growth and political power increasingly take responsibility for their respective regions. Regional integration becomes an effective means to increase competitiveness.[9]

Undoubtedly, the Kremlin views itself as the regional hegemon, as a *velikaya derzhava* [great power]. This is not a new development. The 2000 National Security Concept of the Russian Federation noted as a national interest "the strengthening [of] its position as a great power and as one of the influential centers of a multipolar world."[10] To this end, "Russia maintained its negative attitude towards the expansion of NATO, notably to the plans of admitting Ukraine and Georgia to the membership in the alliance, as well as to bringing the NATO military infrastructure closer to the Russian borders."[11] Deputy Foreign Minister Sergey Ryabkov clearly illustrated Russia's exclusive claim to its Near Abroad when he claimed in 2010 "[Russia] is fulfilling tasks traditional to any state, namely creating a friendly international environment. That space has no room for geo-political games, as the experience in Georgia and Ukraine shows."[12] Russia views perceived inroads made by western states and institutions into the post-Soviet space with disquiet, and it actively polices and chastens the behaviors of its former confederates. Ukraine, for example, tasted the Russian lash in 2006 and 2009 during the so-called gas wars. In 2006, Moscow attempted to gain control over the natural gas pipeline network in Ukraine and its transport pipeline system to Europe, while Ukraine wanted to maintain ownership in order to minimize Russia's ability to use gas exports as a political weapon. In 2009, Gazprom, in which the Russian government holds

9 "Concept of the Foreign Policy of the Russian Federation - Approved by President Vladimir Putin," *The Ministry of Foreign Affairs of the Russian Federation*, February 12, 2013, http://www.mid.ru/brp_4.nsf/0/76389FEC168189ED44257B2E0039B16D (accessed September 5, 2014).

10 "National Security Concept of the Russian Federation," *The Ministry of Foreign Affairs of the Russian* Federation, January 10, 2000, http://www.mid.ru/bdomp/ns-osndoc.nsf/1e5f0de28fe77fdcc32575d900298676/36aba64ac09f737fc32575d900 2bbf31!OpenDocument (accessed September 5, 2014).

11 "The Foreign Policy Concept of the Russian Federation," *President of Russia - Official Web* Portal, July 12, 2008, http://archive.kremlin.ru/eng/text/docs/2008/07 /204750.shtml (accessed September 5, 2014).

12 Sergey Ryabkov, "The View from Moscow: Q&A with the Deputy Minister of Foreign Affairs of the Russian Federation," *Journal of International Affairs* 63, no. 2 (2010): 207.

a 50.1% stake, simply shut off gas supplies to Ukraine over a bill $2 billion in arrears. Bertil Nygren goes so far as to argue that Putin's foreign policy towards former Soviet republics is driven by the goal to re-establish "Greater Russia"—"to re-establish Russian control over geographical areas where it originally established the Tsarist empire."[13] In line with Moscow's polycentric geo-political world view, the Kremlin seeks to direct regional integration favorably to its own interests, using an arsenal of political, economic and military levers. To paraphrase Lord Hastings Ismay's famous dictum on NATO, Moscow's policy towards its near abroad has been to keep the West out, Russia in, and post-Soviet states down. The lead up to the Euromaidan confirms this orientation in Russian policy.

Moscow looked with trepidation and alarm at the Ukraine-European Union Association Agreement—its potential signing posed a direct challenge to Russia's regional economic vision. The 2013 Foreign Policy Concept claimed:

> While respecting its Commonwealth partners' right to build relations with other international actors, Russia stands for the full implementation by the CIS Member States of their commitments within regional integration structures with Russian participation, ensuring further development of integration processes and mutually beneficial cooperation in the CIS space.[14]

As seen from Moscow, the association agreement between Kyiv and Brussels would have compromised Ukraine's ability to fulfill its treaty obligations to Commonwealth members as prescribed by the Commonwealth of Independent States' Free Trade Agreement, signed on October 19, 2011 in St. Petersburg.[15] Ukraine would simply be unable to harmonize domestic laws and policies to satisfy two different supranational economic policy institutions. This process of economic integration, according to Igor

---

13 Bertil Nygren, *The Rebuilding of Greater Russia - Putin's Foreign Policy towards the CIS* Countries (Routledge: New York, 2008), 8.

14 Concept of the Foreign Policy of the Russian Federation - Approved by President Vladimir Putin," *The Ministry of Foreign Affairs of the Russian Federation*, February 12, 2013, http://www.mid.ru/brp_4.nsf/0/76389FEC168189ED44257B2E0039B16D (accessed September 5, 2014).

15 "Most CIS Countries Sign Up to Free Trade Zone," *Radio Free Europe / Radio Liberty*, October 19, 2011, http://www.rferl.org/content/cis_putin_free-trade_zone/2436 4420.html (accessed September 7, 2014). Though the treaty was signed in October 2011, it went into effect in signatory countries on September 20, 2012.

Burakovsky, had from its very beginning a political component.[16] Whereas Russia has consistently tried to transform the CIS into a body of political and military cooperation, Ukraine has sought to limit its involvement to the economic sphere. The Kremlin aimed to "build relations with Ukraine as a priority Commonwealth partner and to contribute to its participation in extended integration processes."[17] Kyiv, however, would rather that integration occur à la carte and in line with its own interests and priorities. The 2009 Eastern Partnership Initiative between, in part, Ukraine and the EU, for example, signalled Kyiv's desire to improve political integration and to enhance economic association and labor mobility between Brussels and Ukraine.[18] Moscow saw such EU expansionism as tantamount to an invasion of Russia's traditional sphere of influence—Russian Prime Minister Dimitriy Medvedev went so far as to call the program useless and unnecessary.[19] Zbigniew Brzezinski famously said that "Ukraine, a new and important space on the Eurasian chessboard, is a geo-political pivot because its very existence as an independent country helps to transform Russia. Without Ukraine, Russia ceases to be a Eurasian empire." To some, Putin's actions regarding Ukraine in 2013 appear to be an attempt to reconstitute the former USSR. At the least, they are designed to maintain Russia's privileged regional position and to wield a level of domestic influence over an ostensibly sovereign state that ensures the Kremlin's voice is heard the loudest in Kyiv policy circles.

Throughout the spring and summer of 2013, statements and actions from the Kremlin clearly telegraphed Russia's displeasure regarding the possibility of the Association Agreement and represented a renewed chill in Russo-Ukrainian relations. Sergey Glazyev, Putin's top economic advisor, divined calamity for Kyiv should it choose economic integration with Europe. But as all good soothsayers know, predicting the future is risky

---

16 Igor Burakovsky, "Economic Integration and Security in the Post-Soviet Space," in *Swords and Sustenance: The Economics of Security in Belarus and Ukraine*, eds. Robert Legvold and Celeste Wallander (Cambridge: American Academy of Arts and Sciences, 2004), 168.

17 Ibid., 169.

18 "The Eastern Partnership: Flagship Initiatives," *European Union External Action*, http://eeas.europa.eu/eastern/initiatives/index_en.htm (accessed September 10, 2014).

19 "Lavrov: Russia could Join Eastern Partnership," *Hurriyet Daily* News, November 25, 2009, http://www.hurriyetdailynews.com/default.aspx?pageid=438&n=lavrov-ru ssia-could-join-eu-eastern-partnership-2009-11-25 (accessed September 10, 2014).

business. Refusing to trust the vagaries of chance, the Kremlin took active steps to ensure a measure of Ukraine's economic misfortune. For example, on July 29, 2013, the Federal Customs Service of Russia risibly banned the import of chocolate confections made by Ukrainian firm Roshen on food safety grounds. The concerns, however, were largely a pretext to pressure Ukraine politicians during a recent ebb in bilateral relations. Flimsy health and safety concerns have become a common weapon in Russia's arsenal; Gennadiy Onishchenko, Russia's chief health inspector, had also banned Georgian and Moldovan wine, Belarusian sugar and milk, and Ukrainian cheese within the previous twenty-four months.[20] In September 2013 during a press conference with Yanukovych, Glazyev claimed that signing the agreement would lead to a decline in living standards and spawn social chaos in Ukraine.[21] In early November at a conference in Kharkiv, he unambiguously stated that "over a dozen articles of Ukraine's draft Association Agreement with the EU violate [the Ukrainian-Russian treaty of friendship and cooperation,]" particularly Article 13 that stipulates that both parties refrain from potentially harmful reciprocal actions.[22] His vague legal and juridical arguments distracted from his fervent belief in the economic, political, and social benefits of the Eurasian Customs Union, a Moscow-dominated free trade pact with Minsk and Astana. In fact, Putin frequently referred to Glazyev's high assessment of the Union and often allowed him to act as the chief Russian representative on the need for Ukrainian membership.[23] Putin frequently wondered aloud about the consequences of Ukraine's closer ties with Euro-Atlantic structures,

---

20 Daisy Sindelar, "Moscow's Latest War On Good Taste: No To Ukrainian Chocolate," *Radio Free Europe / Radio Liberty*, July 30, 2013, http://www.rferl.org/content/russia-ukrainian-chocolate-ban/25060451.html (accessed August 20, 2014).

21 Shaun Walker, "Ukraine's EU trade deal will be catastrophic, says Russia," *The Guardian*, September 22, 2013, http://www.theguardian.com/world/2013/sep/22/ukraine-european-union-trade-russia (accessed August 21, 2013).

22 "Glazyev: Ukraine will fail to harmonize regulations with Customs Union if it signs association agreement with EU," *KyivPost*, November 4, 2013, http://www.kyivpost.com/content/politics/russian-presidential-adviser-sergei-glazyev-ukraine-will-fail-to-harmonize-regulations-with-customs-union-if-it-signs-association-agreement-with-eu-331387.html (accessed August 25, 2014).

23 Anders Åslund,"Sergey Glazyev and the revival of Soviet Economics," *Post-Soviet Affairs* 29, no. 5 (2013): 379.

warning Kyiv about inevitable economic protectionism and higher non-tariff barriers for Ukrainian goods.[24]

Much ink has been spilled regarding Russia's alleged economic blackmail of Ukraine during the fall of 2013. Russian First Deputy Prime Minister Igor Shuvalo noted that Ukraine faced an either-or decision—either sign the Association Agreement and move perceptibly towards free trade and harmonization with the European Union or join the Customs Union and align itself with a Russian-dominated idea of Eurasia.[25] In response, Ukraine's then Minister of Trade Petro Poroshenko went so far to claim that it was "the Kremlin's heavy-handed tactics and threats of a trade war that made European integration inevitable."[26] Warsaw's then-Foreign Minister, Radek Sikorski, one of the founders of the Eastern Partnership Initiative, claimed "it was only when Ukraine was properly allied with Europe that Russia would begin to respect the country." Yet, even the headiest strains of "Eurothusiasm" could not deny the troubles faced by the Ukrainian economy and its already close integration with Russia. The global financial crisis severely affected Ukraine. According to the World Bank, the Ukrainian economy contracted by roughly 14.5% in 2009. In 2012, the gross domestic product increased by an anemic 0.5%, while in 2013 the economy shrank about 1%.[27] During the 2000s, Moscow had invested heavily in Ukrainian industry. In that period, for example, Russian investors accounted for 90% of total foreign direct investment in Ukraine's aluminum industry, over 80% in its oil refining capability, and slightly over 50% of total foreign investment into its telecommunication infrastructure.[28] The collapse of the Soviet Union marked a political disintegration between

---

24 Alexei Anishchuk, "Putin warns Ukraine over Europe Ambitions," *Reuters*, September 19, 2013, http://www.reuters.com/article/2013/09/19/us-russia-ukraine-putin-idU SBRE98I0WB20130919 (accessed August 10, 2014).

25 "Russian deputy premier: Ukraine cannot have both Customs Union and EU free trade zone," *KyivPost*, October 24, 2013, http://www.kyivpost.com/content/russia-and-former-soviet-union/russian-deputy-premier-ukraine-cannot-have-both-customs-union-and-eu-free-trade-zone-330960.html (accessed August 10, 2014).

26 Walker, "Ukraine's EU trade deal," *The Guardian*, September 22, 2014, http://www.theguardian.com/world/2013/sep/22/ukraine-european-union-trade-russia (accessed August 21, 2014).

27 "Country Profile—Ukraine," *The World Bank*, http://data.worldbank.org/country/u kraine (accessed September 10, 2014).

28 Elena Kropatcheva, *Russia's Ukraine Policy against the Background of Russian-Western Competition* (Institute for Peace Research and Security Policy: Hamburg, 2010), 185.

the former federal republics, not an economic one. Economic links were and are strong between the two countries. As seen from the Kremlin, Russian economic interests are best served by Ukraine's continued participation in post-Soviet economic arrangements. Indeed, the practical difficulties that would accompany implementing the Association Agreement would be considerable. Russia and Ukraine already have myriad agreements ranging from engineering standards, veterinary transport, and pharmacology, to a series of reciprocal tariff incentives, similar tax codes, and banking harmonization. Yanukovych has been pilloried for selling out Ukraine's future by turning away from Europe and Putin has been accused of economic extortion. Clearly, Russian interests are served by closer economic integration with Kyiv. However, even the EU admits that the economic benefits accrued to Ukraine from the Association Agreement would only materialize in the long term.[29] Ukraine's producers would eventually have access to the world's largest free trade area and EU rules and protocols could potentially improve the overall business climate. But the country would be required, in return, to introduce difficult and sweeping reforms with the intent to increase transparency, reduce corruption, and raise production standards. Russia's concern over the association agreement stems from its perceived loss of privilege within the Ukrainian market. But a short-term calamity in Ukraine caused by the Association Agreement would be bad for Russian interests, too. Russian investors and banks would be heavily exposed during an economic crisis in Ukraine. Ukraine's roughly 45 million people would also consume fewer Russian imports. Even the most "Russoskeptic" observer cannot deny the degree of economic integration between Kyiv and Moscow and the difficulty that would accompany Ukraine's westward march.

The economic links between the two states and the agreement's potential impact on Ukraine were indeed the basis for Russia's cautionary stance on the association agreement. In 2013, Russia was Ukraine's largest trading partner, in terms of both imports and exports, and its largest source of foreign direct investment.[30] By August 2013, Kyiv's annual budget deficit of $4.4 billion was twice as high as in the corresponding period of

---

29 "Ukraine's Sink or Swim EU Agreement," *BBC News—Europe*, June 27, 2014, http://www.bbc.com/news/world-europe-28044480 (accessed September 5, 2014).

30 "Ukraine Trade Statistics," *United Nations International Merchandise Trade Statistics* 2013, http://comtrade.un.org/pb/CountryPagesNew.aspx?y=2013 (accessed August 25, 2014).

the previous year and was principally financed by Russian bond purchases. Although the Ukrainian public sector was not as heavily indebted as some of its fellow European states, the high budget deficit and relatively short maturity of government debt obligations certainly added to short-term fiscal and foreign liquidity pressures.[31] According to the National Bank of Ukraine, total annual debt repayments amounted to over $60 billion as of June 2013.[32] Not only was Russia the principal buyer of Ukrainian bonds, but efforts to secure monetary tranches from Western institutions have been historically less than fruitful. The Kremlin has frequently served as the lender of last resort to Ukraine. In both 2011 and 2012, Ukraine received no disbursements from its 2010 Stand-By Agreement with the International Monetary Fund because of its failure to implement required structural adjustment and subsidy reduction.[33] A $16.4 billion IMF loan from 2008 was suspended in 2010 when Kyiv raised the national minimum wage and pensions payments.[34]

The composition of the Ukrainian economy also portends a difficult integration within the European Union. For example, metals and mineral products account for almost 40% of Ukraine's exports. Though Russia received roughly a quarter of Ukraine's total exports in 2012, it received roughly three-quarters of Kyiv's metals and mineral production. The largest export sector of Ukraine's economy was certainly tied more closely with Moscow than it was with Brussels. Even value-added products such as

31 "2013 Investment Climate Statement – Ukraine," *U.S. Department of State*, February 2013, http://www.state.gov/e/eb/rls/othr/ics/2013/204754.htm (accessed August 25, 2014). Ukraine's national public debt is 37% of its total gross domestic product. One can compare this to Belgium at 99%, Italy 126%, and Greece at 161%. Source: "Public Debt," *CIA World Fact Book*, 2013.
32 Olga Pogarska, Edilberto L. Segura, SigmaBleyzer Private Equity Firm, and The Bleyzer Foundation, "Ukraine Macro-Economic Situation—October 2013," *U.S.-Ukraine Business Council*, November 11, 2013, http://www.usubc.org/site/sigmableyzer-macroeconomic-reports/ukraine-macroeconomic-situation-october-2013 (accessed August 30, 2014).
33 "2013 Investment Climate Statement—Ukraine," *U.S. Department of State*, February 2013, http://www.state.gov/e/eb/rls/othr/ics/2013/204754.htm (accessed August 25, 2014).
34 Yuri Kulikov and Sabina Zawadzki, "UPDATE 2-Ukraine seeks to overhaul IMF deal, tough talks ahead," *Reuters*, March 24, 2010, http://www.reuters.com/article/2010/03/24/ukraine-imf-idUSLDE62N0U620100324 (accessed August 31, 3014), "IMF Approves US$16.4 Billion Stand-By Arrangement for Ukraine," *International Monetary Fund*, November 5, 2008, https://www.imf.org/external/np/sec/pr/2008/pr08271.htm (accessed August 31, 2014).

machine parts and transportation equipment were more frequently traded with Russia than with the entire European Union.[35] Ukraine, for example, is the world's largest seller of railway freight cars, producing slightly over 50% of global supply; the states of the Eurasian Customs Union import almost two-thirds, 65.49%, of railway cars globally.[36] In September 2013, Kyiv's foreign exchange reserves shrank to under $20 billion, or 2.3 months' worth of imports. As a result, Moody's downgraded Ukraine's government bond rating from B3 to Caa1 and cautioned the possibility of further downgrades.[37] This resulted in a 3.5% increase to the interest rate on a two-year government bond, costing Kyiv an additional $800 million in bond-related interest payments.[38] This move was caused by the "increased political and economic risks [to Ukraine] due to deteriorating relations with Russia, following expectations that Kyiv will sign an Association Agreement with the EU."[39] Indeed, in the short term Ukraine's macroeconomic health would have been better served by the continuation of the economic status quo.

More pointedly, Western institutions often require systemic reforms that demand the purging of naughty elements of political and economic governance, such as corruption and nepotism. In this regard, the Association Agreement placed considerable demands on Ukraine. In 2013, Ukraine was ranked 137th of 185 states in the World Bank's "Ease of Doing Business" index, 161st of 177 in the Heritage Institute's "Economic Freedom" rankings, and 144th of 176 in Transparency International's "Corruption Index" (flanked by Syria and Eritrea).[40] A 2009 report claimed that

---

35 "Ukraine: Country Profile," *Observatory of Economic Complexity*, http://atlas.medi a.mit.edu/profile/country/ukr/ (accessed September 1, 2014).

36 "Railway Freight Cars," *Observatory of Economic Complexity*, http://atlas.medi a.mit.edu/profile/hs/8606/ (accessed September 1, 2014).

37 "Rating Action: Moody's downgrades Ukraine's government bond rating to Caa1 from B3 and places the rating on review for downgrade," *Moody's Investors Service*, September 20, 2013, https://www.moodys.com/research/Moodys-downgrad es-Ukraines-government-bond-rating-to-Caa1-from-B3--PR_282707   (accessed September 5, 2014). Such a rating indicates a 50% possibility of a national default within five years.

38 "Ukraine Bond Yields," *Investing.com*, http://www.investing.com/rates-bonds/ukrai ne-2-year-bond-yield (accessed September 5, 2014).

39 "Rating Action," *Moody's*, September 20, 2013, https://www.moodys.com/research /Moodys-downgrades-Ukraines-government-bond-rating-to-Caa1-from-B3-- PR_282707 (accessed September 5, 2014).

40 "Corruption Perceptions Index – 2012," *Transparency International*, 2012, http://www.transparency.org/cpi2012/results (accessed September 1, 2014).

Ukraine's shadow economy was almost equal in size to its official econo-my.[41] Russian financial assistance, however, demanded neither good gov-ernance reforms nor structural adjustment. The Kremlin's most recent for-eign policy concept calls for "the promotion of Russia's approach to human rights issues," which does not include linking loans and economic assis-tance to domestic democratic reforms.[42] In fall 2013, Ukraine desperately needed additional assistance to conduct the rigorous and unpopular re-forms needed to fulfill the association agreement's prerequisites.[43] The Eu-ropean economy's continued languor coupled with the rise of Euroskeptic political parties in the United Kingdom and Eastern European states pre-empted assistance of the magnitude and duration needed for Ukraine's successful evolutionary transition towards Europe. Ultimately, Yanukovych faced a stark choice: Ukraine could either receive subsidies and loans from Moscow or try to enact expensive self-funded reforms in the hope of accru-ing future benefits from European integration and trade. According to Taras Kuzio, Yanukovych was Ukraine's most pro-Russian president of the post-Soviet era.[44] However, perhaps his choice to suspend the Association Agreement was a short-term act of political pragmatism. Economic realities rather than European aspirations ultimately dominated the calculus in Kyiv. Whereas the European Union demanded costly and sweeping domestic reforms in Ukraine, Moscow, seen through the most imperial and imperi-

41 Boris Davidenko, "Polovina ukrainskoi ekonomiki—v teni [Half of the Ukrainian economy is in the shadows]," *delo.ua*, December 7, 2009, http://delo.ua/ukraine/polovina-ukrainskoj-ekonomiki--134903/ (accessed August 15, 2014).

42 "Concept of the Foreign Policy of the Russian Federation—Approved by President Vladimir Putin," *The Ministry of Foreign Affairs of the Russian Federation*, February 12, 2013, http://www.mid.ru/brp_4.nsf/0/76389FEC168189ED44257B2E0039B16D (accessed September 5, 2014).

43 Taras Kuzio, "Ukraine at Crossroads after Rejecting EU Pact" *Al-Jazeera America*, November 29, 2013, http://america.aljazeera.com/opinions/2013/11/ukraine-at-crossroadsafterrejectingeupact.html (accessed September 1, 2014)."Russia offers Ukraine major economic assistance," *BBC News Europe*, December 17, 2013, http://www.bbc.com/news/world-europe-25411118 (accessed September 1, 2014). The most the EU was willing to guarantee Ukraine was a onetime payment of €790 million ($970.4 million). Laurence Norman, "Barroso Says EU Can Give Ukraine At Most $1 Billion to Pay Bills," *The Wall Street Journal*, October 23, 2014, http://www.wsj.com/articles/barroso-says-eu-can-give-ukraine-at-most-1-billion-to-pay-bills-1414113265 (accessed September 5, 2014).

44 Taras Kuzio, *The Crimea: Europe's Next Flashpoint?* (Washington DC: The Jame-stown Foundation, 2010), 4. Accessed at http://www.peacepalacelibrary.nl/ebooks/files/372451918.pdf.

ous lens, demanded influence over Ukraine's foreign and domestic orientations. Yanukovych pragmatically compromised, delaying European integration until Ukraine returned to macroeconomic health, while negotiating financial assistance from the Kremlin.

Moscow was surely pleased when on November 21, 2013, the Ukrainian Cabinet of Ministers issued a decree that suspended the Association Agreement on the grounds that a more detailed study was needed to quantify its negative economic consequences, such as lost trade with Russia and other states. Moreover, the decree requested "an active dialogue with the Russian Federation and other countries of the Customs Union and the CIS for the revitalization of trade and economic ties with the aim of preserving and strengthening the joint efforts and economic potential of all states."[45] On the same day, the Ukrainian government also announced that it would start to formulate an official regional development strategy for national economic growth.[46] At a press conference in Moscow, spokesman for the Russian Federation Dmitriy Peskov described Ukraine as a "close partner" and welcomed the opportunity to develop closer trade and economic linkages with Kyiv.[47] Within a month of his foreign policy demarche, Yanukovych inked an agreement with Putin that saw the Kremlin agree to purchase more than $15 billion worth of Ukrainian government bonds and slash the cost of Russian gas supplied to Ukraine by more than a third.[48] Then Prime Minister Mykola Azarov claimed that "this will allow us to im-

---

45 "Pravitelstvo prinyalo rasporyazhenie o priostanovlenii protsessa podgotovki k zaklyucheniyu Soglashenyia ob assotsiatsii s EC [The government has adopted an order to suspend the preparations for the association agreement with the EU]," *Department of Communications and Information of the Government of Ukraine,* November 21, 2013, http://www.kmu.gov.ua/control/ru/publish/article?art_id=246866 715 (accessed September 5, 2014).

46 "Pravitelstvo rassmotrit Gosudarstvennuyu strategiyu regionalnogo razvitiya na period do 2020 goda [The government will consider the State strategy for regional development up to 2020]," *Department of Communications and Information of the Government of Ukraine,* November 21, 2013, http://www.kmu.gov.ua/control /ru/publish/article?art_id=246863801 (accessed September 5, 2014).

47 Ian Traynor and Oksana Grytsenko, "Ukraine suspends talks on EU trade pact as Putin wins tug of war," *The Guardian,* November 21, 2013, http://www.theguardian .com/world/2013/nov/21/ukraine-suspends-preparations-eu-trade-pact (accessed September 5, 2014).

48 "Russia offers Ukraine major economic assistance," *BBC News Europe,* December 17, 2014, http://www.bbc.com/news/world-europe-25411118 (accessed September 1, 2014). The new price per cubic meter was also to be applied retroactively to Ukraine's $1.7 billion gas bill.

plement large scale development projects, and undertake industrial and infrastructure upgrades."[49] These sanguine economic predictions, however, did little to mollify the staunch and growing opposition to Kyiv's deceleration of European integration. Moscow looked with increasing alarm as protests increased in intensity and spread throughout Ukraine. Although Russia's 2013 foreign policy concept acknowledges the importance of soft power as "an indispensable component of modern international relations," the Kremlin was notably tone deaf in its early approaches to the Euromaidan. Political and economic competition with Europe, waged in a zero-sum international environment, dominated the Kremlin's early calculus on the Association Agreement and the Euromaidan protests. More sophisticated rationales, entirely consistent with its interests and understanding of global affairs, were quickly forthcoming from Moscow.

Russian Reaction to the Euromaidan

Russian reaction to the Euromaidan protest movement was decidedly negative. Two principal arguments against the protests were pursued simultaneously. The first was a quickly abandoned reasoning on the illegality of the Association Agreement inasmuch as it contravened pre-existing Russo-Ukrainian agreements, while the second was a focus on the undemocratic and the extent of foreign influence in the protests. At a press conference in Trieste with Italian Prime Minister Enrico Letta, Putin expounded this rationale: "If we maintain a free trade zone with Ukraine, we have every reason to believe that goods originating in Europe will directly enter our market, transiting through Ukraine's territory either as European products, or labeled as Ukrainian goods. This poses a serious threat to our economy."[50] Russian Foreign Minister Sergey Lavrov used a similar argument when he stated that the Ukraine-EU Association Agreement would undermine the tariff and non-tariff protections of certain aspects of the economy afforded to Moscow during its ascension negotiations with the

---

49 "Premer-ministr: President Ukrainy dogovorilsya ob ochen vygodnykh usloviyakh kreditovaniya ukrainskoi ekonomiki [Prime Minister: The President of Ukraine has arranged very favorable terms of credit for the Ukrainian economy]," *Department of Communications and Information of the Government of Ukraine,* December 17, 2013, http://www.kmu.gov.ua/control/ru/publish/article?art_id=246924561 (acessed September 5, 2014).

50 "Russian-Italian Interstate Consultations," *The President of Russia,* November 26, 2013, http://eng.kremlin.ru/news/6335 (accessed September 4, 2014).

World Trade Organization. He went on to claim "the creation of a free trade zone between Ukraine and the European Union is incompatible with the privileged regime between [Russia and Ukraine] within the framework of the CIS free trade zone."[51]

Unsurprisingly, such arguments failed to influence protesters in Kyiv. Ukrainian opposition leader and current Prime Minister Arsenii Yatsenyuk implied that the government's decision was state treason—"this is a well-planned scenario by Yanukovych: how to sell the Ukrainian state and to buy himself a seat of the governor of Little Russia as part of the Great Russian empire."[52] Almost as soon as protesters gathered on Independence Square, the Kremlin launched its most sustained critiques of the Euromaidan that focused on alleged foreign interference and manipulation, and the violent and undemocratic nature of the protests. On November 22, 2013, Putin accused the EU of attempting to blackmail Ukraine into the Association Agreement, claiming, "we have heard threats from our European partners towards Ukraine, up to and including promoting mass protests."[53] Putin offered similar arguments in an interview with RIA Novosti on December 2, 2013 when he claimed that the Ukrainian opposition was attempting to destabilize the country's legitimate rulers in order to achieve victory in the 2015 elections.[54] During a press conference with Armenian President Serzh Sargsyan, Putin provocatively compared the so-called revolution to a "pogrom" and denied its pro-European orientations, declaring it a front for extremist elements.[55]

In response to *Berkut*'s failed attempt to disperse the Euromaidan on December 11, 2013, and the presence of foreign politicians on the square, Russian Prime Minister Dimitriy Medvedev warned of a "tectonic split" in

---

51 "Interview by the Russian Foreign Minister Sergey Lavrov to RIA Novosti news agency, Moscow," *The Ministry of Foreign Affairs of the Russian Federation*, December 20, 2013, http://www.mid.ru/bdomp/brp_4.nsf/e78a48070f128a7b4325699 9005bcbb3/b507ffc4347e4fdc44257c4e0059d4fc!OpenDocument (accessed September 4, 2014).

52 "Ukrainians rally over government's snub to EU," *BBC News Europe*, November 22, 2013, http://www.bbc.com/news/world-europe-25050202 (accessed September 10, 2014).

53 Ibid.

54 "Putin: aktsii v Kieve podgotovleny izvne, eto ne revolyutsiya, a pogrom [Putin: Events in Kyiv orchestrated from abroad, they are not a revolution but a pogrom]," *RIA Novosti*, December 2, 2013, http://ria.ru/politics/20131202/981344124.html (accessed September 5, 2014).

55 Ibid.

Ukrainian politics due to "crude interference" from Western states.[56] For example, Medvedev had in mind US Senator John McCain's statements on the square that "[the United States] supports [the protesters'] just cause" and that Putin views Ukraine as the "crown jewel" in the post-Soviet "near abroad."[57] In an interview with a Russian broadcaster, Lavrov unapologetically declared that "our Western partners seem to have lost their sense of reality [and this] makes [me] very sad."[58] He criticized Europe's greed and interventionism and rationalized Western interference on the grounds that the European Union was luring Ukraine because of its lucrative markets "which would be flooded and wiped out by more competitive EU products."[59] During the tumultuous days in December 2013, the Kremlin tried to position itself as a concerned though respectful partner of Ukraine. In his State of the Nation address, Putin declared "we do not impose ourselves on anybody… and I very much hope that [Ukraine's] political forces will be able to negotiate [their] accumulated problems."[60] Moscow clearly did not anticipate the intensity and duration of the protests; however, it seems that key figures in the Kremlin also failed to grasp the underlying *cri de coeur* of Euromaidan participants.

As seen from the Kremlin, the initial stages of the protest movement involved the European aspirations of a disaffected minority. Yanukovych's actions were grounded in traditional power politics—Russia and the European Union battled over Ukraine, and, as one British analyst put it, "[the EU] went to knife fight with a baguette."[61] Russia won. What the Kremlin

56 "Ukraine court frees protesters held after Kiev clashes," *BBC News Europe*, December 13, 2013, http://www.bbc.com/news/world-europe-25367770 (accessed September 5, 2014).

57 "John McCain tells Ukraine protesters: 'We are here to support your just cause'," *The Guardian*, December 15, 2013, http://www.theguardian.com/world/2013/dec/15/john-mccain-ukraine-protests-support-just-cause (accessed September 5, 2014).

58 "West has 'lost sense of reality' over Ukraine: Russia," *Tengri News*, December 14, 2013, http://en.tengrinews.kz/politics_sub/West-has-lost-sense-of-reality-over-Ukraine-Russia-24729/ (accessed September 6, 2014).

59 "Provocations, EU's financial interests behind Ukraine protests—Lavrov," *RT*, December 14, 2013, http://rt.com/news/lavrov-ukraine-criticism-provocations-243/ (accessed September 5, 2014).

60 "Presidential Address to the Federal Assembly," *President of Russia*, December 12, 2013, http://eng.kremlin.ru/news/6402 (accessed August 15, 2014).

61 Robert McConnell, "Ukraine in the News 3-21-14 Vol. I / Issue 100," *U.S.-Ukraine Business Council*, March 21, 2014, http://www.usubc.org/site/recent-news/ukraine-in-the-news-3-21-14-vol-i-issue-100 (accessed September 1, 2014).

failed to understand was the depth and strength of Ukrainian dissatisfaction. After the first attempt to clear the square with violence on November 30, 2013, the movement was no longer principally about a pro-Europe orientation. Rather, according to one observer "the villainy belongs solely to Yanukovych, whose government [protestors] regard as something like a cross between a Mafia family and a Soviet puppet regime."[62] Yanukovych, in this reading, simply decided to sell his country to Russia for his and his cronies' financial aggrandizement. The nature of the Euromaidan turned from a protest movement into a revolutionary movement when faced with state-sanctioned violence. Ukrainians' perception of their state as an economic and political southern rump to its northern hegemon was scarcely tolerable; when the kleptocracy loosed violence on peaceful protesters, its already tenuous legitimacy collapsed. As during the Orange Revolution of 2004–05, the Kremlin initially misjudged the nature of the protests. When the protests intensified, the Kremlin realized that though it had significant influence over Ukraine's political elite, it lacked adequate levers to control the country as a whole. When the Kremlin realized the limitations on its power, it altered its message in two important ways.

First, the Kremlin started to label segments of the protestorate as ideological radicals and ultranationalists. According to Andreas Umland and Anton Shekhovtsov, "Russian officials, [Russia's] leading diplomats, pseudo-journalists, and Western lobbyists, extensively use hyperbolic half-truths and alarmist messages regarding the radical right of Ukraine in order to discredit the Euromaidan as, at least in part, fascist."[63] Speaking at the Munich Security Conference, Lavrov chided European leaders who failed to condemn "those who have occupied and still hold administrative buildings, attack policemen, set them on fire, use racist, anti-Semitic and Nazi slogans."[64] Russian state propaganda frequently labelled and demonized

62 Andrey Slivka, "Rage in Ukraine," *The New Yorker*, December 11, 2013, http://www.newyorker.com/news/news-desk/rage-in-kiev?utm_source=www&utm_medium=tw&utm_campaign=20131211 (accessed September 7, 2014).
63 Andreas Umland and Anton Shekhovtsov, "Ukrainskie pravye radikaly, evrointegratsiya i neofashistskaya ugroza [Ukrainian right-wing radicals, European integration and the neo-fascist threat]," *Polit.ru*, May 21, 2014, http://www.polit.ru/article/2014/05/21/ukraine/ (accessed September 6, 2014).
64 "Speech by the Russian Foreign Minister, Sergey Lavrov, at the 50th Munich Security Conference," *The Ministry of Foreign Affairs of the Russian Federation*, February 1, 2014,

political groups and accused them of staging attacks against Russian speakers and Jews.[65]

Marta Dyczok's contribution in this collection explains Russia's attempt to frame the production of information about the Euromaidan and its participants, particularly the anti-Semitic and fascist character of the protesters. This is entirely consistent with the 2008 and 2013 Foreign Policy Concepts that state "Russia will seek to ensure its objective perception in the world, develop its own effective means of information influence on public opinion abroad, and strengthen the role of Russian mass media in the international information environment providing them with essential state support."[66] She argues that Western media outlets largely took Moscow's bait and instead of focusing on the origins and grievances of the revolution were preoccupied with the unsavory ideological aspects of a minority of protesters who represented an even smaller minority of the total population.[67] To be clear, *Svoboda* and *Pravyi Sektor*, the small but highly visible nationalist groups frequently cited in western and Russian media, could easily be labeled as radical, non-democratic movements without European sympathies. Both groups valorize Stepan Bandera, a highly polarizing Second World War-era Ukrainian nationalist who fought against the Red Army. For Ukrainian nationalists he is a hero beyond reproach who used guerrilla tactics against the Soviet Union for Ukraine's freedom. Problematically, however, his Organization of Ukrainian Nationalists-B battalions also participated in the slaughter of Jewish and Polish civilians. According to Umland, "Russian historians portray him as a fascist ally of the Nazis, while Ukrainian historians praise him without reserve."[68] Hanna Kozlowska contends

http://www.mid.ru/bdomp/brp_4.nsf/e78a48070f128a7b43256999005b cbb3/90c4d89f4bf2b54344257c76002ace67!OpenDocument (accessed September 1, 2014).

65 Maria Danilova, "After Ukraine protest, radical group eyes power," *AP*, March 14, 2014, http://bigstory.ap.org/article/after-ukraine-protest-radical-group-eyes-power (accessed August 30, 2014).

66 Concept of the Foreign Policy of the Russian Federation – Approved by President Vladimir Putin," *The Ministry of Foreign Affairs of the Russian Federation*, February 12, 2013, http://www.mid.ru/brp_4.nsf/0/76389FEC168189ED44257B2E0039B16D (accessed September 5, 2014).

67 Marta Dyczok, "Mass Media Framing, Representations, and Impact on Public Opinion," in *Ukraine's Euromaidan—Analyses of a Civil Revolution*, eds. David R. Marples and Frederick V. Mills (Stuttgart: *ibidem*-Verlag, 2015), 77-94.

68 Andreas Umland, "Ukraine, Russia and the EU," *Le monde diplomatique*, December, 2013, http://mondediplo.com/blogs/ukraine-russia-and-the-eu

that the Kremlin succeeded in painting these groups as powerful neo-Nazi forces intent on taking over Ukraine, though their electoral results clearly highlight the fringe nature of these political forces.[69] Moscow's media management and misdirection advanced its interests and Russia was able, to a certain degree, to influence the international narrative on the Euromaidan protests.

Second, and building on this narrative of Euromaidan radicalization, the Kremlin began to label the protesters as dangerous while positioning Moscow as a potential stabilizing force. In a question-and-answer session with reporters in Novo-Ogaryevo, Putin stated "if we see this lawlessness starting in eastern regions [of Ukraine], if the people ask us for help, then we reserve the right to use all the means we possess to protect those citizens."[70] Moreover, Putin has positioned Russia as the defender of its ethnic Diaspora in the post-Soviet space. The 2013 foreign policy concept claims that the Russian Diaspora is an international partner and that the protection of its rights and interests fall within the purview of the Kremlin.[71] Russian reportage certainly portrayed the protesters as a horde of hooligans funded by the West to topple Ukraine's legitimate government and sow chaos.[72] Consistent with Russia's right to extraterritoriality when ethnic Russians are in danger, Kremlin-run state media also linked developments in Ukraine to civilizational arguments against European integration. Protesters posed a concrete danger and represented an existential threat to innocent civilians. The Kremlin's argument was based upon values, par-

---

(September 1, 2014).

69 Hanna Kozlowska, "The Fascists Are Coming, the Fascists Are Coming!," *FP*, February 6, 2014, http://foreignpolicy.com/2014/06/02/the-fascists-are-coming-the-fascists-are-coming/ (accessed September 1, 2014). Dmytro Yarosh, leader of *Pravyi Sektor*, received just 0.7% of the popular vote in the May 2014 Presidential Election.

70 "Putin: Deploying military force is last resort, but we reserve right," *RT*, March 4, 2014, http://rt.com/news/putin-statement-ukraine-russia-743/ (accessed September 5, 2014).

71 Concept of the Foreign Policy of the Russian Federation – Approved by President Vladimir Putin," *The Ministry of Foreign Affairs of the Russian Federation*, February 12, 2013, http://www.mid.ru/brp_4.nsf/0/76389FEC168189ED44257B2E0039B16D (accessed September 5, 2014).

72 Claire Bigg, "Ukraine's 'Euromaidan' Through the Lens of Russian Television," *Radio Free Europe / Radio Liberty*, December 9, 2013, http://www.rferl.org/content/u kraine-euromaidan-russian-media/25194912.html (accessed September 1, 2014).

ticularly the moral decadence and degeneracy of the West. Dmitriy Kiselyev, the director of the state-run Russian media conglomerate *Rossiya
Segodnya* and a noted homophobe who once said that if gays were killed
in car crashes "their hearts should be buried in the ground or burnt as unfit
for helping to prolong anyone's life," successfully weaponized gay rights
and turned them against the process of European integration. For example, Kiselyev derisively dismissed Vitalii and Volodymyr Klychko as legitimate Ukrainian politicians because they met with the gay former German
Foreign Minister Guido Westerwelle.[73] Snyder claims that Yanukovych's
government pursued a similar strategy when it claimed that closer relations
with the European Union demanded recognition of gay marriage in
Ukraine.[74] Highlighting the degree to which these lies infiltrated Ukrainian
society, William Risch's chapter in this collection recounts a conversation
he heard at a birthday party in Donetsk in which attendees were concerned
about European integration because it would unleash same-sex marriages,
lower education standards, and diminished respect for authority figures.[75]

The Kremlin's value-based objections to the Euromaidan stem, in part,
from a worldview known as "Eurasianism", which was first developed in the
1920s by Russian emigrants to Europe and the United States who merged
elements of anti-liberalism, nationalism, and anti-Semitism. Ingo Mannteufel contends that until recently "these were marginal views, held by political crackpots and conspiracy theorists."[76] However, in Putin's remarks
and policies since 2011, echoes of Eurasianism have become increasingly
apparent.[77] At its core, the Eurasianism put forward by academics like Ale-

---

73 Bigg, "Ukraine's 'Euromaidan'," *Radio Free Europe / Radio Liberty*, December 9,
    2013,   http://www.rferl.org/content/ukraine-euromaidan-russian-media/25194912.h
    tml (accessed September 1, 2014).

74 Timothy Snyder, "Ukraine: The Haze of Propaganda," *The New York Review of
    Books*,   March   1,   2014,   http://www.nybooks.com/blogs/nyrblog/2014/mar/01/uk
    raine-haze-propaganda/ (accessed August 20, 2014).

75 William   Risch,   "EuroRevolution: A   Historian's   Street-Side   Observations,"   in
    Ukraine's Euromaidan—Analyses of a Civil Revolution, eds. David R. Marples and
    Frederick V. Mills (Stuttgart: *ibidem*-Verlag, 2015), 107-122.

76 Ingo   Mannteufel,   "Putin's   Dangerous   Eurasian   Idea,"   *DW*,   May   29,   2014,
    http://www.dw.de/opinion-putins-dangerous-eurasian-idea/a-17670509   (accessed
    September 20, 2014).

77 Timothy Snyder, "Fascism, Russia, and Ukraine, " *The New York Review of Books*,
    March   20,   2014,   http://www.nybooks.com/articles/archives/2014/mar/20/fascism-
    russia-and-ukraine/ (accessed August 20, 2014), Paul Pryce, "Putin's Third Term:

ksandr Dugin, a popular figure within Putin's inner circle, idolizes medieval Muscovy, places considerable importance on the role of Orthodoxy within Russian society, emphasizes Russia's Eurasian civilizational foundation, and is deeply patriarchal.[78] It rejects both Western entreaties for partnership and the notion that Western liberalism has relevance for Russian society. Dugin's magnum opus *The Foundations of Geopolitics: The Geopolitical Future of Russia*, used as a foundational text in the General Staff Academy of the Russian Federation's Armed Forces, argues that Ukraine should not be allowed to remain independent as it represents an "enormous danger" for all of Eurasia.[79] Though the Kremlin never spoke in such frank language, it is clear that its interests were not served by Ukraine's gravitation westward.

Conclusion

Looking south from Red Square, the events of the Euromaidan certainly undermined Russia's influence in Ukrainian politics. Putin may have won an initial victory by offering Kyiv much needed economic inducements to turn away from Brussels, but Moscow's opportunity to consolidate its gains was ephemeral. The Kremlin clearly acted to ensure that other states did not materially or strategically benefit at its expense; Russia, in the words of noted political theorist Kenneth Waltz, acted "not to maximize power, but to maintain its position in the international system."[80] However, as the size and demands of the Euromaidan movement grew to challenge the legitimacy of the Yanukovych regime, Russian actions escalated to simply maintain its position in the international system vis-à-vis Ukraine. Yanukovych's flight first to Donetsk and then to Moscow signalled the collapse of Russia's influence over Ukrainian developments. To prevent the further encroachment of European institutions westward, Putin decided first to send Russian Special Forces into Crimea and then to destabilize Ukraine further by training and arming the separatist fighters of the self-declared

---

The Triumph of Eurasianism?," *Romanian Journal of European Affairs* 13, no.1 (March 2013): 27–29.

78 Ibid., 30.

79 Cited in: John B. Dunlop, "Russia's New and Frightening 'Ism'," *Hoover Institution*, July 30, 2004, http://www.hoover.org/research/russias-new-and-frightening-ism (accessed September 10, 2014).

80 Kenneth Waltz, *Theory of International Politics* (Reading: Addison-Wesley, 1979), 24.

Donetsk and Luhansk People's Republics. Some reports claim that as early as February 2014, Russian *Spetsnatz* forces were operating in Ukrainian territory.[81] Ultimately, Putin viewed the Euromaidan movement as both a crisis for Russian policy and an opportunity for Russian interests. The Kremlin, though unable to maintain a controlling influence over Ukrainian affairs, was able to implement a series of policies aimed at strategic denial. Russia's approach denied Western institutions an opportunity to strengthen their foothold in the largest and most important Soviet successor state, save for Russia itself, while also limiting the viable options available to Ukrainian policy makers. Russian decisions denied the political aspirations of a large cross-section of the Ukrainian population, certainly with tragic results. As seen from the Kremlin, the hard logic of power and influence underpins arguments about the legality of the coup that ousted Yanukovych and the rhetoric of national self-determination for Ukraine's ethnic Russian minorities. For as long as Moscow perceives the pursuit of power and advantage as a zero-sum game, the view from the Kremlin southward will be favorable. In this regard, Ukraine and the West will be forced to compromise with Russian interests.

---

81 Ewan MacAskill, "Does US evidence prove that Russian Special Forces are in Eastern Ukraine?," *The Guardian*, April 22, 2014, http://www.theguardian.com/world/2014/apr/22/-sp-does-us-evidence-prove-russian-special-forces-are-in-eastern-ukraine (accessed September 10, 2014).

Contributors

Anna Chebotariova is a Ph.D. candidate at the Polish Academy of Sciences. She received a Master's Degree in Sociology and Social Anthropology from the Central European University in Budapest and the Ivan Franko National University of Lviv. Since June 2012 she has worked as a researcher at the Lviv Center for Urban History in East Central Europe. Her academic interests include collective memory studies, Holocaust studies, Jewish heritage management in East Central Europe, and qualitative methods of sociological research. Among her recent publications is "Galizien im neuen Jahrtausend: Debatten um (post)moderne Identitätsprojekte in der polnischen und ukrainischen Presse" bei *Galizien. Peripherie der Moderne - Moderne der Peripherie?* Herausgegeben von Elisabeth Haid, Stephanie Weismann, und Burkhard Wöller (Marburg: Verlag Herder-Institut, 2013).

Marta Dyczok is an Associate Professor in the departments of History and Political Science, University of Western Ontario, and a Fellow at the University of Toronto's Munk School of Global Affairs. She has published three books, including *Media, Democracy and Freedom: The Post Communist Experience* (co-edited with Oxana Gaman-Golutvina, 2009), and articles in various journals including *The Russian Journal of Communication* (2014) and *Demokratizatsiya* (2014). Her new book, *Ukraine Twenty Years After Independence: Assessments, Perspectives, Challenges* (co-edited with Giovanna Brogi and Oxana Pachlovska) will appear in 2015. Her doctorate is from Oxford University and she researches media, memory, migration, and history.

Aya Fujiwara holds a PhD from the University of Alberta and was a Postdoctoral Fellow at the L.R. Wilson Institute for Canadian History, McMaster University, Hamilton, Canada. She was also a Research Analyst for the Japanese Embassy in Canada. Currently, she is a Research Associate with the Prince Takamado Japan Centre for Teaching and Research and Adjunct Professor in the Department of History and Classics, University of Alberta. She is the author of *Ethnic Elites and Canadian Identity: Japanese, Ukrainians, and Scots, 1919-1971* (Winnipeg: University of Manitoba Press, 2012).

Olesya Khromeychuk teaches the history of Ukraine, Russia, and the Soviet Union at the School of Slavonic and East European Studies, University College London. She also teaches the history of Russia and the Soviet Union at the University of East Anglia, and the Ukrainian language at the University of Cambridge. In 2011 she received a Ph.D. in history from University College London. She is the author of *'Undetermined' Ukrainians. Post-War Narratives of the Waffen SS 'Galicia' Division* (Oxford: Peter Lang, 2013).

Svitlana Krasynska is a Ph.D. student in Leadership Studies, with a specialization in Nonprofit and Philanthropic Management, at the University of San Diego. Her most recent publications are "Contra Spem Spero: The Third Sector Resilience in the Face of Political Turbulence and Legislative Change in Ukraine" in *Nonprofit Policy Forum* (forthcoming) and her co-edited book, *The Nonprofit Sector in Eastern Europe, Russia and Central Asia: Civil Society Advances and Challenges* (Boston: Brill Publishers, forthcoming).

Taras Kuzio is a Senior Research Associate at the Canadian Institute of Ukrainian Studies, University of Alberta, Senior Fellow at the Chair of Ukrainian Studies, University of Toronto, and a Non-Resident Fellow at the Center for Transatlantic Relations, School of Advanced International Studies (SAIS), Johns Hopkins University. He is currently writing a book on the Donbas conflict and his latest books include *Ukraine: Democratization, Corruption and the New Russian Imperialism* (Westport, CT: Praeger, 2015) and *Open Ukraine: Changing Course towards a European Future*, edited with Daniel Hamilton (Washington DC: Center for Transatlantic Relations, 2011).

David R. Marples is Distinguished University Professor and Chair, Department of History and Classics, University of Alberta. His latest book is *'Our Glorious Past: Lukashenka's Belarus and the Great Patriotic War* (Stuttgart: ibidem Verlag, 2014), and his most recent article, co-authored with Eduard Baidaus and Mariya Melentyeva, is "Causes of the 1932 Famine in Soviet Ukraine: Debates at the Third All-Ukrainian Party Conference," *Canadian Slavonic Papers* 56, no. 3-4 (September-December 2014).

Frederick V. Mills is a Ph.D. candidate in the Department of History and Classics at the University of Alberta, Canada. His research interests include the Cold War, Soviet and Russian foreign policy, and the Modern Middle East.

Olga Onuch (D.Phil. Oxford, M.Phil. LSE) is a Lecturer in Politics at the University of Manchester and an Associate Fellow at Nuffield College, University of Oxford. She specializes in the comparative study of protest politics and elections in democratizing states in Latin American and Eastern Europe. Olga is an expert on protests and activism in Ukraine and is the principle investigator of the Ukrainian Protest Project and is co-investigator on a 2014 National Science Foundation-funded project titled "RAPID: Ukrainian Politics Panel Survey" (Henry Hale, Principal Investigator). She is a member of the OSF-funded Strategic Advisory Group, tasked with advising the government and president of Ukraine. Her book *Mapping Mass Mobilizations: Understanding Revolutionary Moments in Argentina and Ukraine* (London: Palgrave, 2014) investigates mass mobilization in Ukraine and Argentina.

Natalia Otrishchenko is a graduate student at the Institute of Sociology, the National Academy of Sciences of Ukraine in Methodology and Methods of Sociological Research. She holds a Master's degree in Sociology, and is a graduate of the History Department at the Ivan Franko National University of Lviv (2012), as well as the MIHuS (Multi-Institutional Individual Humanity Studies) Program (2011) and UGRAD Program (2009-2010). She leads the "UStories: Oral History and Urban Experience" project and co-coordinates the "Voices of Protest and Hope: Kyiv-Lviv-Kharkiv" project at the Center for Urban History of East Central Europe in Lviv. She recently published "'Šios vietos dvasia teikia stiprybės': ukrainiečių protestai Kijevo Nepriklausomybės aikštėje," *Vietos Dvasios Beieškant*. Sud. Rasa Čepaitienė (2014): 295-318 (in Lithuanian). ['There is a spirit here which makes you stronger': Ukrainian Protest at Independence Square].

Uladzimir Padhol is a prominent Belarusian political scientist and journalist. He received a Candidate of Sciences degree in Philosophy from the Belarusian State University in Minsk. He is a member of the Belarusian Popular Front, and was a candidate in the parliamentary elections of 2012, but not permitted to take part. A prolific author, he is best known for his 1997 novel

Pulya dlya presidenta [A bullet for the president], a second version of which appeared in 2004, published in St. Petersburg. He also edited and published *Narodnyi televisor. Tsitaty I baiki A.G. Lukashenko* [People's Television: Citations and Stories of A.G. Lukashenko], which is now in its thirtieth edition.

William Jay Risch is Associate Professor of History at Georgia College in Milledgeville, Georgia. He is author of *The Ukrainian West: Culture and the Fate of Empire in Soviet Lviv* (Cambridge, MA: Harvard University Press, 2011) and editor of *Youth and Rock in the Soviet Bloc: Youth Cultures, Music, and the State in Russia and Eastern Europe* (New York: Lexington Books, 2015). He is currently writing a book on his experiences in the Euromaidan protests in Ukraine.

Tanya Zaharchenko (University of Cambridge / Higher School of Economics) holds a PhD degree in Slavonic Studies from the University of Cambridge. Her monograph on memory, hybridity and blurred boundaries in contemporary literature of Kharkiv, Ukraine is forthcoming from CEU Press. She is currently a Postdoctoral Fellow at the Center for Historical Research of the Higher School of Economics in Saint Petersburg, Russia. Her next position will be the 2015 Einstein Fellowship at the Einstein Forum in Germany.

Index

Munich Security Conference, 255

Myasnikovich, Mikhail, 224

Mykhachyshyn, Yurii, 136

Mykhailivskyi Cathedral, 157

National Bank of Ukraine, 248

National Science Foundation, 32

National Socialist Party of Slavs, 69

Nationalism, nationalists, 33, 52, 57-9, 67-68, 75, 81-2, 86, 92, 100, 111, 116, 151, 208, 211-12, 256, 258; and Gender, 123-45

NATO (North Atlantic Treaty Organization), 18, 50, 111, 214, 217, 224, 230, 242-3

Nayem, Mustafa, 42-3, 189

Nemsadze, Gyvy, 72

New Democratic Party of Canada, 201, 206-07, 210, 213

New Jersey, 194

New York City, 193, 195

New York University School of Law, 196

New Zealand, 194

NGOs (nongovernmental organizations), 44-5

Nicaragua, Nicaraguans, 219

Nikolayenko, Tetyana, 66-7

North Korea, North Koreans, 219

Novitskiy, Yevgeniy, 74

Novo-Ogaryevo, 257

NTV, 226

U.A. Inter Media Group, 78

UDAR (the fist, Ukrainian Democratic Alliance for Reform), 11, 23, 39

Ukraina Hotel, 86

Ukraine Media Crisis Center, 86

Ukraine Without Kuchma, 28, 36, 42, 51, 66, 149

Ukrainian Canadians, 199-215

Ukrainian Canadian Congress (UCC), 199-200, 206, 208-12, 214-15

Ukrainian Canadian Professional and Business Federation, 208

Ukrainian Diaspora, 108, 168, 177-98

Ukrainian Insurgent Army [UPA], 127n

Ukrainian Media Group, 79

Ukrainian Movement Against Illegal Immigrants, 67

Ukrainian National Assembly-Ukrainian National Self-Defense (UNA-UNSO), 52n, 66, 68

Ukrainian National Labor Party, 68-9

Ukrainian Protest Project, 32, 47-8

Ukrainian Self-Reliance League, 208

Ukrainian World Congress, 178, 209

Ukrainka, Lesya, 127

Ukrainska Pravda, 80, 97

Uman, 69

Umland, Andreas, 255-6

UNIAN [*Ukrainske Nezalezhne Informatsiine Agenstvo*], 119

United Nations (UN), 16, 219

United Kingdom, Britain, British, 18, 228, 250

United Nations (UN), 219, 226-7

SOVIET AND POST-SOVIET POLITICS AND SOCIETY

Edited by Dr. Andreas Umland

ISSN 1614-3515

SOVIET AND POST-SOVIET POLITICS AND SOCIETY

Edited by Dr. Andreas Umland

ISSN 1614-3515

ibidem-Verlag / *ibidem* Press
Melchiorstr. 15
70439 Stuttgart
Germany

ibidem@ibidem.eu
www.ibidem-verlag.com
www.ibidem.eu